MAD MOTHERS, BAD MOTHERS, & WHAT A "GOOD" MOTHER WOULD DO

MAD MOTHERS, BAD MOTHERS, & WHAT A "GOOD" MOTHER WOULD DO

The Ethics of Ambivalence

SARAH LaCHANCE ADAMS

Columbia University Press
New York

Columbia University Press
Publishers Since 1893
New York   Chichester, West Sussex
cup.columbia.edu
Copyright © 2014 Columbia University Press

Library of Congress Cataloging-in-Publication Data

LaChance Adams, Sarah.
Mad mothers, bad mothers, and what a good mother would do: the ethics
of ambivalence / Sarah LaChance Adams.
pages cm
Includes bibliographical references and index.
ISBN 978-0-231-16674-4 (cloth: alk. paper)—ISBN 978-0-231-16675-1
(pbk.: alk. paper)—ISBN 978-0-231-53722-3 (e-book)
1. Mothers—Conduct of life.   2. Ambivalence.   I. Title.
BJ1610.L1455 2014
306.874′3—dc23
2013035268

Columbia University Press books are printed on permanent
and durable acid-free paper.
This book is printed on paper with recycled content.
Printed in the United States of America

c 10 9 8 7 6 5 4 3 2 1
p 10 9 8 7 6 5 4 3 2 1
Jacket Design: Jordan Wannemacher
Jacket Image: ©Shutterstock
References to Web sites (URLs) were accurate at the time of writing.
Neither the author nor Columbia University Press is responsible for URLs
that may have expired or changed since the manuscript was prepared.

For Geneva Louise LaChance Adams
& Nancy Bird LaChance

Longing for the further, the higher, the brighter.
"I want heirs," so saith everything that suffereth,
"I want children, I do not want myself."

—NIETZSCHE, *THUS SPAKE ZARATHUSTRA*

A Rain-Brain in a Broom-Room

"Write another one, Mum," she says,
and wriggles her pants to her waist,
and pulls me down to a Henry-hug,
and squinches her soft-nosed face.

Seeing me raise the pen again,
she clasps tiny fingers in delight
and turns up the ends of her rose-bud mouth
and bounces her pudgy knees tight.

Earlier with her mini'ture tool,
She'd set out to sweep up her room,
Needing the dust pan in the back hall asked,
"Why don't you use your broom?"

I'm hoping that someday she'll fully comprehend,
that I'll no longer have to explain,
when using my broom I don't get the smiles
that I get when I'm using my brain!

—NANCY BIRD LACHANCE, 1979

CONTENTS

ACKNOWLEDGMENTS

For Simone de Beauvoir, the realization of freedom is to exceed who one is and who one has been through engaging in projects that change the future in a direction she values. Yet the exercise of freedom is not just the glorious, uninhibited expression of free will. In taking action one is faced with disruptive questions about the boundaries between oneself and others and the implications of one's actions for them. Making use of one's freedom entangles one in the lives of others. Having a child and writing a book are two activities that make this starkly apparent. Doing both at the same time can instill in one enough gratitude to last a lifetime. One cannot do these things alone, but requires comrades, caregivers, collaborators, worthy rivals, people to stand guard over one's solitude and to knock on the door when it is time for a break. My chief hope is that they find the finished product to be worthy of their sacrifices.

I'd like to thank those who funded my dissertation work, conference travel to discuss this work, and the book project: Mount Holyoke College Alumnae Association for the Mary E. Wooley Fellowship; the University of Wisconsin, Superior for a Faculty Development Grant; the Oregon Humanities Center; the Center for the Study of Women in Society; as well as the following fellowships administered by the University of

Oregon Graduate School: the Charles A. Reed Fellowship, the John L. and Naomi M. Luvaas, and Betty Foster McCue fellowships.

I wish to acknowledge my faculty mentors at the University of Oregon, especially Mark Johnson, John Lysaker, Bonnie Mann, and Beata Stawarska.

Fellow graduate students who were integral to my intellectual development and sanity include David Craig, Carolyn Culbertson, Caroline Lundquist, José Mendoza, Lucy Schultz, and Jessica Sims.

Further thanks are owed to my long-distance teachers and advisers: Ted George, Lisa Guenther, Dorothea Olkowski, Brian Schroeder, Eva Simms, Gail Weiss, Talia Welsh, William Wilkerson, and Jason Wirth.

All of my colleagues in the Department of Social Inquiry at the University of Wisconsin, Superior have been incredibly supportive, especially Deb Augsberger, Janet Blair, and Joel Sipress. My gratitude also goes out to Kaelene Arvidson-Hicks and Lisa Mattsson.

Students at University of Wisconsin who have been my philosophical community and genuine interlocutors include Eric Chan Burr, Yasmina Antcliff, Erin Blood, Taylor Gambos, and Benjamin Jesberg.

I'd like to thank Hattie Peterson (and Amber) for loaning me their little cottage on the lake in which to complete the final revisions.

Thank you, Scott Poupore-Haats, for helping me negotiate life's many ambiguities.

The anonymous reviewers for Columbia University Press provided invaluable comments.

A profound debt is owed to my family; including those nearby—Robert Adams, Geneva LaChance Adams, Nancy Bird LaChance; those far away—Joan Adams, Diane LaChance, Danielle Liberty, Elizabeth Parslow, and Kristan Stringer; and those who've passed on—Charles Adams Jr., William Bird Sr., Marilyn Hawkins, Geneva LaChance, Raymond LaChance Sr., and Wayne LaChance. Special thanks to my Mamacita for letting me add her poem to the book.

I feel deeply grateful to my dear compatriots in motherhood, Courtney Bates and Christa Badorek, who bravely share their own complex journeys with me.

Beauvoir writes of the child drawing: "By himself, he would not have dared to put confidence in those hesitant lines." These are the words that most aptly describe how I feel about your contributions to this work. Thank you.

MAD MOTHERS, BAD MOTHERS, & WHAT A "GOOD" MOTHER WOULD DO

One

MAD MOTHERS, BAD MOTHERS, & WHAT A "GOOD" MOTHER WOULD DO

Woman seems to differ from man in her greater tenderness and less self-ishness. Woman, owing to her maternal instincts, displays these qualities toward her infants in an eminent degree; therefore it is likely that she would often extend them toward her fellow creatures.

—CHARLES DARWIN, *THE DESCENT OF MAN,*
AND SELECTION IN RELATION TO SEX

Women make us poets, children make us philosophers.

—MALCOLM DE CHAZAL

On April 14, 2011, just after 7:30 AM, LaShanda Armstrong deliberately drove her minivan into the Hudson River. Her four children, ten-year-old La'Shaun, five-year-old Landen, two-year-old Lance, and eleven-month-old Lainaina, were with her in the van. Only La'Shaun survived; he was able to roll down a window and climb out. He made his way to a nearby fire station shivering and incoherent. By the time rescuers were able to find and reach the vehicle, one hour later, the rest of the family had drowned. In a response to this incident, Cheryl Meyer, coauthor of *Mothers Who Kill Their Children* recently made the "conservative" estimate that, in the United States, a mother kills a child once every three days.[1] Clearly American mothers and children are in a state of emergency that calls for *immediate* action.

Upon hearing of such horrific incidents as that of Armstrong and her children, we must ask ourselves: how could a mother do such a thing? Maternal love and care are supposed to be a given. This is one of those rare, mutual assumptions shared by scientists and poets alike. We would prefer to think that such instances must be rare and pathological, the actions of a deeply disturbed or evil individual. We would like to believe that a mother like Armstrong has nothing in common with "good mothers," that most mothers never share in the feelings and impulses that drove Armstrong to act as she did. However, as I will argue here, this is simply not the case.

In *Mothers Who Kill Their Children*, Cheryl Meyer and Michelle Oberman devote a chapter to cases like Armstrong's, incidents of what they call purposeful filicide. This category is opposed to unintentional killing through abuse or neglect, murders that are assisted or coerced, and neonaticide (within twenty-four hours postpartum). Meyer and Oberman had initially intended to divide purposeful filicide into two categories—cases with mental illness (*mad* mothers) and cases without mental illness (*bad* mothers). However, it soon became apparent that the cases were not so clear-cut. "we realized that these women did not easily fit into a dichotomy (i.e., 'mad versus bad') but represented a diverse continuum, covering the entire spectrum of mental illness, ethnic and cultural group distinctions, and socioeconomic strata."[2] Although in all cases the mother was experiencing some kind of emotional distress, the majority would not meet the legal requirement of insanity—they were or would be considered competent to stand trial—and the majority were deemed legally sane at the time of the murders. Only 8 percent suffered from postpartum disorders. Meyer and Oberman also found that these mothers could not simply be categorized as bad mothers; they were not neglectful, wicked, or uncaring. On the contrary, they were generally very dedicated to their children. Meyer and Oberman write:

At first glance, the mothers within this category seem like premeditated murderers who violently kill their children. However, upon deeper examination one of the most distinctive features of these women's stories was their devotion toward their children. While it may seem like an oxymoron to describe women who kill their children as loving mothers, by all accounts that is exactly what most of them were. The overwhelming majority of them had no history of abuse or neglect toward their children and most people who knew them spoke of their undying love for their children.[3]

This seemed to be the case with Armstrong. In news reports neighbors describe her as a loving mother who was stretched beyond her limits. The twenty five year old was taking classes at a community college, holding down a job, and caring for her four children alone.[4] A supervisor at the children's day care center described Armstrong as under enormous stress. The woman said that when Armstrong picked up her children the day before the murder "the only thing she'd say was that she was so alone."[5] A woman at Armstrong's neighborhood church stated: "Sometimes she'd be holding the baby on her hip, and one child in each hand and trying to walk with her groceries at the same time, and she'd drop the diapers or something on the ground. She couldn't handle everything at once."[6]

Interestingly, out of mothers who committed purposeful filicide studied by Meyer and Oberman, more than half, 68 percent, were murder-suicides. Researchers believe that in many of these cases, women believe they are killing their children to spare them from a worse fate. Lita Linzer Schwartz, author of *Endangered Children: Neonaticide, Infanticide, Filicide*, states that "we see cases where the mother thinks the child would be better off in heaven than on this miserable earth. They think it's a good deed, a blessing."[7] In some cases mothers fear leaving their children to an abusive father or to a broken foster care system. Oberman says that when some mothers feel driven to suicide "she thinks, 'what would a good mother do?'" and killing her children seems to be the lesser evil than leaving them without a mother.[8] Jill Korbin, an anthropologist who has interviewed incarcerated mothers who killed their children, says that many of the mothers she spoke to believed that they were good mothers. Korbin states: "And it's that very ideal of being a 'good mother' that is holding our society back from taking preventive action or intervening in a potentially abusive situation before it's too late."[9]

Indeed, the pregiven fact of maternal love is so widely assumed to be the case that scholars rarely question the existence, structure, and significance of maternal care. They attribute it to the essence of motherhood and/or label it maternal instinct. In so doing, they ignore the complexity of mothers' responses to their children and foreclose inquiry into its significance. Maternal love, in reality, is part of a much more complex picture that includes contradictory impulses and emotions. Philosophers, too, are guilty of frequently trivializing maternity. Many who do consider the mother-child relationship treat it metaphorically, giving little consideration to its lived experience. These accounts idealize the mother's relationship to her child, emphasizing love, connection, and fecundity. In this case, philosophical metaphors of motherhood generally shed more light on long-standing stereotypes than the phenomenon itself. Those who resist this poetic impulse tend to consider pregnancy, childbirth, and mothering as obstacles to women's participation in public life and to their financial independence.[10]

Throughout this book I offer an alternative to the usual treatments of motherhood in philosophy and explore its significance in connection with the philosophies of care ethics, Emmanuel Levinas, Maurice Merleau-Ponty, and Simone de Beauvoir. I move the discussion from abstract notions of the feminine and maternal to consideration of the concrete experiences of mothers. My intention is to provide a more nuanced characterization of the mother-child relationship, one that highlights its conflicted nature. I argue that the ambiguity of human relationships results in an ambivalent ethical orientation, contingent as it is on negotiating the interrelated yet separable interests of the self and the other. Central to this discussion is a phenomenological description of maternal ambivalence (mothers' simultaneous desires to nurture and violently reject their children). My research shows that such feelings are fairly common and are the result of valid conflicts that exist between mothers' and children's interests. I argue that ethical ambivalence is morally productive insofar as it helps one to recognize the alterity of others, attend to the particularities of situation, and negotiate one's own needs and desires with those of other people. The maternal example brings human interdependence into relief while also affirming our independent (and often conflicting) interests. I maintain that it is *because of*, not in spite of, the tensions inherent to mothering that it is an instructive case for ethics. This paradigm example demonstrates our need for an account of ethics situated in a world held in common where self and other share a relation of interdependent co-origination, yet conflict between self and other can still be made sense of. This understanding of *what is* (phenomenologically speaking) allows us to more fairly assert *what ought to be* and how we might get there.

One of my key concerns is how to keep ambivalence from finding its expression in filicide. To better appreciate this problem, I take two overlapping perspectives on the phenomenon—the existential and the social. First, I assert that maternal ambivalence is the result of our existential condition, one that is perhaps impossible (and even undesirable) to change. Nevertheless, there are also certain oppressive social structures at play that heighten ambivalence to mortally dangerous levels. These existential and social factors operate in a dynamic interdependent tension. One cannot be understood without reference to the other; but there is a relationship of *motivation* rather than determination between the two.

In the following chapter I examine the mother as ethical exemplar, as she is portrayed in care ethics. Care ethics invites theorists to expand their concerns to more intimate relationships. They insist we consider the material and social conditions of ethics and embolden us to think beyond atomistic individualism. In some ways my own project is an affirmation of care ethics, but my approach and many of my questions differ. I am concerned with a traditionally feminine enterprise, motherhood, and how this practice can expand our notions of the human being, the good, and the ethical. Since the counterpoint to traditional ethical theory has been so well achieved in feminist ethics already, I do not feel called to address certain questions that have become standard in care ethics. I am not concerned with whether or not mothers are sufficiently feminist or about feminine versus masculine virtues. Using the model of mothers does not imply that I wish to set up standards of care or criteria of ethical behavior. I will assume, however, that some behaviors are ethical and others are not (such as taking care of children versus killing them). I will not debate whether justice or care is more primary or how the two orientations relate to one another.

Although care ethics sets important precedents for my research, it pays inadequate attention to the contradictions of mother-child relationships, especially what might drive a mother to murder a child for whom she deeply cares. In care ethicists' emphasis on interdependence, they sometimes ignore the need for individual flourishing and conflicts of interest between mother and child. We require an ethical theory that accounts for the needs to care, to be cared for, *and* to maintain independence. Although care ethics does not, at this point, provide the full account, I believe that collaboration with feminist phenomenology can fill in some of the blanks. One of my hopes is to provide some new insight and directions for care ethics, and my own ideas about the future of ethical theory and action are compatible with some of theirs.

This book is my contribution to a phenomenology of ethics—an exploration of ethical experience as it appears, paying attention to the meaning that emerges through description and inquiring into its philosophical significance. In chapter 3 I present an account of maternal experience, pointing out some themes and questions that arise from these descriptions. Using sources and examples from first-person narratives, psychiatry, psychology, sociology, anthropology, and history, I provide a description of maternal subjectivity and ambivalence, my claim being that clashes between mother and child frequently act as a rupture within the woman herself between her competing desires to nurture and to be independent. Maternal experience challenges the assumption that subjectivity is singular and reveals that the ethical draw of another can disrupt one's sense of self-coherence. Such conflicts are not unique to motherhood, but are especially intense because of the child's dependence and vulnerability, societal expectations of women (such as their being primarily responsible for children), the shared embodiment between mother and child, and our society's systematic neglect of caregivers and their dependents. It is my contention that ethical theory should be able to encompass the ambiguity of this relationship, including the fact that many mothers resist their impulses to abuse, neglect, and abandon their children in spite of both opportunity and motive to the contrary.

My approach is that of a feminist phenomenologist and has precedent in the works of Simone de Beauvoir, Iris Marion Young, Linda Fisher, and many others.[11] Maurice Merleau-Ponty has also been influential in this branch of phenomenology. In his preface to *Phenomenology of Perception* he writes: "all [phenomenology's] efforts concentrate upon re-achieving a direct and primitive contact with the world, and endowing that contact with philosophical significance."[12] Phenomenologists do not adhere to the point of view of the detached consciousness; instead it is through the first-person perspective that we gain the most basic insights into the world's meaning for human beings. This method is already consistent with some other feminists' manners of proceeding. For example, Sara Ruddick describes her method as follows: "As an 'anthropologist,' I begin by remembering as honestly and deeply as I can my own experience as a mother and daughter and that of my closest friends. I then extend my memory as responsibly as I am able, by eavesdropping, by looking at films, and, most of all by mother-watching."[13] Ruddick's "anthropology" is similar to that of phenomenology in that both are concerned with how individual experiences are shared by those in similar situations and give rise to meanings in common. Linda Fisher affirms this overlap in approaches in "Phenomenology and Feminism: Perspectives on Their Relation": "Phenomenology and feminism share this commitment to descriptive and experiential analysis, where the systematic examination and articulation of the nature of lived experience, along with the attendant theoretical and practical implications, functions as the basis for reflective discourse."[14] The best way to avoid the idealization of motherhood is by turning to its reality. With this in mind, I find it essential to consider the accounts of a number of mothers. They will be the measure of the theories' validity. As Edmund Husserl advocates, we must continually go "back to the things themselves": women's experiences as mothers.[15]

When the issue of maternal ambivalence arises, an immediate question that many people pose is "What is the cause of maternal ambivalence?" In both popular culture and scholarly work, maternal rage is frequently considered either a result of postpartum hormones, the product of a more pervasive pathology, or the consequence of living in a racist, heterosexist, and classist patriarchy that idealizes the nuclear family. These diagnoses shed necessary light on the hard facts that women confront, the situation they are responding to, and thus add to our understanding of their experiences. However, to begin the inquiry in this way invites us to *diagnose* maternal ambivalence. This assumes that maternal ambivalence is first and foremost an atypical *problem* to be overcome. Instead, I see it as primarily a phenomenon to be understood, one that can shed light on fundamental structures of our relationships with others. In considering this as a problem from the outset, too much has been decided beforehand. That is, we miss out on looking into its potentially positive, creative aspects. Moreover, I believe that pointing to specific causes of human behavior and feelings is suspect. I am skeptical that causes, whether linear or complex, can be adequately proven when it comes to our own "nature." At best, I think that we can point to a propitious environment or a potential motivation. To diagnose a problem or to look for its cause from the outset is to move beyond the phenomenon at question. It is to look underneath it to find out "what is really going on." In taking such an approach one forecloses the search to understand the inner coherence of the phenomenon itself, what it means to the person who is experiencing it and what is it that *inherently makes sense* about this phenomenon in and of itself. Ultimately, if we jump to a search for causes, we forget to provide an account of the thing itself.

This is different from saying that the phenomenon can be separated from the situation in which it arises. We cannot take the threads from a fabric and still have a pattern within it. Situation includes all the material and social conditions in which a phenomenon arises. Without the situation, there is no phenomenon, but this is not to say that the situation *causes* the phenomenon any more than threads can *cause* the pattern in fabric to emerge. In both cases the resourcefulness, creativity, and agency of the human beings involved must be recognized. This is not to be ahistorical, to decontextualize the phenomenon. We must assume that context and history are vital and looking more deeply into a phenomenon ought to shed further light on the context itself.[16]

Some of the complexities of maternal life can be understood through the philosophy of Emmanuel Levinas, as I explain in chapter 4. Levinas argues that to be a subject is to be incessantly undermined by one's proximity to the other. Yet, in spite of this nearness, one cannot overcome the insurmountable alterity of the other. He asserts that we are drawn to respond ethically when we witness infinity and vulnerability in the face of another and illustrates his theory with images of femininity and maternity. While Levinas accurately depicts the ambiguous intersubjectivity described by mothers, he fails to acknowledge the practical significance and context of their conflicted ethical stance. He portrays the mother as an ethical prototype, a natural and willing "hostage" in his ideal of infinite responsibility; in his universe, maternal filicide is impossible.[17] Levinas's philosophy advocates values that essentialize gender roles as they have been prescribed by patriarchy and elevates them to an ethical imperative. In addition, his emphasis on the powerful call of the face of the other, while important, denies the subtle interplay of active and passive ethical agency. Deliberative agency, I argue, is especially necessary to account for our ability to resist violence even when we feel a compulsion toward it. Finally, Levinas ignores the practical limitations to caring for others and fails to explore how one might negotiate conflicting interests. I conclude that his principle of infinite responsibility places an unfair burden on the individual as ethical agent, as it minimizes the importance of social and material factors.

What remains extremely important in Levinas's account for our understanding of maternal experience is that *having dependents* is a key factor in what makes us capable of ethics. Care ethics has thoroughly demonstrated that *to be dependent* is central to being human and that the philosophical tradition has overlooked this. However, I contend, with Levinas's support (or more precisely with the support of Lisa Guenther's reading of Levinas), that *having dependents* is perhaps even more threatening to our sense of enjoyment and independence. One's own dependence can be somewhat more easily concealed, and the feminist exposé of the philosophical cannon, and of patriarchy more broadly, demonstrates this quite well.[18] Historically, men have quite comfortably concealed their own dependency on the work of women and slaves, as wealthy countries continue to conceal their dependency on nature and exploited countries. However, I think that it is much more difficult to shake the dependence of others upon oneself. As Levinas aptly describes, the face of the other keeps popping up at the most inopportune moments. One is watching a late night movie and the ASPCA commercials with their neglected and abused animals comes on, or a Save the Children commercial with an impoverished child in Africa, India, or Latin America interrupts one's relaxation. Or one is out on a date and the homeless drunk asks for change. These interruptions are temporary, but, whether we decide to help or not help, their faces tend to linger. The reason they inspire ire is because they impose needs on us that are far greater than what we can fulfill, even if we gave them everything we have. They force us to confront our own perpetual ethical failure. As Levinas teaches, they impose on our self-centered enjoyments, sense of personal integrity and make us feel hostage to their needs. To have dependents is something that is simultaneously psychologically threatening and necessary for our full humanity.[19] One need not have children to feel the dependence of others upon oneself, but they are what I call the primal parasite that makes this dynamic undeniably visible.[20]

To deepen our understanding of intersubjective ambiguity as a promising way to connect it with the ethical ambivalence that mothers experience, I next turn to the work of Maurice Merleau-Ponty. Merleau-Ponty claims that each person experiences a prereflective coherence between herself and the world, between himself and others. In his later work he deems the things of the world, including people, to be expressions of one sensible flesh. While flesh establishes our continuity, it also involves an inherent dehiscence between the sensing and the sensed, and between the self and the other. Merleau-Ponty uses metaphors of maternity to illustrate these concepts, which do accurately capture the fundamental ambiguity of mother-child relations. Moreover, in his lectures on child psychology and pedagogy he makes empirical claims about maternal experience that are consistent with my findings. Upon comparing maternal experience to Merleau-Ponty's notion of the flesh, I propose that maternity can be aptly characterized as a case of dehiscence in the flesh.

To elaborate on his notion of ambiguous intersubjectivity and counter some of his critics, I explicate Merleau-Ponty's use of Hegel's "immanent logic of human existence." I also refer to the Hegelian-style logic at work in Merleau-Ponty to demonstrate the manner in which alterity and interconnection relate in our ambiguous relations and how this is a more nuanced and useful view over those held by Levinas, Jean Paul Sartre, and Antonio Damasio. I claim that, although he neither wrote an ethics nor prescribed a vision of the good life, Merleau-Ponty does describe a lifeworld that comprehends intersubjective ambiguity, provokes the question "What should I do?" and indicates that the answer will often be conflicted and founded in ambivalence.

While Merleau-Ponty looks at intersubjectivity in concert with our embodiment, Beauvoir adds to this hearty consideration of the social and material conditions of our ethical relations. This is the subject of chapter 6. Beauvoir argues that, when freely chosen, motherhood is a vital commitment to care for another and, moreover, that a person's ethical standing is indicated by how she negotiates the ambiguity between her independence and her responsibility to others. Motherhood heightens the possibilities for "existential evil," since it provides the opportunities to dominate a vulnerable person and/or to escape one's freedom in devotion to another. Whether or not the mother will be able to carry out her obligation depends greatly on how she responds to a typically highly constraining situation. Beauvoir posits that individuals and society as a whole should embrace an active responsibility for children; mothers must have opportunities to engage in other meaningful, enduring activities. I assert that having reliable support will not eliminate maternal ambivalence, but will enable mother and child to negotiate mutual existential transcendence.

Of all the philosophers discussed herein, Beauvoir provides one of the most important contributions to understanding the ethical life of mothers; she explicitly acknowledges the likelihood of ethical failure. The romanticizaton of maternity has divided mothers into the categories of either naturally good or pathologically bad. This has meant that mothers feel an exaggerated guilt over the slightest feeling of aggression or impulse toward violence against their children. In contrast, Beauvoir realizes that our ethical obligations often outstrip our ability to meet them, that others tax our reserves, and that one may *justifiably* need to assert one's own well-being over another. Recognition of this possibility for failure need not lead to despair. It is the beginning of considering how to reasonably meet competing demands when possible. It is to affirm that it is often unclear what choice should be made before examining the complex relationships involved.

Throughout this book I consider feminists' engagements with each of the central figures. I aim to highlight the lively dialogue between feminists and existential phenomenology and to showcase feminist phenomenology. I often disagree with both critics and supporters on each of the figures. For example, in Beauvoir's case, I oppose critics who deem her account overly strife ridden and supporters who minimize the importance of conflict to Beauvoir's philosophy as a whole. In contrast to this, I maintain that Beauvoir's conflicted account of maternity (and of intersubjectivity more generally) is neither in deference to Sartre's philosophy nor is it a rhetorical strategy; it is an insightful recognition of maternity's joint potential to enrich and to devastate. In this case, the firsthand accounts of mothers provide support for Beauvoir's theory and breathe new life into the debates in secondary scholarship.

For Levinas, Merleau-Ponty, and Beauvoir, ambiguous intersubjectivity is the context of our ethical life, and it has a number of consequences we find to be true in the case of mothers. The needs of the other are integral to one's own, since my well-being is wrapped up in hers. I am compelled to respond to her cries and become almost helplessly drawn to meet her needs. Yet her desires will conflict with mine. I revolt against her demands and/or struggle to balance them with my own. This results in an ambivalent ethical orientation; I want to both care for and abandon the other. In this instance passive responsiveness is insufficient. Conscious effort, skill, resources, and thought are all required to negotiate our competing, yet intertwined, needs. Levinas, Merleau-Ponty, and Beauvoir each provide an integral piece of this account.

I view philosophy as a hermeneutic dialogue across generations (in the manner that Han-Georg Gadamer describes in *Truth and Method*). The works of a philosopher have a special relevance in the time and place they were conceived, but also have a unique potential to open up the meaning of contemporary concerns. In this investigation I seek to enable mutual critique and enlightenment between maternal experience and existential phenomenology. Bringing them into dialogue both tests and demonstrates the concrete relevance of philosophy to everyday experience. Attention to mothering reveals paradoxical truths that require a complex logic to comprehend them. In this regard, philosophy may be a critical player in challenging and expanding our conceptions of motherhood in society. Therefore, although I favor an interdisciplinary approach to understanding motherhood, I think that philosophers can have an especially important role in challenging long-standing misconceptions.

Children's vulnerability is profound and obvious; their dependence is undeniable and seems justified to even the staunchest individualists. Care ethics places such dependency relations at the foundation of ethical theory. They find that the mother-child relationship can help us recognize important factors we may overlook in other cases. We are all fragile bodies that require the goodwill and generosity of others. Human bonds are essential to human life, but those bonds also place us at risk. The boundaries between self and other are often unclear, but this can be more easily overlooked in the supposedly "autonomous" adult. Recognizing our interdependence helps us to understand the true context for ethical life. As Kelly Oliver states, "When the relation between self and other becomes ambiguous, when identity is an exchange between self and other, only then can we begin to talk about ethics. Ethics requires a relationship between two that are neither identical nor autonomous."[21] When considered in the context of the mother-child relation, because it can be among the most intimate and the most conflicted, our intersubjective ambiguity and ethical ambivalence come into most striking relief.

Two

THE MOTHER AS ETHICAL EXEMPLAR IN CARE ETHICS

E arly movements for women's emancipation sought specific rights for women, such as those for suffrage and the right to own property. Since the 1960s women have waged a more comprehensive battle for inclusion in public and political life. As a part of this struggle, feminists undermine the myth of binary genders that serves to separate us and our concerns from public notice. We fight against the fallacy that emotion, nature, and caretaking are the strict purview of women and that only men use reason in their affairs. We insist that the personal is political, that what happens in the political realm impacts the personal and vice versa. For example, feminists claim that domestic violence should be prevented by legislation and police enforcement and argue that when women are systematically denied access to education and finances they are not able to develop at full capacity. While women seek freedom from the imprisonment of feminine roles, we also point out that the domestic realm is ethically and politically significant; this work had been devalued in spite of the fact that all people rely on it.

Drawing on the same claims as the wider women's movement, the feminist revolution also changed the field of ethics. Innovations first began as grassroots applications and then worked their way into academia.

The term *feminist ethics* came into use in the 1970s and 1980s. Today feminist ethics continues to challenge androcentrism in the ethical tradition through attention to a wide range of issues: the idea that women cannot be full moral agents, the fact that virtues traditionally attributed to women (for example, obedience and nurturance) give advantages to men, the devaluation of the domestic realm and its ostracism from the political, ignorance of the need to care for dependents, and traditional ethical theory's contradiction with "a distinctively feminine moral experience or sensibility."[1]

In 1982 a new branch of feminist ethics, care ethics, began with the publication of Carol Gilligan's influential and hotly debated book, *In a Different Voice*. In it Gilligan presents a challenge to Lawrence Kohlberg's moral stage theory by noting differences in the ethical orientations of males and females. According to Gilligan's studies, men and boys emphasize individual rights and consider *interference* with another to be the primary violation. Meanwhile, women and girls tend to believe that ethical wrongdoing is the failure to take care of another in need; noninterference is a greater offense than interference. As such, the girls and women in Gilligan's studies repeatedly give voice to "the ethics of care": "Her world is a world of relationships and psychological truths where an awareness of the connection between people gives rise to a recognition of responsibility for one another, a perception of the need for response."[2] With this work Gilligan inaugurated a concern with uncovering and affirming a quintessentially feminine approach to ethics.[3]

While there is great diversity among care ethicists, they agree on several fundamental principles: caring is assuming an ongoing responsibility for and commitment to another. As Joan Tronto states succinctly, "caring involves responding to the particular, concrete, physical, spiritual, intellectual, psychic, and emotional needs of others."[4] These theorists affirm a relational ontology; relationships are deemed more primary than individuals. Individual rights, therefore, become secondary to responsibilities between people in relationship to one another. Care is based on interpersonal connection and can neither be performed from a detached, objective perspective nor deduced from abstract principles or hypothetical situations. They further posit that it involves taking on the point of view of another and cannot be generalized from one's own experience. Most care ethicists do not attribute this "feminine" approach strictly to women, but do agree that it emerges in the context of practices that are historically a woman's domain, especially caretaking of children, the infirm, and the elderly; women's traditional roles have made them more aware of the prevalence and importance of interpersonal dependence.[5] Care ethicists encourage us to rethink personal and social accountability on the basis of an ethics of care and have brought this perspective to larger political and societal concerns. The addition of this perspective to international relations, for example, has enabled care ethics to propose innovative solutions to problems such as global poverty, environmental degradation, and widespread incarceration that a justice or rights-based perspective overlooks.

The fact that women have often been forced into the caretaking role has caused some feminists to worry that care ethics is a "slave morality."[6] They argue that differences between feminine and masculine ethics are induced by men's dominance of women and that to affirm these differences is to affirm the injustice that caused them. Nevertheless, every human being needs to be taken care of by someone else, at least in infancy. This is a basic fact of human existence, and, as I will continue to argue throughout this book, it is the *denial* of the need for human care that allows care work to become as exploitative as it has been. For this reason, it is one of the major concerns of care ethics to make this hidden truth visible.[7] This is the first step toward affirming the needs and rights of caretakers and fighting for the just treatment and support of both dependency workers and their charges. If this work is recognized as essential to the good of both individuals and society, shared more equitably and compensated fairly, then caregiving need *not* be equated with slavery. In this case, the values of care ethics neither have to arise under nor contribute to oppressive circumstances; women's affirmation of care need not be a kind of Stockholm syndrome that is "transforming vices of subservience into virtues of redemption."[8] On the contrary, care ethics insists that ethical theorists consider the material and social conditions that both constrain and enable ethics and emboldens them to think beyond the staunch individualism of the past. This more honest conception of the human being enables ethical theory to be more realistic, practical, and expansive. As long as theorists acknowledge the historical and contemporary contexts in which "caring" has been a mechanism of oppression, these changes in ethical theory will contribute to the emancipation of women.

The conception of the human being as autonomous has provided for an impractical conception of ethics in which detachment and objectivity have been considered the only proper ethical orientations. While a human being might die alone, it is preposterous to say that anyone is born alone. We do not pop out of the ground like mushrooms as Thomas Hobbes would have us imagine, but out of the womb of a woman. Without a mother, or someone acting as a mother, no human infant would survive for a day. Thus, in care ethics, the example of mother and child appears time and again as the prototype for a caring relationship. What happens if we do not start with a mushroom mythos, but with the plain fact that we are all of woman born? What difference does this make for our ethical, social, and political thought if we recognize that our 'independence" is made possible through reliance on others?

Theorists have taken this tenet in several directions. Virginia Held employs the mother-child relationship in a thought experiment to challenge beliefs about the structure of relationships in our society. She finds that this relation, once it occurs, is not contractual or voluntary; it does not presuppose symmetrical reciprocity; the individuals involved are not strictly separate entities; harmony, love, and cooperation are valued; and a policy of noninterference is obviously morally insufficient. With different suppositions about relationships, the goals and motives of our society and its ethical theory can be rethought as well. Attention to mothering brings the value of care more clearly into view and advocates an ethical paradigm in which interdependence and engagement are the appropriate points of departure for theory and practice.

Eva Kittay proposes a principle around which such a paradigm might be constructed. She argues that since we are all "some mother's child," each person is worthy of care and respect. This first principle recognizes the necessity of acknowledging the value of the caregiver's work. Those who are most vulnerable need respect and assistance, but so do their care-givers. Caregiving unfolds in a far-reaching social situation. The dependent individual is the catalyst for building an edifice of care in which caretakers serve as the pillars, but are themselves in need of the foundation of supportive friends, family, and society. The caregiver will not be able to help others if she does not receive sufficient nurturance. This apparently obvious point is frequently ignored to the detriment of everyone.

One of the most detailed and well-known considerations of maternal ethics is Sara Ruddick's *Maternal Thinking: Toward a Politics of Peace.* Mothers, she claims, are those women or men who meet a child's demands for preservation, growth, and social acceptability. These demands lead to the mother's activities of preservative love, nurturance, and training. She argues that reason arises in the contexts of particular practices and thus maternal practice encourages a unique brand of thinking. Since maternal practice relies on *both* emotion and reason, maternal ethics mends the schism found between them in most traditional ethics. Although Ruddick asserts that mothers garner a distinctive intelligence, she is cautious not to romanticize them: "Mothers are not any more or less wonderful than other people—they are not especially sensible or foolish, noble or ignoble, courageous or cowardly."[9]

While there is considerable consensus among maternal ethicists, some important disagreements remain. Of particular concern is the question of whether or not mothers are naturally inclined to care for their children. Nel Noddings is especially insistent that natural inclination is the original impetus for all moral behavior and prescribes our understanding of the good. Again and again, Noddings affirms that natural caring is epitomized in the mother's response to her child: "Responding to my own child crying in the night may require a physical effort, but it does not usually require what might be called an ethical effort. I naturally want to relieve my child's distress" (17). "Mothers quite naturally feel with their infants" (31). The example of mother love, above all others, is used to reaffirm the distinction between her idea of natural caring and principle-oriented morality. Reason, the ethics of the father—"the detached one"—only becomes necessary when inclination fails (2). But, even then, our ideals are always grounded in a previous "pre-conscious" affirmation of caring (28). She claims that it is the father's objectivity that would have allowed Abraham to kill Isaac. "But for the mother, for us, this is horrendous" (43).

As I'll demonstrate more fully in the next chapter, Noddings's squishy conception of maternal care is a quintessential example of a destructive (nonfeminist) feminine ethics. Her supposedly pivotal, mind-exploding ethical question, "what if this were my child?" (36) is in foolish refusal of the obvious—that real mothers, good mothers, do not always seamlessly care for their children. She underestimates the complexity of maternal emotion and the necessity of maternal thinking. As she depicts it, there is no actual ethical *conflict* in need of resolution. She maintains the same old tiresome dichotomies of masculine versus feminine and reason versus emotion. Finally, her view is pitifully stereotypical. She depicts mothers as joyful and bottomless founts of loving compassion and thus places no limit on the care that one can or should provide for another.

Noddings's formulation is not just simpleminded; it is dangerous. If maternal care simply comes naturally, then there is little reason to advocate for the support of mothers. Noddings's "natural inclination" assumption is oblivious to familial, cultural, and social factors that enable or disable women's caring. Secondly, she does not recognize that providing care may require the use of *all* available human faculties, including reason and deliberative choice. She might as well side with Immanuel Kant in denying women access to education because the development of their ability to reason will only interfere with the services they provide to the family. Third, in naming the father "the detached one" she effectively denies men's nurturing, discourages them from developing these capacities, and ignores the fact that emotional distance and care are not always mutually exclusive. In fact, detachment may be the *best* response of a loving parent. In moments of rage, as we will see in the next chapter, a mother may disconnect from her emotions as a coping mechanism to prevent her from harming herself or her child.

Fortunately, most care ethicists are not so naive. They are cautious not to reinforce the oppression of women by romanticizing women's traditional roles. For those who read her carefully, Gilligan deftly undercuts this potential criticism. Some of her subjects are women considering abortion, and Gilligan claims that for some of them a greater degree of ethical maturity coincides with the decision to have an abortion. While Gilligan does not necessarily advocate abortion as a caring practice, she also does not eliminate it. Abortion remains an option because Gilligan rightfully acknowledges that a mature and sustainable ethical position must include self-care. Even mothers must secure their own oxygen masks before helping another.[10]

Ruddick provides further options for thinking about the structure of maternal care outside of natural inclination. She declares that "mothers" are not necessarily women; a mother is anyone who meets a child's needs for preservative love, nurturance, and training. Furthermore, she thinks there is no necessary reason why mothers care for their children upon birth. She opposes the idea of a state of fusion often associated with mother and child,[11] insisting that women have a *need* for individuation from their children.[12] Instead of describing birth as a moment of sympathy between mother and infant, she emphasizes that it is a separation. Given this division of mother and infant, Ruddick believes that any mother's care depends on her "adoption" of the child—an event after which she feels a lifelong commitment to care for it.[13] This notion of adoption asserts that choice is involved in the care of a child; it is not automatic, immediate, or necessarily grounded in nature. It is a commitment that must recur repeatedly. As a mother who legally adopted her son writes: "Thankfully, you can't get arrested for your private thoughts (I would have been behind bars long ago). I've since learned that loads of new parents—both the adoptive and biological variety—fear that they've ruined their lives at some point as their children evolve. Somehow, perhaps because all kids eventually will fall asleep and ultimately will grow up, you sign on for another day. And then another."[14] Ruddick does not oversimplify or make light of this responsibility. As Kittay also affirms, it is a bond, a duty, and a commitment all in one. It is both voluntary and compelled, both reasoned and felt. The concept of adoption supports Ruddick's claim that reason and inclination do not need to be pitted against one another in order to affirm that the practice of mothering has something unique to offer ethics.[15]

Ultimately, what does it mean to take the mother and child as presenting an exemplary ethical relationship? Kittay says that the mothering relation is meant to be an *analogy* "for social relations in which vulnerability is central."[16] The analogy affirms a connection-based equality—we are equal on the basis that we are all "some mother's child" and it is on this ground that we are entitled to care. For Held, the mother-child paradigm is a *thought experiment* demonstrating that the competitive dominance-driven notion of the human does not cover all moral relations.[17] Both these approaches are viable. Still, we must keep in mind that to make an analogy is not the same as declaring equivalence. Even when some common features can be identified, distinctions will remain between different types of relationships. While Held's thought experiment is also a useful approach in some respects,[18] as I show in chapter 3, the mother-child relationship can also be competitive. That is, there can be very real conflicts between the needs and desires of mothers and those of her child.

In fact, it is not because the mother-child relationship is typically harmonious that it is an instructive case for ethics. Contrary to the idea that maternal care is primarily "natural" stands the well-known fact that mothers abuse and neglect their children. Such occurrences are commonly deemed aberrations. Noddings argues that in such cases the woman is either sick or in pathological circumstances, but this analysis lacks subtlety. First, it is true that conflicts are heightened because of conditions such as racism, poverty, ignorance, mental illness, and so on. However, even sane, loving, middle- to upper-class mothers with supportive families and communities may have shaken a baby or slapped a teenager. Second, maternal abuse, neglect, and discontent occur in varying degrees. Is a frustrated mother who occasionally yells at a child to be deemed mentally unsound? Clearly such occurrences need further investigation, but the negative aspects of mothering are not given enough consideration in maternal ethics.[19]

Held says that she is not concerned about perpetuating an idealization of motherhood as long it is not "more severely idealized than the relation between rational contractors that it is to replace; for the purposes of my exploration, it does not need to be less of an idealization."[20] This should raise an alarm. The romanticization of mothering can be difficult to resist. Motherhood carries heavy symbolism and mothering/being mothered is a significant formative experience for most people. Still, mothers are not straightforward moral figures. They are subject to the same failings as other people. And although they are charged with the social training of children, they are often still in the process of figuring out their own value system; raising children can cause them to question their beliefs even further.[21]

Care ethics theorists must remain vigilant against generalizing about the family and idealizing its relations. They must take into account the complexity and diversity of family relationships and social environment. If they cannot address injustices within and about the family, then they will reinforce them. It is also important to recognize that there are unique features to the mother-child relationship. The child's needs and demands are distinctive, the child is unequal to the parent in skills and knowledge, the parental role is a teaching role, the parent must tolerate and accept behavior that would be unacceptable in another adult, parents are responsible for children's well-being and not the reverse, parents are supposed to behave better than children, and they must sometimes make executive orders over their children.[22] All of this means that any discoveries regarding the mother-child relationship cannot be blindly applied to all relationships. However, we also cannot assume that an asymmetrical ethics is always suitable even in this relationship.

In order to act as a useful example, this relationship must be understood as thoroughly as possible. This is why I strongly advocate an interdisciplinary approach to studying mothering. We ought to be making use of all available perspectives and avoid relying on popular assumptions about motherhood or on the experiences of a few if this investigation is to be adequate from a feminist point of view. None are harmed more by the maternal ideal than mothers and children.[23]

As I will demonstrate more fully in the following chapters, attention to the phenomenon of maternal ambivalence brings to light some questions that maternal ethics does not address: Human beings *do* rely on each other for survival, but what are the ramifications of this for the self that is constituted in these relations? If mothers recognize human interdependence, then why do they often crave freedom and independence? If mothers are more inclined, as some would believe, toward a care-oriented perspective, then why do they sometimes abuse, neglect, and kill their children? Given that mothers sometimes feel hatred and rage toward their children, why do they frequently act in contradiction to these emotions? If mothers need to *adopt* their children, what motivates them to do so?

When these questions are considered, new aspects of mothering will emerge. One discovery that will have ramifications for ethics as a whole is the fact that mothers need independence from their children—including alone time, a sense of boundaries, and opportunities to flourish outside of mothering activities. In its emphasis on interdependence, care ethics often ignores the need for personal flourishing. However, maternal accounts reveal a fundamental ambiguity for all human beings; we have *simultaneous* needs to nurture, to be nurtured, and to maintain independence. This tension between ourselves as independent and ourselves as entangled in indissoluble bonds with others becomes acutely apparent in maternal ambivalence. The conflicts that can arise between caring for another and preserving one's independence can be exceedingly distressing. Even women who had previously been very independent typically find their participation in public life and the pursuit of their own projects, at least temporarily, curtailed. This seems especially difficult for women who have fought hard for their emancipation. Even those who are freed of the rule of the father may find themselves chafing under the yoke of children.

Care ethics validates the inquiry into familial relationships against traditional philosophical disinterest in these concerns. They require us to rethink the sources of moral values and interactions by expanding our notion of the origins of morality to include nurturance and care. Some theorists rest care ethics on the maternal relationship, making it the quintessential model for our ethical attitudes, motives, and acts. One problem with this approach is that philosophers lack an adequate understanding of mothering itself. On this point, care ethics would benefit from greater collaboration with other disciplines in the humanities and social sciences. Most vitally, we must attend to the voices of more mothers on this topic. If mothering is to be a useful example for ethics, we need to understand how the nurturance of children happens for diverse groups of women. As I will demonstrate in the next chapter, the experience of maternal ambivalence reveals a more nuanced account of our interpersonal relationships than that provided by care ethics. Its existence demonstrates that one can act ethically (at the minimum, not kill one's child and give it what it needs to survive another day) in spite of the overwhelming desire to do otherwise.

Care ethics and traditional rights-based ethical theory seem to serve different masters. Care ethics provides for the person in need and for her caretakers. Traditional theory enables the individual to pursue her own ends without interference. Maternal experience points to the value of *both* of these approaches. In accounts of maternal ambivalence we witness an ambiguous subject who finds herself caught in a bind; providing for the other can frustrate her own pursuits, yet satisfying the needs of the other can be as vital to her as fulfilling her own. Thus this enigmatic experience reveals implications for ethical theory more broadly—the need to reconcile care with individual freedom. It shows that doing the right thing does not always come naturally; thought and sometimes the resistance of impulse are necessary. It affirms the needs to care, to be cared for, *and* to maintain independence. We need an ethics that argues for the value of all three. No simple amalgamation of care ethics and traditional ethics will bring these two aspects of the human condition together. What is needed is a third approach that can conceive of the *ambiguity* between these apparently contradictory motives. Such an ethics will be aware of the fundamental ambiguity at the heart of our existence; it will contend with the fact that distance and relation with other people is always being negotiated.

Three

MOTHERHOOD'S JANUS HEAD

For finding your mother
There's one certain test.
You must look for the creature
Who loves you the best.

—DAVID KIRK, *LITTLE MISS SPIDER*

I did realize before [I had children] that people come up to you and say silly things like how can anybody ever batter children? I would say that it must be the easiest thing in the world.

—GILLIAN HARTLEY, QUOTED IN OAKLEY, *BECOMING A MOTHER*

At the Uffizi Gallery in Florence there is a series of six panels by the Renaissance painter Antonio Pollaiolo. Each one depicts a different virtue as a woman—prudence, faith, hope, justice, temperance, and charity. Charity is the only one of these figures who holds a child. Women have been idealized in many ways, but the mother is the ultimate model for generosity, compassion, and altruism. She is counted on to help the helpless, even when it is to her own detriment. On the other hand, it is common knowledge that mothers sometimes neglect, abuse, and even murder their own children. Such incidences generate feelings of disgust, horror, and severe judgment. Mothers like this are thought to be abominations, pathological, violations of the very definition of *mother*.

In this chapter I will describe the experiences of women who are neither self-immolating saints nor pathological murderesses. Their feelings about their children are mixed and varied—not just from woman to woman but within the selfsame woman. A loving mother can be mean, a giving mother can be selfish, a content mother can be filled with rage. In accounts of maternal ambivalence, women describe a passionate love for their children paired with fantasies of suicide, infanticide, or accidental death as the only way out of motherhood. They wish they could, somehow, reverse the fact of their child's existence:

> I could remember little except anxiety, physical weariness, anger, self-blame, boredom, and division within myself: a division made more acute by the moments of passionate love, delight in my children's spirited bodies and minds, amazement at how they went on loving me in spite of my failures to love them wholly and selflessly. . . . My children cause me the most exquisite suffering of which I have any experience. It is the suffering of ambivalence: the murderous alternation between bitter resentment and raw-edged nerves, and blissful gratification and tenderness. Sometimes I seem to myself, in my feelings toward these tiny guiltless beings, a monster of selfishness and intolerance. Their voices wear away at my nerves, their constant needs, above all their need for simplicity and patience, fill me with despair at my own failures, despair too at my fate, which is to serve a function for which I was not fitted. And I am weak sometimes from held-in rage. There are times when I feel only death will free us from one another, when I envy the barren woman who has the luxury of her regrets but has a life of freedom and privacy.[1]

> I sometimes think she's a cow. I *hated* her at first, not so much in hospital, but the first week or two here: I just wished she'd never been born, couldn't *bear* her. It was a mixture really, half and half, I'd be either madly in love with her, she's ever so good, dear little baby, terribly protective and all that,

and then sometimes I'd think oh: I'd wake up and remember there was a child there . . . I just felt *so* miserable . . . I just wanted to die. I would happily have committed suicide.[2]

Romantic ideals of motherhood tell us that our children bring out the best in us. True enough, I've done things for my kids that I never would have dreamed I was capable of doing; they've showed me my deep capacity to love, to value someone else's life more than I value my own. But . . . I wish there wasn't a but. Who can imagine feeling hatred for one's own child? Who can imagine anger—not just fleeting anger but a smoldering rage—toward an infant? I didn't know it was possible until I experienced it. . . . Sometimes mothers are mired in regret over the decision to have a child. Good mothers. Normal mothers. Mothers who don't hit or starve their children, who never lock them in the closet or leave them in the car while they go into the store. Some mothers who love their children also hate them.[3]

I was becoming convinced that I was the only mother in the world who had such hateful feelings for the child I also loved so intensely, who wished over and over that it had never happened, who, finally, could understand those women I had met when working for the Welfare Department who had burnt their babies' arms, beat their faces, killed them. But I would never breathe a word of such identification, I decided. I would hide my real feelings in order to avoid the terrible looks which say, I am not like you nor have I ever been.[4]

Accounts of maternal ambivalence, depression, and aggression can be found in a variety of sources—first-person narratives, psychiatry, psychology, sociology, anthropology, and history. Each one attests to the hidden prevalence of these responses to motherhood. In *The Mother Knot,* her memoir of the first year of motherhood, Jane Lazarre writes: "The only thing which seems to me to be eternal and natural in motherhood is ambivalence and its manifestation in the ever ongoing cycles of separation and unification with our children."[5] In *Maternal Desire,* psychologist

Daphne de Marneffe writes of ambivalence: "What is remarkable about these moments is not that they are a rarity or crisis, but rather that they are so routine. If there is any feature we can reliably assign to the experience of mothering, it is that it will encompass extreme states of feeling."[6] In *Mothers: Their Power and Influence*, psychiatrist Ann Dally argues that maternal ambivalence is widespread, but such feelings are so unacceptable that many women cannot consciously admit them: "Mothers are not infrequently distressed by sudden desires to injure or torture their babies, and they are not necessarily bad or unsuccessful mothers. Other mothers have similar thoughts but are unable to acknowledge them as their own. The hostile ideas seem to come out of the blue and from elsewhere. Such mothers usually feel a great need to reassure others that they love their babies, that such thoughts are 'utterly alien' to them and so on."[7] In *Of Woman Born*, poet and feminist theorist Adrienne Rich also notes the commonness of such feelings. She describes an evening meeting of women poets in 1975 who discussed Joanne Michulski—a mother of eight who had murdered and decapitated her two youngest children on her suburban front lawn. Rich comments that "every woman in that room who had children, every poet, could identify with her."[8] In "Normal Motherhood: An Exercise in Self-Control?" Ann Oakley, a sociologist, explains that two-thirds of mothers in her study "expressed negative feelings and ambivalence."[9] In *Becoming a Mother* she also saw a strong correlation between being a mother and feeling depressed: "Surveying the mental health of women, researchers in London have found that one in three women have definite psychiatric symptoms of depression and that the likelihood of becoming depressed is crucially related to motherhood."[10]

A number of scholars have discovered maternal aggression and neglect in diverse historical and cultural contexts. In *Mother Love: Myth and Reality*, historian Elisabeth Badinter disputes the existence of maternal instinct or any inevitable desire among women to care for and love children. She cites the many forms maternal indifference has taken throughout history. A sampling of these are insensitivity to the death of a small child, the refusal to nurse, and sending infants off to be raised by strangers (where their chances of survival were very poor).[11] Badinter concludes that, before the end of the eighteenth century in Europe, parental care was erratic at best.

In *Mother Nature: Maternal Instincts and How They Shape the Human Species*, Sarah Blaffer Hrdy, an anthropologist and primatologist, provides an analysis of maternal hate and infanticide from the perspective of evolutionary biology. Hrdy notes the widespread denial of maternal ambivalence: "Many people snatch at implausible straws so as to cling to the conviction that the emotional ambivalence many mothers feel about investing in infants is 'unnatural,' and hence very rare, and completely separate from more common, or 'normal,' maternal emotions."[12] Hrdy affirms that the murder and abandonment of children are not an historical or cultural anomaly:[13]

> I still recall the crisp autumn day in the old cathedral city of Durham, England, when at a conference on abandoned children, the full extent of a phenomenon I had been aware of for years sank in. The talks were routine scientific fare. Overhead projectors flashed graphs and charts onto a screen. The black lines sprawling across the grid summarized data from European foundling homes, tracking changes in infant mortality rates over time. As the morning wore on, the phenomenon of child abandonment was described, country by country, epoch by epoch, for England, Sweden, Italy, even Portugal's colony in the Azores. Gradually it dawned on me that this phenomenon affected not tens of thousands or even hundreds of thousands of infants, as I had long assumed, but millions of babies.[14]

To say that maternal aggression, depression, and ambivalence can be found in a variety of times and places is not to claim its universality; it is not to deny a relationship to cultural pressures and constraints. Perhaps there is one happy land where mothers are so well supported that they never experience a negative feeling toward their children. However, in this research, which spans cultures, classes, races, and historical time periods, maternal ambivalence is found to be pervasive. Even if it is impossible to assert universality, it nevertheless *does* contradict the pervasive denial of maternal ambivalence, the tendency to label ambivalent mothers unnatural or pathological, and the taking of mothers' love and care for granted. Ultimately, I claim that maternal ambivalence results from mother's efforts to achieve both intimacy and separation in relation to their children and that this is likely to be an aspect of all mother-child relationships. Nevertheless, it is critically important to recognize the role of situation in either exacerbating conflicts between mother and child or supporting women in their attempts to negotiate them.

PSYCHOLOGY AND PSYCHOANALYSIS

Detailed theories about the structures of maternal ambivalence come largely from psychology and psychoanalysis. Rozsika Parker's *Torn in Two: The Experience of Maternal Ambivalence* is the definitive contemporary resource on maternal ambivalence. Parker, a clinical psychologist, draws on her psychotherapy practice, interviews, personal experience, and feminist and psychoanalytic texts in her account of maternal ambivalence: "I refer to the fleeting (or not so fleeting) feelings of hatred for a child that can grip a mother, the moment of recoil from a much-loved body, the desire to abandon, to smash the untouched plate of food in a toddler's face, to yank a child's arm while crossing the road, scrub too hard with a facecloth, change the lock against an adolescent, or the fantasy of hurling a howling baby out of the window."[15] Parker states from the outset that while maternal ambivalence is experienced by all mothers at some point,[16] their reactions to it vary broadly: "There is, however, a spectrum of maternal feeling, from thoughtful containment to retaliatory abuse, a spectrum from pulling a zipper roughly to outright acts of violence. It is perhaps reassuring to think in neatly bifurcated terms of those mothers who contain and those who retaliate, but small moments of aggression will well up and pepper even the most caring of mothers . . . I am suggesting that most mothers do indulge in small acts of revenge."[17]

Early psychoanalysts also recognize the pervasiveness of maternal animosity. In "Hate in the Countertransference," D. W. Winnicott draws a comparison between the psychoanalysts' work with a psychotic and a mother's relationship to her baby, defining the infant as one who "cannot understand what he owes to his mother."[18] Winnicott declares, "The mother . . . hates the infant from the word go" and gives a list of eighteen reasons why she would, including: "The baby is a danger to her body in pregnancy and at birth. . . . He is ruthless, treats her as scum, an unpaid servant, a slave. . . . He is suspicious, refuses her good food, and makes her doubt herself, but eats well with his aunt. . . . If she fails him at the start she knows he will pay her out forever."[19] Winnicott shows respect for the difficulties of motherhood, but does not acknowledge that mothers sometimes fail to contain their frustration: "A mother has to be able to tolerate hating her baby without doing anything about it. . . . The most remarkable thing about a mother is her ability to be hurt so much by her baby and to hate so much without paying the child out, and her ability to wait for rewards that may or may not come at a later date."[20]

In *Totem and Taboo*, Sigmund Freud identifies not only the existence of maternal enmity, but true ambivalence:

> Every psychoanalyst knows how infallibly this anxious excess of tenderness can be resolved even under the most improbable circumstances, as for instance, when it appears between mother and child, or in the case of affectionate married people. Applied to the treatment of privileged persons this theory of an ambivalent feeling would reveal that their veneration, their very deification, is opposed in the unconscious by an intense hostile tendency, so that, as we had expected, the situation of an ambivalent feeling is here realized.[21]

Freud explains that mothers may display excessive affection toward their children as a reaction formation to conceal their hatred. This by no means *resolves* a mother's ambivalence; her animosity remains concealed in the unconscious.

Melanie Klein is well-known for her account of infantile ambivalence. She thinks that the infant regards his mother as two separate people—the mother who gratifies his needs (the good breast) and the mother who frustrates them (the bad breast). Meanwhile, the *mother's* feelings toward her child are not a reflection of her current relationship with that child, they reflect her childhood feelings toward her own mother: "We already know that this early relationship is characterized by the conflicts between love and hate. Unconscious death-wishes which the child bears towards her mother are carried over to her own child when she becomes a mother."[22] While Klein recognizes the existence of maternal ambivalence, she minimizes its significance and force. She claims that a girl's desire for a baby, present from early childhood, diminishes the aggressive tendencies she might feel toward her actual baby. Her child's helplessness and vulnerability fulfill her lifelong desire to offer "more love than can be given to any other person."[23]

The most detailed psychoanalytic account of maternal ambivalence is provided by Helene Deutsch in the second volume of *Psychology of Women*.[24] In chapter 9, which is devoted to the mother-child relation, Deutsch declares that "woman's two greatest tasks as a mother are to shape her unity with the child in a harmonious manner and later to dissolve it harmoniously."[25] Yet the chapter details the many pitfalls mothers experience in attempting to achieve this "harmony," and much attention is given to mothers' various neuroses.

In spite of these few examples treating maternal ambivalence, classical psychoanalysts rarely consider the psychic life of the mother. The mother-child relationship is considered in retrospect, from the point of view of the child and for the sake of diagnosing adult pathology. Ambivalence is typically attributed to the infant, child, neurotic, and/or psychotic.

In "A Case of Obsessional Neurosis," Freud declares that "in every neurosis we come upon the same suppressed instincts behind the symptoms . . . hatred kept suppressed in the unconscious by love."[26] In "Thoughts for the Times on War and Death," he makes a similar claim: "It might be said that we owe the fairest flowering of our love to the reaction against the hostile impulse which we sense within us."[27] Ambivalence is one of Freud's explanations for equinophobia in the case study of Little Hans. Freud thought that horses were a substitute for Hans's father, toward whom he was ambivalent. Little Hans's negative feelings toward horses were copresent with feelings of curiosity and esteem. Although classical psychoanalysts regard emotional ambivalence as a predictable element of psychic life, when repressed it is to blame for fixations, phobias, and obsessions.[28]

Nevertheless, ambivalence also has a constructive potential. As Parker correctly asserts, maternal ambivalence is neither a moral nor a psychological failure; it can positively contribute to the relationship between mother and child and enhance the mother's own psychological development. However, before presenting these conclusions, it is necessary to provide a more thorough description of maternal ambivalence.

THE TWO FACES OF MATERNAL AMBIVALENCE

Most simply, maternal ambivalence can be described as the simultaneous and contradictory emotional responses of mothers toward their children—love and hate, anger and tenderness, pity and cruelty, satisfaction and rage. But it would be incomplete to think of maternal ambivalence as simply an emotional reaction. It can be better understood through Martin Heidegger's concept of *Befindlichkeit*. *Befindlichkeit*, sometimes translated as mood, more literally means "how you find yourself in the world."[29] It is not just an internal state, but emphasizes that *how you find yourself* is in your orientation to the world; it is your relationship to people, events, and facts. Consider the way one relates to the world when depressed. Everything is exhausting, hopeless, and ugly. It is not just the *person* who is depressed, that person's *world* is depressed. It is, *in fact,* more arduous to take action in the world. Depression is not just a subjective perspective on the world; it changes *who one is* in relation to the world and how *the world is* in relation to oneself. Similarly, the ambivalent mother is not just an internal subject who is having a feeling about the objective world. When we consider maternal ambivalence as *Befindlichkeit*, we ask how the ambivalent mother *finds herself*. *Where is she* in relationship to her children?

The ambivalent mother finds herself in two opposite orientations toward her child(ren).[30] They share both a relationship of conflict and a relationship of happy mutuality. On one side, both mother and child receive some reward from the relationship. Their interests and desires are held in common; what benefits one, benefits both. We can see this positive reciprocity when a child asks to be held and the mother wants to hold her, when both enjoy an outing together, or during a mutually enlivening conversation. On the other side, the interests of mother and child are at odds with one another, e.g., when a child needs help with homework, but the mother has her own work to do, when a mother needs to relax after a long day and a child wants to tell a rambling story about her day, or when a baby wakes her exhausted mother in the middle of the night. In some cases it is impossible for both mother and child to get what they want and/or need. They interfere with each another, and their feelings are discordant.

Yet even this portrayal is too straightforward. Mothers often feel as though their own desires are directed against themselves when they are in opposition to their children's needs and wishes. When one's beloved child cries in despair at one's departure, one may *both* want *and* not want to leave. When the mother simultaneously desires intimacy and distance in relation to her child; when she feels the impulses to both harm and protect, to both abandon and nurture; this is when maternal ambivalence is at its perplexing height. At these moments a woman can feel most displaced by motherhood, as she simultaneously looses and finds herself in relation to her child. First, I will discuss each of these moments—of mutuality and of conflict—individually and then I will describe how they come together in an ambiguous intersubjectivity within which the child is experienced as both intimately tied to oneself and as a stranger.

MUTUALITY—MY CHILD, MYSELF

To suffer with and for and against a child—maternally, egotistically, neurotically, sometimes with a sense of helplessness, sometimes with the illusion of learning wisdom—but always, everywhere, in body and soul, with that child—because that child is a piece of oneself.

—ADRIENNE RICH, *OF WOMAN BORN*

The maternal body seems perhaps more permeable than most. However, all bodily boundaries are permeable by necessity; the skin and orifices provide means of exit and entry for food, air, drink, lovers, and children. This penetrability means the body is open to both danger and pleasure—viruses, wounds, sex, and so on. In spite of the body's accessibility, it typically maintains its integrity and provides a relatively stable location for the sense of self. In *The Feeling of What Happens*, Antonio Damasio argues that "things are [either] in or out of you" and that for each body there is no more than one person.[31] The idea that "one body goes with one self" is what he calls the first principle of the singularity of self: "One key to understanding living organisms, from those that are made up of one cell to those that are made up of billions of cells, is the definition of their boundary, the separation of what is *in* and what is *out*.[32] The structure of the organism is inside the boundary and the life of the organism is defined by the maintenance of internal states within the boundary. Singular individuality depends on the boundary."[33] Damasio's claim seems obvious enough, but maternal experience complicates this ostensibly straightforward "first principle."

From the perspective of a pregnant mother, another person, literally, inhabits her body with her. In "Pregnant Embodiment," Iris Young considers the fact that in pregnancy another person exists within the boundaries of one's body. She contemplates how the presence of the fetus within the mother challenges the unity of the mother's body by conflating her sense of interiority and exteriority. Young states,

> The integrity of my body is undermined in pregnancy not only by this externality of the inside, but also by the fact that the boundaries of my body are themselves in flux. In pregnancy I literally do not have a firm sense of where my body ends and the world begins.[34]

> The pregnant subject, I suggest, is decentered, split, doubled in several ways. She experiences her body as both herself and not herself. Its inner movements belong to another being, yet they are not other, because her body boundaries shift and because her bodily self-location is focused on her trunk in addition to her head.[35]

Young points to the fact that, to some degree, to share one's body is to share one's self. To muddle the physical boundary of the self is to muddle the psychological boundary between self and other. Damasio is correct that "singular individuality depends on the boundary," but in pregnancy it is not accurate to say that "things are either in or out of you." In pregnancy, neither subjectivity nor the body is singular.

This intertwining between self and other is also experienced in breast-feeding. Through nursing, two bodies share one physiological process. Consider these descriptions of this alliance between mother and child:

> Faith [the author's daughter] is the consumer, and I am the consumed . . . I am milk. My milk is me. When Faith cries for me, she cries for milk, for the breast stuffed into the mouth. It is all the same thing. I am eaten. I have never felt more alive. I am eaten. I have never felt more abolished. The oneness of breastfeeding is totalizing. . . . We even sleep and wake in tandem, my eyes opening just before she begins to stir in the bed next to me. I pull her down to my breast, check for a wet diaper. I'm getting good at this. We drift back to sleep, conjoined.[36]

> The day after Lea was born I watched her sleep next to me on the big bed. Even before she stirred I could feel the milk come down into my breasts. Lea whimpered, opened her eyes, and I picked her up. Greedily she nuzzled around for the target, locked on, and began sucking.

> The need of a mother for her baby to consume the milk she produces is a very strange phenomenon. My body was ruled by her need, her need called forth from it an immediate and uncontrollable response. . . . I made milk, smelled like milk, was sticky with this stuff that was me, but not me, that produced in me the need to give it away. . . . The miracle is that she and my body were one, that she, more than myself, controlled what my body made in milk. . . . I often looked at her and marveled that even though she had left my body, she still grew through it. Milk was the line that tied us together.[37]

After only several days of his life, we both felt that the breast was his. As he drew milk out of me, my inner self seems to shrink into a very small knot, gathering intensity under a protective shell, moving away, further and further away, from the changes being wrought by this child who was at once separate and a part of me. Frightened that he would claim my life completely I tried to cling to my boundaries. Yet I held him very close, stroked his skin, and imagined that we were still one person.[38]

Many mothers revel in the embodied connection of nursing. Even in times of extreme alienation and crisis in the relationship, it can provide a bond:

But what nobody understood was that the breast-feeding was my only real connection to the baby. If I were to eliminate that, I might have no hope of coming through this nightmare. I was hanging on to the breast-feeding as my lifeline. It was the only thing that made me unique in terms of caring for her, and it created an undeniable connection, even if only a physical one. Without it, she might be lost to me forever. If I continued, maybe I would eventually become less cut off from my own flesh and blood. I wanted to recede into the distance, but her mouth on my body kept forcing me to be present. I refused to quit.[39]

The thoughtful responsiveness of these women to their infants mirrors the way nursing mothers' and babies' bodies reply to one another. Mother and child *together* create the possibility for making milk. The breast responds to the baby's hunger by producing the amount that she needs. Operating by supply and demand, the breast is "a self-replenishing vessel."[40] Nursing also can help to suppress ovulation in the mother (preventing another pregnancy from occurring too soon) and to contract the uterus to its prepregnancy size. Meanwhile, breast-feeding does much more than simply feed the child. The breast-fed baby receives the mother's *live* white blood cells capable of killing giardia, trichomonad protozoans, dysentery amoebas, and E. coli bacteria on contact (231). Many of the changes that breast-feeding brings impact both mother and child for the rest of their lives. Women who breast-feed dramatically reduce their chances of getting ovarian or breast cancer (228). Breast milk also contains chemical signals that direct the baby's development and impact every system in the child's body (234). This can best be observed in the health advantages enjoyed by breast-fed children into adulthood. They have fewer respiratory, gastrointestinal, urinary tract, and ear infections. Nursing also dramatically reduces their chances of getting bacterial meningitis, high blood pressure, allergies, asthma, juvenile diabetes, Crohn's disease, ulcerative colitis, juvenile rheumatoid arthritis, and Hodgkin's lymphoma (225–228).

The times of pregnancy and nursing are brief and cannot simply stand in as symbols for the entirety of motherhood. But mothers attest that embodied mutuality exists beyond the physiological collaborations of pregnancy and breast-feeding:

> Lovers make you a gift of your body; so do children. The body again becomes distinct, edged, a marvel you'd forgotten, retrieved by the unexpected: your belly slimy with gel. . . . Or your newly shaved leg, buffed by the smooth ecstatic face of a sybaritic three-year-old. . . . My daughter, now two, has started licking me. The start of a hug, arms around my neck; or I'm bending down, picking up little plastic kitty cats off the floor, and her tongue laps my cheekbone, flicks the crater of my eye. . . . Her licks have the power to completely alter my mood, capture my full attention, put me under her spell, which is no doubt part of the reason she loves to lick me. . . . As a young woman, I thought about my body all the time: how to disguise it, to shape it, to present it, to comfort it; what everyone else thought of it. Motherhood taught me to live in it.[41]

A child can get under one's skin (in a positive *and* negative sense) regardless of their age: "Eight years in, I can't always tell the difference between my children's needs and my own. . . . The needs of our children and our world and our selves merge and divide and merge again, until sometimes you can't tell one strand from another."[42]

The "undeniable connection" described by mothers cannot be reduced to mere mother-child enmeshment. As a healthy child develops, every milestone achieved is a step toward a more independent existence. Mothers are certainly aware of this fact. Even as they cherish the intimacy with their children it is already slipping away. "Now that she sits up, has cut two bottom teeth, and is beginning to enjoy solid food, I know my milk supply will wane as more and more of her calories come directly from the rest of the world, unfiltered through my body. I'm beginning to perceive motherhood as a long, slow letting go, of which birth is just the first step."[43]

To some women, however, the first step in this differentiation is actually conception. Julia Kristeva, for example, considers pregnancy to be, first and foremost, a rupture within the mother's body:

> My body is no longer mine, it doubles up, suffers, bleeds, catches cold, puts its teeth in, slobbers, coughs, is covered with pimples, and it laughs. . . . There is him, however, his own flesh, which was mine yesterday. . . . There is this other abyss that opens up between the body and what had been its inside: there is the abyss between the mother and child. What connection is there between myself, or even more unassumingly between my body and this internal graft and fold, which, once the umbilical cord has been severed, is an inaccessible other? My body . . . and him. No connection. Nothing to do with it. . . . I confront the abyss between what was once mine and is henceforth but irreparably alien. Trying to think through that abyss: staggering vertigo. No identity holds up. A mother's identity is maintained only through the well-known closure of consciousness within the indolence of habit, when a woman protects herself from the borderline that severs her body and expatriates it from her child.[44]

For many women, the sense of differentiation from the fetus increases as their pregnancy progresses. They sense an individuated intentionality in the infant's movements. They feel a difference between a kick, hiccup, or a stretch, and believe that the fetus's touch communicates something to them—annoyance, boredom, playfulness, and so on. They say that the baby touches them from within and they know whether it was a foot, a hand, or an elbow that touched them. Furthermore, the fetus seems to reply to the mother's voice, music, a poke to the belly, rubbing the belly, and so on. This responsiveness is interpreted by some mothers as the purposefulness of another human being:

It's exciting when the baby kicks. I just love it! Each kick has a different meaning to it. You can really feel it stretching out, or when you are in an uncomfortable position for it, it will give you a different type of kick from anything else.[45]

Before the baby is born you know the personality. With Danielle I couldn't sleep at night because at night the baby woke up. Even from the beginning, I could feel her flutter at night.[46]

It's really strange. When the baby started kicking, all of a sudden it seemed real and I could believe it. Like you said, when the baby's active, he's doing this and that. . . . It's one thing to be pregnant and it's another to start thinking about who's in there.[47]

Nor, in pregnancy, did I experience the embryo as decisively internal in Freud's terms, but rather, as something inside and of me, yet becoming hourly and daily more separate, on its way to becoming separate from me and of-itself. In early pregnancy the stirring of the fetus felt like ghostly tremors of my own body, later like the movements of a being imprisoned in me . . .[48]

Research has confirmed mothers' intuitions that a fetus can hear, move voluntarily, swallow, taste, and touch. Fetuses respond to pressure and pain and loud or soothing noises. They establish patterns of rest and movement in the womb.[49] This means the responsiveness of a fetus to her mother is indeed both possible and likely.

There is another sense in which the pregnant mother engages in interaction with her fetus as a separate person. Many women respond differently to their own bodies when they realize there is a distinctly other presence within them. Kristan Stringer, a mother of four, describes a sudden change in her self-care as a result of being pregnant. "When I first became pregnant with Elizabeth, I was involved with drug use at the time. Then, suddenly, I was pregnant. A baby breathes through you and digests your food. I felt more responsible to my body."[50]

When a woman takes care of her body differently in pregnancy, she is not just taking care of herself in a new way; she is taking care of her baby to be. In "Women's Experiences of Pregnancy: A Tapestry of Joy and Suffering," Teresa Bondas and Katie Eriksson explain that Stringer's changed attitude toward her own health is a typical response to being pregnant.[51] The fact that many women become extra vigilant toward their health during pregnancy and do not maintain this stance afterward suggests that their healthful behaviors are largely directed toward the developing fetus and less so toward themselves. They seek to give their child a chance at healthy development, not an abstract medicalized conception of a fetus, but the specific baby developing within her. Francine Wynn states that "although the birth-giver can take care of the fetus by taking care of herself, the point of her caretaking, and some of her details, depend upon the specific needs of the potential infant to whom she aims to give birth."[52]

Perhaps mothers are accused of mindless enmeshment with their children because the pleasure of caring for a child can be a visceral and ecstatic experience. From playing with a young child to having an adult conversation, the joy of mothering is lived in the body. In *Maternal Desire*, Daphne De Marneffe describes the carnal character of this experience: "I feel it in my throat, in my belly, in my involuntary smile, and in a startling, ridiculous welling up of tears. . . . I am not in command of my own joy. . . . It seems that on the simplest level, the desire to mother is rooted in this experience—the expectation of it, the living of it, the longing for it. It is a rush of connection, a feeling that both deepens and exceeds us."[53]

Connection to one's child is not merely that of one monad to another, but can lead to a blissful (even if temporary) self-forgetting. Children, especially young children and infants, live a direct relation to the world, unmediated by reflection and judgment. Eva Simms, a developmental psychologist, describes it this way: "The newborn lives the pre-reflective and unmediated subjectivity 'wild Being' of the flesh, which adults experience consciously only in moments of great ecstasy or breakdown of the cogito, but which nevertheless remains the continual substratum of adult experience."[54] In moments of communion with their children, mothers can connect to this immediacy and spontaneity. It is not surprising that some women describe it as akin to a religious experience: "When I saw him and heard him cry, I was overwhelmed with emotion, and when the nurse placed him in my arms, I felt that I had *knowledge* of something very powerful that made life completely comprehensible. I remember feeling very light, as if every burden was lifted from me. It made me understand why some people search for ecstatic experiences of revelation in religion."[55] While this woman describes holding her child after giving birth, others have the same response to first meeting their adopted child.[56]

Antonio Damasio argues that "the tendency toward one single self and its advantage to the healthy mind are undeniable."[57] Yet the experiences of mothers gesture toward a self that exceeds simple singularity. While the body is, indeed, the location of the self, this is a body that is pregnable in more ways than one. As Simms eloquently explains, human embodiment is fundamentally intertwined with others: "It is through understanding our fundamental housedness in the flesh and the dance we are engaged in with the (m)other that we can see human consciousness and selfhood arising out of its bodily, co-existential substratum."[58] Although intertwining begins in the womb, it is not merely infantile. For a physically typical human female, part of what it means to become an *adult* is to be capable of interdependent embodiment, to develop breasts and to ovulate, to be equipped for pregnancy and breast-feeding. Yet coexistence is not only a matter of physiological symbiosis. Temporarily forgetting oneself, yielding to the needs of a child, being swept away by passionate love—these are experienced in the body and can occur with children of various ages. This "undeniable connection," "totalizing oneness," "staggering vertigo," and "rush of connection" are not blind enmeshment; they occur across the abyss between mother and child. This is why it is so surprising and wonderful when, within the flux of these ever-shifting borders, mothers encounter the ecstasy of mutuality.

CONFLICT—EITHER THE KID GOES OR I GO

It's a good thing we love Carter, or else we'd be banging him on the floor.[59]

While feminists have sought to increase women's opportunities for independence and self-determination, they have also argued that women exist in relation. In *The Reproduction of Mothering*, Nancy Chodorow claims: "that women experience a sense of self-in-relation that is in contrast to men's creation of a self that wishes to deny relation and connection. . . . Chief among the conscious outcomes of these processes are the ways in which many women feel intuitively connected to others, able to empathize, and embedded in or dependent upon relationships, on the one side, and on the other side, many men's counterphobically asserted independence and anxiety about intimacy if it signals dependence."[60] Chodorow is undeniably correct in her assertion that relationships are fundamentally important to women. However, she seems to ignore that women also feel anxiety about their interdependence and that this anxiety is well founded. Dependence on others and their dependence upon oneself can seriously impede one's plans and ambitions.

Mothers do not always revel in the self-forgetting and sacrifices that frequently characterize motherhood. A mother may have a longing for independence that is at odds with caretaking, revolt against the relentless empathy with one's child, and mourn the loss of her maiden self. Depending on the age and needs of the child and other adults involved in the child's life, a mother's self-assertion and desire for distance can be a real detriment to the child. Yet even if a mother *wants* to care for her children, when she loses freedom of movement, guilt-free work time, recreation, adult-interactions and alone-time, this is a serious deprivation that can drive her to despair.

A mother's sense of conflict with her child can begin as early as pregnancy. Many women attest to experiencing the fetus as a monstrous *Other* who threatens her body, eats away at her vitality, upsets her sense of self, invades her home, and ultimately seeks to commandeer her life. In these cases the child may appear in dreams, fantasies, or in her thoughts as a parasite or other monstrous figure. One pregnant woman had the recurring dream that her infant sat in the middle of a playpen doing nothing and that the locus of the child's subjectivity—the face—was missing.[61] Some women describe pregnancy as "a kind of hijacking—an invasion from within . . . as if by some oversight one has put on the wrong skin."[62]

Other mothers feel a sense of harmony with their pregnancy, but upon the birth of the child feel as though it is a threatening stranger. One woman said of her newborn: "I feel that there is this intruder in the house who is never going to go away."'[63] Another admitted that her daughter seemed "like a complete alien." [64] As Parker notes, these feelings of alienation may come as a surprise to the new mother:

> Immediately after giving birth, most women expect to experience a joyful sense of love and oneness with their baby: some do but many don't and warnings that it may not happen tend to fall on deaf ears. For women carry babies for nine months within a culture which represents the postnatal mother-child social relationship as if it replicated the intrauterine state of antenatal union. The nineteenth-century tradition of presenting a new mother with a pincushion bearing pins arranged to spell out the words "Welcome Little Stranger" was in many ways a more appropriate representation of the state of affairs.[65]

The pregnant or breast-feeding mother provides her child's sustenance from her own body and this can exhaust and deplete her. On average, a mother will spend six hours a day nursing a baby who does not eat solid foods yet.[66] The lack of appropriate places to feed a baby means that breast-feeding mothers are often isolated in the private sphere. Breast-feeding my newborn daughter took about ten hours a day. It can seem that the baby is not just sucking nutrients from the mother, but her vitality as well: "The maiden 'I' sometimes has to weep with the sure, coming death of the maiden-self, the self that could 'arise and go' at will; *the self that is not food for others, but eats and drinks the world.*"[67] The sublime violence of childbirth or a cesarean section can also cause a woman to feel that she has been more of a hostage than a host to the child and that she will be left a deflated husk of her former self: "I pictured the scene in *Alien* when the guy's chest opens up and the creature comes out. . . . Had I fulfilled my purpose here, and in life? Was I purely a vessel, a pod, and now I was no longer necessary?"[68] Some mothers feel that their children, like young cannibals, threaten to consume them:

> My life right now is just all theirs. Sometimes it's a depressing thought because I think "Where am I? I want my life back." . . . I mean, they are totally selfish. It's like an ice cream. They just gobble that down and say, "Let me have the cinnamon roll now."[69]

> The children remind me of a litter of kittens. They would rather have a starving dead mother than allow her to go away and feed. It doesn't matter how long that cat has been lying there without eating, when she gets up and moves away, the kittens feel she is a bad mother. And she feels she's a bad mother. As soon as I feel OK about myself going and doing something for myself, they make me feel I've abandoned them. And the sense they give me of being a rotten selfish mum destroys whatever ability I have to do anything besides being a wife and mother.[70]

> When Martin was a year old he would only go to sleep if he could hold my hand. I would sit there by his [crib] and lose all sense of myself. My physical boundaries would feel to be disintegrating. I would want to scream at him "Give me my space." I felt desperate for physical space, let alone time for myself.[71]

An image often stayed in the forefront of [one mother's] thoughts, of a teapot tilted over, with the proverbial last drop hanging from its lip: "Tip me over and pour me out," the motto beneath it might read. Other times she imagined herself to be a little generator with another tiny appliance plugged into her, sucking energy. And yet her own power source had been disconnected.[72]

Mothers responses to these feelings vary, but many describe an impulse to either fight or flight. They have a sudden urge to kill their child, to run away, to kill themselves, or otherwise reverse the fact of their child's existence.

I can remember going in one night, going in where she was in the middle of colic [and saying] "Take this baby before I throw it through the window."[73]

If I hadn't had anyone to help me, I mean these girls that *do* turn against their babies, I think it would be quite easy to do it. . . . I mean I think if I'd been left on my own I would have just *left* him."[74]

Sometimes . . . I feel my child has destroyed my marriage. Sometimes I want my child to disappear so I can have my husband back.[75]

I hit traffic on the drive home and started getting the terrible feeling that I was going to ram the car into the wall on the side of the freeway. The baby was in the back, and though I didn't think of hurting her, I wanted to smash violently through the window myself.[76]

Usually in the first few months you feel pretty down about things. It's just trying to cope with less sleep and feeling like a zombie, and not being able to speak to people properly because you're too tired to think. . . . You teeter on the edge and come back a bit, and then back to the edge and think, oh, will you jump or not?[77]

At other times, during and after feedings, he would cry and scream. . . . Sometimes I hated him for rejecting me so completely; "Shut up! I'll kill myself if you don't shut up!" I'd yell. Then I would try to shove my nipple into his mouth and he would push it away, his face distorted with pain.[78]

I have felt many times over the years that I was capable of hurting him. I have not done this yet. Or at any rate, I have hurt him only a little—I have spanked him a few times, yanked him and grabbed him too hard. I have managed to stay on this side of the line. . . . At one of my lowest points, a friend—a teacher—told me that she looks at her child and thinks: I gave you life. So if I kill you, it's a wash.[79]

Many of these testaments to maternal rage feature pregnant mothers or mothers of infants. This might lead one to think that they are simply examples of postpartum depression, that these responses to mothering are the result of pregnant and/or postpartum hormones. Depression is known to be the foremost cause of disease-related disability among women.[80] Pregnancy and new motherhood are well-known risk factors, significantly increasing the likelihood that a woman will be depressed; studies have estimated that postpartum depression is very common, affecting as many as 5 to 25 percent of new mothers.[81] Nevertheless, there is no strong consensus on the cause of postpartum depression. No correlation to the hormonal changes of pregnancy has been substantiated.[82] In addition, some new parents who were never pregnant display the same symptoms, including fathers and adoptive parents.[83] Numerous Web sites provide resources and support for parents suffering from postadoption depression (though it is not an accepted diagnosis by the American Psychiatric Association).[84] As one mother discusses, adoption brings its own added complications to maternal ambivalence:

Grateful though we should be, adoptive parents are not always. I was anything but grateful one night when my son was two. It had been a three-tantrum day, and there he was in his high chair, throwing spaghetti directly at my face. I could feel the tomato sauce sinking into my hair and can remember thinking the most horrible thoughts: Who is this kid? Where did he come from? Are we dealing with a bad seed here?

If he's this angry now, wait till he understands that he was adopted, that he doesn't look a thing like his parents. What will he throw at me then? Would my biological child have flung spaghetti at me? And worse: Can we return him?[85]

Mothers of adolescents and young adults have also described such feelings. The mother of an adolescent boy says: "I feel torn in two. I want to be a loving mother and to offer him a good home. Yet, at the same time, I just want him out of here."[86] Suffice to say that negative responses to motherhood cannot be univocally reduced to a single diagnosis or biological cause.

Anne Oakley argues that maternal depression is related to the expectation that motherhood requires abnegation of the self.[87] She believes that, in part, "postnatal depression is a form of bereavement reaction in which a woman mourns her former identity" and that motherhood seems "to lead to a sense of lowered ('depressed') self-worth: children take the centre of the stage; the mother is merely a supporting player. Her role is static, theirs dynamic: having no time to herself, her self is quiescent."[88] Indeed, many mothers' lives are directed around the lives of their children:

I would feel the futility of any attempt to salvage myself, and also the inequality between us: my needs always balanced against those of a child, and always loosing.[89]

My outings are [limited]. I'm excited when I have to go grocery shopping. Everything I pick up is what they eat, everything they like, or what they should eat. Me, I'm just *there*. I'm there for them. I feel that I'm here for them.[90]

One sometimes forgets that one is actually a person other than [the child's] mother.[91]

Being a mother is a terrible thing. It ruins your relationship with your husband. It ruins your life. You can't leave them because you love them and when you're with them you hate them. I used to be a damn good nurse. Very competent. I've nursed people all over the world. I ran an entire ward in Boston. Now I'm a mother, and that means that I'm nothing.[92]

Yet, even when mothers have other activities and interests, many women may still feel that motherhood undermines the identity that they have spent a lifetime creating. Quoting from her pregnancy journal, Rich says that she fears "the crumbling to death of that scarcely-born physiognomy which my whole life has been a battle to give birth to—a recognizable, autonomous self, a creation in poetry and in life."[93]

Jane Lazarre's breathtaking memoir, *The Mother Knot*, explores the misery of this loss:

> I turned to that self inside of me, that girlwoman who had once been all I needed to know of myself, whom I had fought to understand, to love, to free—I turned to her now and I banished her. Into a protective shell tied in a knot, she retreated, four, five, six times a day, whenever Benjamin wanted to nurse. Soon, even when I sought her, she would not come, but began to stay out of reach longer and longer, sometimes not reappearing for whole days. For if she was present when the baby needed me, she was of necessity pushed aside, sent to go hungry. She who had been in my life, whom I know I had to nourish daily in order to be fed in return, hid for weeks, hoarding her gentleness and her strength, placing no gifts in my outstretched hands.[94]

Naomi Wolf also describes this loss of self as peculiar to maternity:

> I realized that my identity was about to be cloven in two, my independence cut by half. It was the first time I could see it spelled out for me in all its sweetness and regret, in all its ambiguity. . . . The tension was this: I was mourning, protesting a point of departure in the road that I could never retrace. An "I" would go forward, swept irrevocably on by the tide of the natural order. . . . And the "I" would reconfigure eventually around [the baby's] need, and take joy in it, and spin a new identity. But it would never again be the "I" it had been before.[95]

There are times when a woman's self-determination is deferred in favor of the child's concrete and immediate needs. Wolf describes one of these moments:

> On another day, I became engaged in writing again for the first time in months. It was one of those rare good days when a writer can lose herself in time. Caught up in my excitement, I stayed too long at the office. It meant that I was late for a feeding. By the time I snapped out of my state of concentration and raced out of the building to run the few blocks to cross the street to reach our house, I was very late indeed. Christine, our new caregiver, was standing on the other side of the busy boulevard, holding the baby, on her way over to come get me. The wind was whipping Christine's hair and skirt, and the baby was howling. I tried to lunge across, but with six lane of traffic roaring between us, I couldn't. I felt guilty almost to the point of crying at the baby's hunger, but in the midst of my guilt, intertwined with it, was a sheer vexation, almost a childlike anger, at having had to interrupt my work. It wasn't just the one interruption, but the realization that this was a condition: interruption was now my life. I was crying because I could not win. Because, as a worker, I was turning away from my work at exactly the most important moment; yet at the same time, as a mother, I had already stayed too long at the fair.[96]

Wolf's desires and her child's needs are not in straightforward opposition. While she feels a yearning for uninterrupted concentration, she also describes "a longing for caring," even a desire to run into traffic to reach her daughter. Whereas her desires used to be more strictly her own, her child's needs have an irresistible pull. There is no simple solution to this contradiction. More time away from one's child is not necessarily a feasible or attractive option. Wolf does not want to sacrifice either work or motherhood, as both are deeply meaningful to her. Thus the problem of her "self-sacrifice" is not just a matter of yielding to the child's demands over her own. Lazarre, too, describes this aspect of the conflict:

> For two days every week I would be in New York attending classes. For two days and one night every week I would be away from Benjamin. I felt

peaceful and expectant standing alone, frightened and exhilarated by this attempt to embrace once again my own life. But the deepest part of me leaned toward that moment on the following afternoon when I would return to my baby: I was changed forever . . . except for the two days I am in New York, there is a real danger of losing faith in my existence.[97]

For Wolf and Lazarre, becoming a mother means that they yearn in two opposite directions. In wanting time to themselves, they are also directed against that part of themselves that wants to be with their children. The conflicted aspect of maternal ambivalence is not just a fissure between the mother and her child; it is a rupture within the woman herself, between her own competing desires, between equally valued parts of herself. Many women find this conflict to be a disturbing splitting of their self-coincidence. In her study of maternal identity across economic classes, sociologist Martha McMahon comes to similar conclusions: "To these women, motherhood, I argue did not mean self-sacrifice. Rather it meant the 'death' of an earlier self and the emergence of a new self through a process of moral reform. In this context, the notion of self-sacrifice for one's child is rhetorical in that the self has been transformed in ways in which self and other are integrated. Thus when women spoke of self-sacrifice, it was the sacrifice of other selves rather than the self as mother to which they were referring."[98]

In Wolf's narrative, Wolf-the-writer must contest with Wolf-the-mother. Whereas Wolf's identity used to be based primarily on her own achievements, actions, and qualities, this is no longer the case. For a loving mother, her sense of self, groundedness, and well-being are, at least in part, dependent on meeting the needs of her child. In such cases, one who obstructs her self-determination is also integral to her sense of self. Though one is never fully transparent to oneself, self-alienation is dramatic when one is in symbiotic relation to one's saboteur.

Where women expect to have an independent identity and yet, as mothers, are fundamentally intertwined with their children, there may be no way to avoid feeling torn. De Marneffe agrees with this analysis: "From time to time, we try to fortify ourselves in our choices by disowning our competing motivations: by elaborately insisting on our contentment at home with children, or our belief in the importance of mother's work. But the reality for most of us is that we are torn, and we live with a sense of conflict, sometimes flickering, sometimes flaring, hour by hour, day by day."[99]

There is both internal and external pressure for women to be creative and unique individuals (at least in Western culture). Yet opportunities for self-expression frequently mean hours away from children. Mothers are, of course, blamed for any neglect of children, whether actual or imagined. But women also suffer separation from their children: "One professional woman I know spends her Monday mornings in her office, like clockwork, crying over leaving her children for another work week."[100] The mother who works, whether out of necessity or desire, misses opportunities to develop the relationship with her children, to teach them about the world, and to contribute to who they are becoming. If being a mother means to engage in the practice of mothering, then being away from one's child for long hours can be a threat to that identity.

Mierle Laderman Ukele, a performance and environmental artist, deals with this conflict. In her self-titled "Maintenance Art," Ukele showcases daily life-sustaining activities that generally go unnoticed. In a performance titled "Handshake and Thanking Ritual," she shook the hands of all eighty-five hundred New York City sanitation workers and said "Thank you for keeping New York City alive." Ukele's earliest work deals with maternal care. For example, in a photograph titled "Maintenance Art: Rinsing a B.M. Diaper," she is shown rinsing a cloth diaper in the toilet.

While Ukele's thesis is that our daily care activities can be art, she also deals with the conflicted aspect of being both an artist and a mother. In: "Some Kinds of Maintenance Cancel Others Out, Keep Your Head Together—1,000 Times, or Babysitter Hangup—Incantation Ritual," a performance at the Institute of Contemporary Art in Boston, she carried out the following "procedure":

1) Begin: Call New York long distance & ask babysitter if babies (3) are o.k.? o.k.

2) Hang string back and forth across full length of gallery (30 ft.).

3) Read each set of statements out loud on each page.

4) Stamp each page with Maintenance Art Stamp.

5) Clip it to string.

6) Move on to next identical page.

7) Fill up whole space with words and sheets, move up the stairs and out-side to boundary of I.C.A—street.

8) If I say it enough times, (maybe) it will come true.

9) Call N.Y.C. and ask babysitter if children are o.k.? o.k.

END

(Repeat approx. 500 times)

Ukele calls the babysitter a total of one thousand times to ask if her children are OK. According to art theorist Andrea Liss, Ukele acts out her anxiety over leaving her children with a babysitter in New York.[101] Ukele is not just asking if the children are OK, but if it is OK to leave them with a babysitter. As the "mantra" in number 8 reveals: "If I say it enough times, (maybe) it will come true," it really does *not* feel ok to leave her children so far away. Liss claims that Ukele's art, "poetically and unabashedly addressed maternal issues and created a feminist statement in its acceptance that children are individual human beings both connected to and distinct from their mothers. To make such a statement is an admission of love, a succumbing to difference, and a difficult acceptance of the ambiguity of intimacy within the mother-child bond . . . the secret code of the mother's mourning."[102]

In order to flourish, or even to survive, young children are dependent on someone's intense investment in them. So often, this responsibility rests on the shoulders of the mother. Conflict arises when caring for children competes with women's self-care, development, and expression. But, for the mother who derives at least part of her identity from her relationship with her child, this struggle is not just directed toward her child; it is part of her self-relation. This is further complicated by the fact that a child's successful development typically leads to increased independence. From the time one begins to care for a child, whether through pregnancy or adoption, he is taking steps away. Even as the mother longs for independence, her child is already leaving. The "secret code of the mother's mourning" is that the relationship with her child, even when it is experienced as an invasion, is already an uneasy letting go:

> I see the accelerating future approach. I've done this already, after all, with two boys—grieved for the silly three-year-olds, the gap-toothed six-year-olds, the willowy nine-year-olds. They've died and will never return, and I grieve. . . . I remember the world fading into the universe made by Two, and I remember how it shatters when that ends—and then, how it begins again, brand new. So much to do, so many mistakes to make for the first time. And what is there to regret? This is how the world goes, this is how it must be. I don't grieve for her—I grieve for me, sitting by some poolside in a few years, pretending to read so my sunglasses hide my hungry, tearful eyes as she glides by, oblivious.[103]

Mothers identify innumerable moments that signal the ongoing, increasing loss— from childbirth, to starting school, to the rebellions of adolescence:

> Zachary's body isn't mine anymore, not like it once was. We've been moving in this direction since the day he was born, when I held him swaddled in flannel and watched every possible emotion roll and brighten and twitch over his face, like a symphony warming up, like clouds passing in front of the moon.[104]

> From this point on, I knew, our separation would continue to grow over the years, as she experienced things in her life that I wouldn't even know about. Imagining her in the world without needing the protection of a mother's body, I felt a small moment of panic, a sudden, clenching cramp, not unlike the muted pain experienced at her birth.[105]

> "Stay close by," I call to her as she runs. "Stay by Mama." Each day, she runs a little farther away, turns her head and laughs."[106]

And there is also the possibility that one's child will die:

> A woman carries a baby in her body and when that child dies, no mat-
> ter how old he or she is, the mother feels that something has been cut
> out from inside her—the loss is as permanent and profound as becom-
> ing a parent. I asked Rose and Suzanne how childbirth and child death
> changed their lives. "A woman named Elizabeth Stone wrote that having
> a child is 'to decide forever to have your heart go walking around outside
> your body,' Suzanne says. "That's what becoming a parent is like. And now
> I've lost that piece of myself."[107]

Even an intimate moment can highlight the child's departure:

> Carefully, very consciously, gauging my reaction, he lowers his soapy head
> to my chest, leaning his chin on my breast and looking up into my face,
> then lifts his hand from the water and places it over my heart. A trigger
> of concern goes off in my brain—physical boundaries: when to impose—
> but when he sees my even expression (my poker face, hitched to genuine
> pleasure at the closeness of my child), I'm just his mommy gazing back at
> him, and all the tension goes out of his body. He knows he's my little boy,
> curled up with his mother in the bathtub for one of the last times; we both
> know it, and relax.[108]

> Eyes closed, her tiny fists clenched, she mewled and rooted against my
> breast, already instinctively searching for reconnection. Exhausted, I was
> overwhelmed with the force of her perfection and individuality: a tiny be-
> ing separate from and yet still so intimately tied to me.[109]

Connection and loss are the yin and yang of motherhood and, nevertheless, make it difficult to achieve a sense of balance, coherence, and
unity. If the woman, as a more or less singular individual, is sacrificed to
motherhood, then what is it that takes her place? The mother who finds
herself joined to her child's needs, joys, and pains (whether this is the
source of pleasurable mutuality or painful conflict) has increased herself

in number. She is more than one. But, to the extent that her child is at the center of herself, she has lost her self-coincidence, and she is less than one. How are we to conceive of this dichotomy?

AMBIGUOUS INTERSUBJECTIVITY— MORE AND LESS THAN ONE[110]

In "On the Maternal Order," an interview with biologist Hélène Rouch, Luce Irigaray considers the placenta as a model for the relationship between mother and child. Rouch and Irigaray note that, contrary to the psychoanalytic idea that mother and fetus are fused, the placenta is a vital intermediary that preserves differentiation within the relationship. Indeed, the placenta is an amazing example of symbiosis, central to the survival of both pregnant woman and fetus. Its growth is initiated by the embryo, but it is made up of tissues from both individuals.[111] Rouch states:

> On the one hand, it's the mediating space between mother and fetus, which means that there's never a fusion of maternal and embryonic tissues. On the other hand, it constitutes a system regulating exchanges between the two organisms, not merely quantitatively regulating the exchanges (nutritious substances from mother to fetus, waste matter in the other direction), but also modifying the maternal metabolism: transforming, storing, and redistributing maternal substances for both her own and the fetus' benefit. It thus establishes a relationship between mother and fetus, enabling the latter to grow without exhausting the mother in the process, and yet not simply being a means for obtaining nutritious substances.[112]

While a woman is pregnant, the placenta controls her hormone production. This ensures that the fetus is recognized as an other, but not as a hostile other to be rejected (as in the case of a transplanted organ). According to Rouch, "there has to be a recognition of the other, of the non-self by the mother, and therefore an initial reaction from her, in order for placental factors to be produced. The difference between the 'self' and other is, so to speak, continuously negotiated. It's as if the mother always knew that the embryo (and thus the placenta) was other, and that she lets the placenta know this, which then produces the factors enabling the maternal organism to accept it as other."[113] Sandra Steingraber compares the placenta to the symbiotic relationships between organisms and the synergetic ecology of a forest:

> The placenta is made up of the cells of two individuals—indeed, it is the only mammalian organ with this characteristic. In that sense, it is like the lichen. . . . Part fungus, part algae, lichens represent a symbiosis so complete that the two organisms are, for all intents and purposes, one creature. Likewise, a placenta is an intertwining of mother and child in the closest kind of embrace biologically possible. Yet, because the child's portion of the placenta is made up of cells genetically different from those of the mother, it should be identified as non-self by the mother's body and rejected, like any other implanted tissue.[114]

In fact, the internal anatomy of the human placenta closely resembles a maple grove: the long column of cells sent out by the embryo into the uterine lining during the first few weeks of pregnancy quickly branch and branch again until, by the third month of pregnancy, the treetops of an entire forest press up against the deepest layers of the womb. Meanwhile, the open taps of the uterus's spiral arteries send jets of blood spurting between those arboreal structures. As the mother's blood trickles through the canopy of placental branches all kinds of important transactions take place. Most notable, carbon dioxide and metabolic wastes are swapped for oxygen, water, minerals, antibodies, and nutrients. This is the same process by which the blood inside our own capillaries is cleansed and refueled but with one major difference: rather than relying on simple diffusion, the placenta actively pumps much of what it needs out of the percolating raindrops of maternal blood . . . Many larger molecules transported into the placenta are picked apart before they are allowed to cross the border between mother and child. Some proteins, for example, are disassembled and carried over brick by amino-acid brick. Then they are rebuilt on the other side.[115]

Steingraber describes pregnancy as a "subtle hijack[ing]."[116] "In all cases, a pregnant woman aids and abets her own infiltration."[117] Meanwhile Irigaray refers to this relation as a "placental economy" and deems it "almost ethical."[118]

Why is placental economy *almost* ethical? For some biological mothers, being disinherited from their bodies in pregnancy initiates this process in their lives as a whole. However, biological processes cannot stand in for conscious and deliberative acts. The exact relationship between the reflective mind and prereflective body, especially within pregnancy, is insufficiently understood. It could be that the body's reaction to pregnancy is already affected by the mother's attitude toward it. For example, in "Being Torn: Toward a Phenomenology of Unwanted Pregnancy," Caroline Lundquist notes that in denied pregnancies the "normal symptoms" of pregnancy, such as weight gain and morning sickness, are suppressed or reduced. This seems to imply that the mother's conscious acknowledgment of her pregnancy is necessary in order for it to take its "normal" course. In addition, denied fetuses are frequently underweight. This is an extraordinary finding since, as Lundquist also notes, the human female is unique in that, when they are limited, her body will direct resources toward the fetus first. This means that an unwanted fetus cannot be deliberately starved; the mother's body will be deprived first. Yet, in denied pregnancy, the fetus often *will* be denied vital nutrients, even when there are enough for both. Clearly, ethical mothering is not merely a compliance with biological precedents, but it is interesting to recognize that the body has its own way of negotiating the ambiguity between mother and child. Pregnancy, as ambiguous intersubjectivity, mirrors the relationship between a child and the mother(s) who raise(s) her. In *The Mask of Motherhood*, Ann Maushart comes to similar conclusions: "Indeed, by its very nature pregnancy is ambivalence made flesh. It's the classic instance of 'to have and have not,' 'to be and not to be.' The blurring of the boundaries of selfhood, of where 'I' leaves off and 'You' begins, is a primary biological fact of pregnancy. Later it will become the primary emotional reality of parenthood. The delicate yet strenuous agenda of symbiosis—to exist at once separately and in seamless, self-less merger with another—is the central paradox of motherhood."[119] The biological aspects of motherhood do not *cause or explain* ambivalence, but they are one more manifestation of the ambiguity between mother and child.

Due to the enigmatic nature of ambiguous intersubjectivity, many women attempt to understand it through creative nonfiction, poetry, and art. Rishma Dunlop does so in the essay "Written on the Body" and in the poem "Child": "Child of mine. Separate and strange. Separated in the beginning by childbirth, yet inseparable from my flesh. The recognition of the abyss between mother and child."[120]

> In my baby's eyes,
> I am locked
> in self-extension.
> I do not know
> where I finish
> and she begins;
> she is my pact
> with life and death
> and I must dance for her,
> so she will know the
> uncommon
> steps.[121]

Creative work, even when it is concerned with motherhood, often confronts the irony that reflecting on motherhood requires a step back from it. This is true at a practical level because children can be a tremendous impediment to thoughtful concentration. Ruth Nemzoff describes this in the following poem:

> My one-year-old peed on the floor
> My seven-year-old threw-up in the car

My nine-year-old has chicken pox
And I wonder
"Why can't I write my thesis?"[122]

However, a mother's creativity and her relationship to her children are not always in plain opposition when both are central to who she is. One mother courageously tries to explain this dynamic to her daughter:

> Adriane, age four, would sidle up to me: "Do you still love me when you're doing that work?" Or, more confrontationally, at age seven: "Which do you love more—me or your work?" I've been told that I was seriously remiss in my answer to the latter. But I had made a pledge of honesty to my daughters from the very beginning. And so I would say, "You can't make me choose. I have to do my work, not just for money but for me. But I have to be with you too. I love you and I love my work." My answer is deeply etched in memory by the surrounding cultural guilt that told me there was only one right answer: "I love you most of all my darling." But I was obdurate in my pledge to be honest. Truly, I loved my work, even as my daughters were at the core of my being.[123]

In her essay on maternal subjectivity, Mielle Chandler also describes the complexity of this dynamic. Chandler explains that the *act* of writing about motherhood, not just *what* is written, is an exploration of ambiguous intersubjectivity:

> To write a paper is to leave mothering, or, rather, it is to leave the type of subjectivity I engage in while mothering. A clean break is neither possible nor desirable, mothering being my topic, and so integral to my identity. Indeed, to leave it would be to become someone completely different. As I write, a child is asleep in the next room, part of me is still on duty, ready to battle dream monsters or change wet sheets, making a mental note to tell the babysitter (that is, the stand-in mother whose labor affords me, temporarily, a paper-writing subjectivity) that the child can't go swimming tomorrow (I'm worried the cold might turn into an ear infection), adding

granola bars to the shopping list. The process is one of traveling between an individuated and separated subjectivity which allows me to write, and an actively in-relation subjectivity (if it can be called a subjectivity) which is born of mothering. It is an existence fraught with tension, for while each site demands my attention, the former requiring quiet sustained concentration, the latter the alertness of a catcher behind home plate, neither allows me to inhabit the other adequately.[124]

Perhaps the most brilliant demonstration of a mother living out ambiguous intersubjectivity through writing is Julia Kristeva's "Stabat Mater." This piece is actually two intertwined essays: one presents a reasoned argument against the conceptions of motherhood as they are posited by science and Christianity and the other enacts the experience of being a mother poetically. The first account is often interrupted mid-sentence by the poetic, not to be taken up again until a few pages later. In this way, Kristeva presents the interconnected, yet contradictory nature of what she calls the symbolic (formal aspects of signification, such as judgment, grammar, and structure) and semiotic (rhythms and tones that discharge bodily drives, that channel the unconscious and provide catharsis). For Kristeva, to be a mother is to be on intimate terms with the semiotic, to have one's symbolic thought constantly interrupted. Recall Wolf's writing being halted by the hungry wails of her infant. In "Stabat Mater," Kristeva brilliantly demonstrates this disruption for the reader. What is more, Kristeva argues that the ongoing development of the symbolic requires intrusions of the semiotic. Thus, for Kristeva, maternity is not a mere disruption; it is the well of prereflective, unconscious, and embodied understanding from which the symbolic must drink.

Kristeva, a psychoanalyst and philosopher, highlights the great creative potential inherent in mothering, but classical psychoanalysis gives little consideration to its transformative powers. The mother is typically a static figure in tales of children's development who either enables or impedes separation.[125] A good mother provides care and stability; she holds on, but with enough slack so that the child can achieve gradual, age-appropriate independence. Having a child has largely been considered the pinnacle of her life, rather than instigation to further development. However, accounts of maternal ambivalence repeatedly affirm that motherhood entails dramatic transformations of the self. In particular, conflict with one's child guards against a potentially consuming intimacy and brings the mother's need for differentiation into view. Rich affirms that a mother must "struggle from that one-to-one intensity into new realization, or reaffirmation, of her being-unto-herself. . . . The mother has to wean herself from the infant and the infant from herself. In psychologies of child-rearing the emphasis is placed on 'letting the child go' for the child's sake. But the mother needs to let it go as much or more for her own. . . . It is not enough to let our children go; we need selves of our own to return to."[126] Maternal aggression is often a sign that the mother is in need of literal and psychological distance. Regarding the mother whose son will only sleep while holding her hand, Parker says: "But what she does not consider is the possibility that her desire to pull back, to reclaim her sense of bodily boundaries, may also signify an appropriate and productive move towards separation on her part as a mother."[127]

Negotiating the double binds of mothering can lead to homicidal and/or suicidal depression and acts of violent retribution or neglect. Yet Parker repeatedly asserts that maternal ambivalence, though painful, can be a psychological *achievement*.

> The mother's achievement of ambivalence—the awareness of her co-existing love and hate for the [child]—can promote a sense of concern and responsibility towards, and differentiation of self from, the [child]. Maternal ambivalence signifies the mother's capacity to know herself and to tolerate traits in herself she may consider less than admirable—and to hold a more complete image of her baby. Accordingly, idealization and/or denigration of self and, by extension, her baby, diminish. But the sense of loss and sorrow that accompanies maternal ambivalence cannot be avoided. Acknowledging that she hates where she loves is acutely painful for a mother.[128]

Insofar as she imagines mothering to entail only a picturesque mutuality, as long as she cannot reconcile herself to the full 360 degrees of her responses, ambivalence increases a mother's denial and rage. In a society that alternately romanticizes and condemns mothers, it is a brave overcoming of cultural denial to recognize the duality of maternal experience. The ability to think through ambivalence and ambiguity seems to make all the difference in whether or not a mother's rage can be checked. When reflection is possible, a woman can begin to understand herself and her *actual* child through their interactions, rather than trying to be the perfect mother. The child comes into relief as a particular, *concrete* other as one whose needs, desires, and perspective change radically as she develops. The acknowledgment of ambivalence makes possible this genuine discovery of relationship as it unfolds and sensitivity to the developmental needs of both mother and child; but the mother who denies her own complexity cannot expect to recognize her child's.

Reflection's importance to mothering tells us that being a mother is far more than being a womb, a placenta, or a breast. While these organs share a kind of symbiosis with a biological child, this is insufficient for appropriate responsiveness to a child. It does not keep one from responding to a child out of one's own projected desires. Furthermore, a child, no matter how beloved, is also radically other with discrepant needs, experiences, and desires. A sense of *unanimity* with one's child may motivate an ethical response, but *dispute* forces recognition of interpersonal divergence. When taken together, these attitudes entreat a mother to expand and practice self-knowledge, sound judgment, and problem-solving abilities in order to respond appropriately to her child.

Sara Ruddick provides a detailed account of maternal deliberation in *Maternal Thinking*. Ruddick believes that thought develops in the context of a given practice. Since each practice is directed toward particular ends, thought is cultivated in deliberating about the means to those ends. Over time, a certain style of thought will prove to be more conducive to achieving the ends of a given practice. In this way, mothering, as a practice, will engender a unique manner of thought in its practitioners—maternal thinking.

Mothering entails meeting three demands, according to Ruddick: to preserve the lives of children, to foster their physical, emotional, and intellectual growth, and to teach them to be socially acceptable. Thus maternal practice involves preservative love, nurturance, and training. To accomplish the tasks of mothering, mothers must strategize about how to meet the demands of caring for children. They make judgments, attempt to ask appropriate questions, assume certain standards for truth, consider their own methods, set priorities and aims, and consciously affirm certain values, thereby developing their intellectual capacities. Indeed, studies indicate that parenting stimulates brain activity and development in the prefrontal cortex.[129] It has been noted that women typically have a more developed prefrontal cortex, the part of the brain associated with complex thinking. But research suggests that men who are actively involved in child rearing can improve their own capacity in this area.

Maternal thinking involves the use of seemingly opposed faculties: reason, passion, and love, challenging the idea that reason is detached and impersonal. Reason is not there simply to dominate and control emotion. Emotion can be thought provoking, but it is also thoughtful and reflective in itself. The practical nature of motherhood's ends encourages concrete thought over abstraction. Dilemmas, conflicts, and struggles do not detract from this process, but rather they prompt the need for further thought.

Examples of how the practice of mothering encourages maternal thinking can be seen when we consider the complexities of training a child to be socially acceptable. To avoid ostracism, a child must be able to understand and get along with others in their society. However, a mother's own values may often be at odds with the dominant culture. Thus the dilemma may arise as to how she can train her children to be socially acceptable, while also teaching them to be people whom she herself will like and respect. This is further complicated by the fact that a mother's own values are not necessarily stable and may be brought into question by the very practice of mothering. In addition, a mother often finds that, as a child matures, her values may come to conflict with hers. For instance, the daughter of a pacifist mother may join the military, or a mother who values taking care of one's belongings may have a son who finds this to be materialistic. In such cases a mother must consider how she can respect her child's values while feeling passionately opposed to them.

Quoting the experience of Julie Olsen Edwards, Ruddick tells a striking story of maternal ambivalence to illustrate the importance of maternal thinking. Edwards looked forward to having her baby. Ruddick quotes her as saying: "You were such a wanted baby. I would rub my belly in awe of your growing. Sit motionless waiting for your kicks and stretches. Think of you, wonder about you, wait for you—totally caught in the miracle of your coming to life. First child, child of hope, child of commitment."[130] When born, however, the baby was sick with croup and bronchitis and could not sleep. Since the father had to both work and study, Edwards was frequently left alone with the baby. One night when the father could not come home and the baby was up yet again, Edwards woke up and went into her room:

> My knees buckle beneath me and I find myself huddled on the floor. "Please do not cry. Oh child I love, please do not cry. Tonight you can breathe, so let me breathe." And I realize my chest is locked and I am gasping for breath. I picture myself walking towards you, lifting your tininess in both my hands and flinging you at the window. Mixed with my choking I can almost hear the glass as it would smash and I see your body, your perfect body, swirl through the air and land three stories below on the pavement.[131]

Ruddick continues the story: "Sickened by her vision, Julie vomited and then felt calmer. After changing the baby's diaper and propping a warm bottle so that she could drink, Julie shut the door to the baby's room, barricading it against herself with a large armchair. Later that night, she carefully wrapped her daughter in blankets, carried her downstairs and rode a bus from one end of the city to another, 'thinking you would be safe with me if we were not alone.'"[132] Ruddick presents this example to demonstrate that, in mothering, passion works in concert with careful thought, attention, judgment, and deliberation. In extreme cases mothers may need to strategize to protect the lives of their children, even from themselves.

We have seen examples of mothers *thinking through* their conflicted feelings toward their children via art, nonfiction writing, and poetry. When

I use this expression *thinking through*, I mean to indicate that the emotions themselves contain an understanding, even if it is not yet fully formulated. This engagement between reason and passion is not a hierarchical relation. The emotions themselves must be contemplated and turned over in order to gain greater understanding of them. Yet it is not the place of reason, in these accounts, to merely squelch unruly emotions. As Kristeva has asserted, the unformulated semiotic can be a fount of insight, telling us things that our rational accounts have hitherto overlooked. Maternal thinking assists women not only to get past specific instances of conflict but also to understand the ambiguity of their needs for both distance *from* and intimacy *with* their children. This is true at all stages of parenting. Regarding successfully negotiating the efforts of adolescent girls toward differentiation from their mothers, de Marneffe says: "On closer view, the necessary balance between separation and connectedness relates, again, to the capacity for reflectiveness so basic to satisfying relationships between children and caregivers. The core of reflectiveness is the capacity to perceive the difference between one's own mind and another's and ultimately to be able to think about, and respond to, one's own and other's needs and desires . . . interpretive space, or the room for surprise, or the discovery of the other—is the heart of true relating."[133]

As psychiatrists Michael Kerr and Murray Bowen observe in *Family Evaluation*, it seems to be a common problem that when one person in a relationship withdraws the other person pursues. Likewise, if one person pursues, the other then withdraws. Kerr and Bowen's fundamental assumptions are that all people crave both intimacy and distance, but usually only recognize the need for one or the other at a time. The attainment of either more distance or more relation creates an appreciation for the other. The achievement of both intimacy and distance simultaneously is a paradox, but one that can be embraced nonetheless. A dyad has unlimited alternatives for dealing with this paradox, including achieving a satisfying balance within their relationship, vacillating between extremes, or finding their equilibrium in establishing a triangle with a third person. This tension, however, can also cause much pain and confusion, especially when it appears as a force beyond their control.

In "Distance and Relation," Martin Buber takes this thought further. He believes that in order for a connection to occur between two individuals, they must set each other at a distance. "One can enter into relation only with being which has been set at a distance."[134] This means that, paradoxically, the more aware a mother is of her child's separateness, the more striking their intimacy will be. Likewise, if she loses sight of their separateness, her enjoyment of their intimacy will be jeopardized. "One cannot stand in relation to something that is not perceived as contrasted and existing for itself."[135] When a mother realizes her child's impending departure, it is conducive to their current closeness. The briefness of childhood can make a mother's awareness of the end even more pressing. Buber says:

> Here and now for the first time does the other become a self for me, and the making independent of his being which was carried out in the first movement of distancing is shown in a new highly pregnant sense as a presupposition—a presupposition of this "becoming a self for me," which is, however, to be understood not in a psychological but in a strictly ontological sense, and should therefore be called "becoming a self with me." But it is ontologically complete only when the other knows that he is made present by me in his self and when this knowledge induces the process of his inmost self-becoming.[136]

The child's independence from the mother, the many occasions when she misunderstands her, the shortness of their time together, the mother's powerlessness to protect the child, and the permanent separation they will someday suffer are all partially responsible for the child's "becoming a self for/with" the mother. In recognizing the interpersonal abyss, a mother can induce the "process of [her child's and her own] inmost self-becoming."

Mothering imparts harsh lessons about the boundaries of the self— the constraints on what one can give to another, the limits of self-determination, and the way that others can become integral to the self.

These borders may remain permeable and ambiguous, expanding and constricting throughout the life of the relationship. When a mother is able to face her conflicted feelings and recognize the distance between herself and her child, then the tumult indigenous to mothering invites a *thoughtful* response to her child. Reflection helps to mediate between mothers' murderous fantasies toward their children and their commitment to protect them. Undermining the usual idealization of maternal self-sacrifice, it gives attention to the concrete and specific needs of a unique child and mother and thus supports both their efforts toward intertwined individuation.

Attention to maternal ambivalence brings to light more than mothers' contradictory emotional responses (love and hate) and impulses (to nurture and do violence). These mixed feelings—passionate rage, love, profound boredom, ecstasy, and so on—are not mere reactions. They contain wisdom of their own that tells us what is going on in a given situation and they act as forces that can bind as well as liberate. The impulse to shove a child away indicates the need for space, just as the desire to hold him close points to the awareness of abyssal separation. Rather than suppressing these lessons, we need to turn them over in our minds and conversations. It is time we realized, on a broad cultural scale, that if we care for the well-being of children we *must* care for the well-being of their caregivers.

Motherhood is an especially striking example for ethical theory because of the child's intense dependence and vulnerability, society's high expectations of mothers, and the shared embodiment between mother and child. Yet, as I will explain more fully in the coming chapters, the insights of maternal ambivalence are relevant beyond the mother-child relationship. Such claustrophobia, ecstasy, and longing are present in other relationships as well; and this teaches us that *both* intimacy and individuation are vital. Motherhood demonstrates, even in cases of cherished nearness, that one cannot overcome the insurmountable alterity of the other. Although there is a prereflective coherence between self and other, there is also an inherent dehiscence. Maternal experience also illustrates the possibilities for existential good or evil—we can dominate vulnerable people and/or escape our freedom in devotion to them. Nevertheless, whether or not one will be able to carry out her obligation depends on the larger political, cultural, and material context. Both individuals and society as a whole must embrace an active responsibility for the defenseless and provide caregivers with opportunities to engage in other meaningful activities. Our ambivalence toward others teaches us that the failure to help them is always a risk, but, recognizing the possibility of this failure, is itself a critical part of an ethical orientation.

In contrast to Pollaiolo's Charity, I propose the Janus head as a more accurate image of maternity. Janus, the Roman god of entrances and exits (especially those of the home), is a figure with two faces looking in opposite directions. The ambivalent mother holds two perspectives at once; this part of the comparison seems obvious. However, Janus is most like a mother in that he is always positioned at gates or doorways; he oversees new beginnings, paths and journeys; he has the gift of seeing both past and future. The maternal body is less a container for the self than a threshold for her own life and the life of another. As her "heart goes walking around outside," her self is both internal and external to her body. As her body also envelopes another, it both encircles and exceeds her. As she anticipates the expiration date on childhood dependence, the mother inhabits both the *here* of intimacy within and between bodies and the *there* of physical distance and the future. It is rooted in the present, but always anticipating that which does not yet exist. It is a relation of becoming. As the mother attempts to live in these contradictions, she may feel that she is suspended across a chasm. But true relating requires this simultaneous sympathy and reflective distance. It compels the recognition that while the mother's body is the child's first home, it is also her passageway to the wider world.

In the next three chapters I engage Levinas, Merleau-Ponty, and Beauvoir because they include key elements missing in a care ethics approach to mothers' ethical orientations. Each one contributes to a robust account of ambiguous intersubjectivity and describes (or suggests, in Merleau-Ponty's case) ethical life as inherently conflicted in a manner consistent with maternal experience. In the works of these three philosophers the subject is always already in relation. This is, of course, a claim already made by care ethics, but it is not explored in the depth that we see in existential phenomenology. The other is a primordial disturbance in any selfsameness I might enjoy. Our relationships to others are so intimate that they pervade us to the core, influencing our very perceptions. Moreover, this closeness is not only cause for mutuality and care but also rebellion, frustration, and even rage. Perhaps this ambiguity is even a central factor in the high percentage of murder-suicides in cases of purposeful filicide. Yet there is also a chasm between self and other, a radical alterity that Levinas has placed at the origin of ethics, a divide that keeps us from ever being one and the same. As in the 32 percent of cases in which a mother kills her children and *not* herself, the other might die while I live on.

Four

MATERNITY AS VULNERABILITY IN THE PHILOSOPHY OF EMMANUEL LEVINAS

Over the thirty years span in which Emmanuel Levinas wrote *Time and the Other* (1947), *Totality and Infinity* (1961), and *Otherwise Than Being or Beyond Essence* (1974), the feminine and maternity became increasingly central to his ethics. Feminist scholarship has demonstrated that there is tremendous ambiguity in his philosophy, including multiple solid interpretations of his work that are nevertheless at odds with one another. This makes it quite difficult to evaluate the feminist potential of his philosophy. Differences in interpretation frequently stem from whether or not Levinas is taken as describing real, empirical women or if he explains aspects of the feminine and maternal that could be present within everyone. When read as a descriptive phenomenology, his account is incomplete and may even be used to justify the submission of women and their isolation in the home. Were women to recognize themselves in his account of the feminine, they would find themselves in a merely supportive role. His depiction of maternity reveals a profound ignorance of its diverse forms and of the central importance of a mother's situation in her ability to care for her child. Nevertheless, I think that whether or not Levinas intends to describe real women may not be the most important question. Regardless of his intent, we can see a very clear appropriation of some patriarchal ideals in his philosophy. As he talks *about* femininity (whether or not he means women), he frequently fails to *address women* and their concerns.[1]

When read as a prescriptive (even if non-normative) ethics, the damage may be even worse. Since Levinas affirms the need to care for the other, even to the extent of self-abnegation, his ethic of infinite responsibility advocates a destructive asymmetry. Women traditionally hold the responsibility for care giving at the sacrifice of their own needs and are especially vulnerable to being oppressed under this ideal. Contrary to Levinas's expectation and intention, mothers find that when they live toward such an unbalanced servitude, it devastates their capacity to care for their children. His solution to conflicts of interest—submission to the needs of the other—denies his own great insight into intersubjective intertwining. And, although he sheds necessary light on the passive element in ethical agency, he does so at the cost of denying the importance of deliberative agency. Given this passivity—that, according to Levinas, being compelled by the epiphany of the face is *the* ethical motivator—and his acknowledgment that one may also feel incited to violence by others' vulnerability, it is unclear how he expects the peaceful impulse will win.

So why include Levinas in this book at all? Levinas's philosophy contains some vital insights as well as some critical half-truths that will contribute to a robust view of ethics. Chief among these is the coercive power that others' needs and vulnerability exert over us. This helps to make sense of why we might rebel with hostility against the dependency of others. Levinas also describes the radical alterity of others, which points to the insufficiency of mere empathy in meeting other's needs. This aggression and radical divergence between self and other receive insufficient attention in care ethics, but are starkly prevalent in accounts of maternal ambivalence. Ruddick's notion of adoption could also be augmented through consideration of the anachronistic temporality of ethical obligation described by Levinas. Both birth and adoptive mothers describe a baffling temporality to their commitment; it hesitates, resists, jerks forward, repeats itself, and yet also finds itself to be always already in place. While care ethics focuses on connection between mothers and children, Levinas makes sense of the feelings that children disrupt our enjoyment and self-possession. Care ethics understands that it is human to be dependent, but they do not make it as explicit that we depend on our dependents to make us ethical creatures.

A SKETCH OF FEMININITY AND MATERNITY IN LEVINAS

Levinas's Early Work

In *Time and the Other*, Levinas claims that solitude, which is "an absence of time," is overcome in the relationship with the other.[2] "The other is the future. The very relationship with the other is the relationship with future" (77). After a brief discussion of eros, Levinas concludes that one cannot overcome solitude via the erotic alone (84–90). The subject remains a subject; communication fails (88). Eros remains important, however, in that it leads to fecundity and "time is essentially a new birth" (81). That is, another's natality can give one time, the future. This birth is construed as the birth of a son to a father:

> How can the ego become other to itself? This can happen only in one way: through paternity. Paternity is the relationship with a stranger who, entirely whole being Other, is myself, the relationship of the ego with a myself who is nonetheless a stranger to me. . . . I do not *have* my child; I *am* in some way my child. But the words "I am" here have significance different from an Eleatic or Platonic significance. . . . The son is an ego, a person. Lastly, the alterity of the son is not that of an alter ego. Paternity is not a sympathy through which I can put myself in the son's place. It is through my being, not through sympathy, that I am my son.
>
> (91)

It is because the son is so similar to the father, because he seems to be the father himself, that the father identifies with him. However, the father also realizes that the son is not himself, he is a distinctly *other* person who will inhabit a future that the father will never know. This ambiguity in the relationship between father and son causes the father to recognize his own ambiguity in relationship to himself. Just as his son is both self and other to himself, so he too is self and other to himself. This is how the father discovers the truth of his subjectivity, that he is a stranger to himself.

In *Totality and Infinity*, Levinas recognizes women more explicitly than in previous work, although little is added to the feminine role in ethics. In this later book he identifies the feminine with voluptuosity and hospitality. Feminine voluptuosity is important to ethics because its *telos* is the birth of the son, and this birth initiates the father into ethical responsibility. Still, the feminine beloved appears without a voice and without a face, which means, in Levinas's scheme, that she has no ethical standing and no personhood.

> The beloved is opposed to me not as a will struggling with my own or subject to my own, but on the contrary as an irresponsible animality which does not speak true words. The beloved, returned to the stage of infancy without responsibility—this coquettish head, this youth, this pure life "a bit silly"—has quit her status as a person. The face fades, and in its impersonal and inexpressive neutrality is prolonged, in ambiguity, into animality. The relations with the Other are enacted in play; one plays with the Other as with a young animal.[3]

In this passage, the feminine other is a plaything, not taken seriously in her face or voice, having no will, an irresponsible nonperson.

While feminine hospitality is vital to ethics, it does not admit women to participate in ethics. Hospitality is important, according to Levinas, because it prepares the place for the welcoming of the needy stranger. The woman provides that which the man has to offer—good soup, a warm fire. Yet ultimately it is the man's place to invite the stranger into the home, while the woman remains invisible and inaudible: "And the other whose presence is discretely an absence, with which is accomplished the primary hospitable welcome which describes the field of intimacy, is the Woman."[4] Though the absent-presence of the woman is essential, she remains an ethical nonentity. She is neither receiver of the stranger, nor is she received. She sets the stage in her domestic service and then fades into the background.

In this exposition I have referred to the feminine as interchangeable with empirical women, however, feminist scholars actively debate whether or not the feminine represents *women* for Levinas. [5] Some scholars argue that he is not referring to concrete women but to a principle that can be found, to a greater or lesser extent, in every person. There is some support for this interpretation in *Ethics and Infinity* (1982). Speaking of *Time and the Other*, Levinas says: "Perhaps, on the other hand, all these allusions to the ontological difference between the masculine and the feminine would appear less archaic if, instead of dividing humanity into two species (or into two genders), they would signify that the participation in the masculine and the feminine were the attribute of every human being."[6] This statement seems to indicate Levinas's own uncertainty about the meaning of the feminine and the masculine. Even though it was spoken by Levinas eight year after the publication of *Otherwise Than Being*, many scholars see it as an invitation to rethink the meaning of the feminine in his work. Diane Perpich argues: "In fact, the feminine is nowhere identified by Levinas with concrete, really existing beings. It is not a set of characteristics or qualities attributed to a certain class of beings (namely, women); it is not a *type*, of which individual women would be tokens."[7]

However, I argue that there are passages in which Levinas may be identifying the feminine with empirical women. Consider this translation of a quote from "Judaism and the Feminine" (1969) in which the feminine, woman, and wife are described interchangeably:

> To light eyes that are blind, to restore to equilibrium . . . should be the ontological function of the feminine [*du feminine*], the vocation of the one "who does not conquer." Woman [*La femme*]does not simply come to someone deprived of companionship to keep him company. She answers to a solitude . . . the strange flow of gentleness must enter into the geometry of infinite and cold space. Its name is woman [*femme*]. . . . The wife [*La femme*], the betrothed [*fiancée*], is not the coming together in

a human being of all the perfections of tenderness and goodness which subsist in themselves. Everything indicates that the feminine [*le feminin*] is the original manifestation of these perfections, of gentleness itself, the origin of all gentleness on earth.[8]

La femme has been translated alternately as the wife and woman. It could also be that Levinas intended *la femme* as an archetypal (rather than empirical) woman. However, the translation of *la femme* as wife, when it is juxtaposed with *fiancée*, is appropriate; and this would seem to point toward actual women. Ultimately, the idea that the feminine is the origin of all gentleness on earth, whether it is intended as archetypal or empirical, is problematic is either case. I disagree with Perpich that Levinas is not describing a set of characteristics attributed to women, since his description is perfectly in line with a historical, patriarchal image of women. Real women are continually held up against these ideals. Thus, regardless of Levinas's *intention*, he perpetuates a limited view of woman as nurturer, erotic beloved, idealized wife, and mother. Woman's kindness, her passivity, and her conjugal vocation to be the precondition for all virtue.[9] On this view, women's engagements in activities outside the kitchen, bedroom, and nursery are a threat to the very existence of ethics; women's submission is an ethical imperative. This becomes even more disturbing when paired with Levinas's statements that exclude women from participation in the ethical relation. Recall that the feminine beloved's face "fades," that she has "quit her status as a person."[10] As Irigaray says, "For him, the feminine does not stand for an other to be respected in her human freedom and human identity. The feminine other is left without her own specific face. On this point, his philosophy falls radically short of ethics."[11] If Levinas's philosophy is to be read in this light, then it would not just be inadequate as a theory of ethics, but would be, itself, unethical. It not only validates but also enforces the traditional feminine role that has been oppressive to so many women. Moreover, since women are without a "face," this leaves them no recourse to seek justice in response to their exploitation.

Tina Chanter acknowledges a slippage between Levinas's references to the feminine and to women. "So while Levinas cannot be accused of definitively or intentionally marking the inferiority of the feminine sex, there are ways in which this inferiority is marked in his texts, despite his best intentions."[12] In spite of this equivocation, she believes that Levinas ultimately intends to upset the traditional values of egoism and male dominance.[13] Donna Brody affirms that Levinas can be read along either interpretation (feminine = woman, or feminine = an aspect of everyone), but that each is problematic in its own way. If we read Levinas as referring to women when he speaks of the feminine, then we must condemn his patriarchal characterization. But if we interpret the masculine and feminine to be aspects in each of us, then he lacks any theory of sexual difference. Given Brody's estimation that he vacillates between these two positions, it would seem that Levinas remains *dually* problematic for feminism.

Some scholars applaud Levinas's ethics as providing a necessary *feminine* counterpoint to the overly masculine history of ethics for its emphasis on care, charity, and the home; but ultimately the concern remains that it may not be sufficiently *feminist*. Levinas's account is problematic whether he intends to speak of actual women *or* of a feminine principle. His characterization of femininity is anachronistic; it evokes and affirms conditions that feminists have rightly denounced as oppressive. Levinas maintains that he does not want to "ignore the legitimate claims of feminism."[14] Yet I see no evidence that Levinas is even familiar with their arguments. Feminists have many landmines to negotiate within his texts because he draws on sexist portrayals of women for his characterization of the feminine. In his early works, Levinas writes from a heterosexual, patriarchal point of view.[15] The significant players are all masculine; the feminine and maternal are always depicted from a masculine point of view. In *Time and the Other*, the father's relationship to the son is the central human relation; woman's most important function is to provide a son. Mothers and daughters do not participate in egoism or ambiguity, in time or the future. In this work Levinas disappoints women in the classic way, he fails to acknowledge their participation in humanity. *Totality and Infinity* adds little to improve this. Even though Levinas seems to try to honor women in his descriptions of hospitality, they are still regarded within their traditional restrictive role. Furthermore, his characterizations of voluptuousness are overtly sexist; insofar as the feminine beloved is voluptuous for Levinas, she has no ethical status.

Otherwise Than Being, or Beyond Essence

In *Time and the Other* and *Totality and Infinity*, ethics and the emergence of self-understanding begins with the birth of a son; in *Otherwise Than Being*, they begin before birth, in the maternal body. In contrast to Levinas's previous focus on the *"concrete situation"* of paternity,[16] he turns to maternity *as a metaphor*: "The evocation of maternity in this metaphor suggests to us the proper sense of oneself. The oneself cannot form itself; it is already formed with absolute passivity. In this sense it is the victim of a persecution that paralyzes any assumption that could awaken it, so that it would posit itself for itself. This passivity is that of an attachment that has already been made, as something irreversibly past, prior to all memory and recall."[17] Levinas is not referring to the fetus or child when he says that the self is passively formed via maternity in a time irrevocably lost to memory. While the mother gives physical existence to the child, the child bestows the mother with the "proper sense of oneself," "complete being 'for the other'" (108). It is the mother (with child) who is this absolute passivity, the "victim" who is the prototypical ethical subject, the sufferer of this inevitable amnesia; and *pregnancy*—"the gestation of the other in the same"—is the archetype for responsibility (105). In this view, to be a mother means to be "devoted to the others, without being able to resign," "incarnated in order to offer itself, to suffer and to give" (105). The maternal metaphor helps Levinas to make clear how subjectivity, properly understood, is "an irreplaceable hostage"; how as ethical beings we are *all* victimized, held captive, and persecuted (124). He believes that serving the other in this way is not an alienation from oneself because "I am summoned as someone irreplaceable" (114). That is, ethical responsibility is the true foundation of the self; the self is epiphenomenal to its responsibility for the other. Thus, in this text, pregnancy and motherhood are the image of all ethical relations. It is significant, however, that maternity is invoked by Levinas specifically *as a metaphor*. Men are not excluded from these relations as women were from the "concrete situation" of paternity in the earlier works.

Why does Levinas shift his focus from paternity to maternity? In *The Gift of the Other: Levinas and the Politics of Reproduction*, Lisa Guenther points out that by introducing maternity Levinas addresses his previous "neglect of the flesh."[18] "The maternal body *gives herself*, her skin stretching to make room for an Other; she not only provides but actually *becomes* a dwelling-place for the stranger. For Levinas, the maternal body gives despite herself, without having chosen to give."[19] It is true that the maternal body gives to the fetus without the mother needing to will it. The very calcium from her bones will be leached for the developing baby if necessary. Empirical facts such as these can support the belief that instances of involuntary generosity exist.[20] The example of maternity also helps Levinas to break more completely from the notion of the independently existing ego than he could before. When Levinas works from the example of the father, the subject always exists (albeit imperfectly) before the child arrives, but the mother embodies permeability to the other. In *Time and the Other*, the self begins in solitude until the other makes communication and, most importantly, *time* possible; in *Totality and Infinity*, the other gives one ethics and freedom. However, in *Otherwise Than Being*, responsibility for the other is the source of one's own uniqueness; the child is conceived before the mother can be born.

There is no simple conclusion about the feminist (or sexist) potential of *Otherwise Than Being*. Initially it might appear to be a dramatic overturning of Levinas's earlier ideas. A relational ontology takes hold. Many feminists have also proclaimed the necessity of such an ontology. Care ethicists, for one, argue that individualist notions of the self stand in stark denial of the mother-child relationship, and of the fact that our existence is dependent on others before we can even entertain the possibility of solipsism. In *Otherwise Than Being*, ethics and intersubjectivity seem to be a matriarchal affair. However, it is a problem that women gain their selfhood and ethical standing through bearing children. Is a woman's identity to be entirely derivative? What about women who are childless by choice, by chance, or because of infertility? What about adoptive mothers who did not gestate the other within? Are they not models of the "proper" sense of oneself? Are women not to be as valued for their other achievements and abilities? Is their independence only a *barrier* to their ethical responsiveness?

Another problem with *Otherwise Than Being* is that its characterizations of maternity seem to be at odds with women's reproductive freedom. For example, Sonia Sikka notes that abortion could never be ethical under Levinas's picture of maternity: "Notice what happens, in this regard, if one introduces, into the portrait of ideal maternity painted by Levinas, the image of a woman who, in order to secure her own well-being, chooses to eject the other whom she harbors within her body. From the perspective of Levinas's ideal mother, must not this latter woman, whether or not her choice is guaranteed by the law of the land, be judged as monstrous? It must, I think."[21] Obviously, the fact that abortion becomes a quintessentially unethical act in Levinas's philosophy would be problematic for many feminists. (I will have more to say about this later in this chapter.) Likewise, if a woman is able to use birth control, give her children up for adoption, or even ask for help with the children, then this gives the "irreplaceable hostage" a way out of her bondage. Even when women *do* want children, they do not necessarily want to become their hostage. In *Maternal Ethics and Other Slave Moralities*, Cynthia Willett expresses concern that the figure of the mother in Levinas is one of a self-sacrificing martyr that "effaces the female self. . . . The verticality of the approach of the Other obliquely renders the mother supine before her infant's every demand."[22] This problem is compounded by the fact that "Levinas never theorizes the maternal subject as the recipient of care."[23]

Levinas's image of the suffering, captive mother looks even worse when we pair it with his language, which is evocative of sexual violence. As Chloé Taylor indicates:

> Evoking as Cynthia Willett has noted, both the "violation" of a feminized subject and "pregnancy against one's will," Levinas writes that the subject

has the other "in his skin," is "penetrated-by-the-other," and this involuntarily, "despite itself," "a sacrificed rather than sacrificing itself." One is "torn up from oneself in the core of one's unity," in a "nudity more naked than all destitution," and "whitens under the harness" in the "form of a corporeal life devoted to expressing and giving. It is devoted, and does not devote itself." Drawing intentionally or otherwise on metaphors of concubinism, rape and involuntary impregnation, this subject is responsible for the other who is not in "his" skin, like a phallus, like a fetus, whether or not "he" chose to have it there.[24]

Even if we assume that Levinas does not intend to advocate violence against women, what is to prevent his philosophy from being used to rationalize misogyny? In light of these concerns, Levinas's nod to feminism in *Time and the Other,* is not very reassuring[25]

Is it possible that, while he invokes women's servitude as a metaphor, Levinas does not intend to enslave women or romanticize their oppression? Certainly, his supporters could argue that he does not intend to single women out. What Levinas says of the mother, he intends for every person: not just mothers' subjectivity, but *everyone's* subjectivity is derivative. It is not that women, in particular, are passive helpers, rather ethical "agency" is constituted in radical passivity and responsiveness to others. Thus, if women appear submissive in Levinas's account, this actually demonstrates that they are ethically empowered. Levinas's allies could argue that although women find themselves in their traditional place in Levinas's writings, he elevates the status of these roles. In this regard, Levinas is in agreement with care ethics theorists who seek to affirm the value of feminine caretaking.[26]

However, it is important to recognize that the call to prostrate oneself has diverse implications for people who are differently situated. While it may be a radical move to obligate a privileged person to serve others, to make this decree to an exploited person or group merely reinforces an oppressive status quo. In this regard, Levinas's ethics can be charged with the same criticism that the valuing of "feminine tenderness" conceals a "slave morality."[27] Some feminists argue that to value feminine ethics is to affirm the oppressive conditions in which they arise. In this view, women's position of social inferiority has damaged them morally, and such women should serve primarily as cautionary tales. What of mothers who do not want to submit to the "proper sense of oneself" according to Levinas? What about women's desires for political freedom and support in caregiving? Is it never justified to desire some independence, to have a life that is not completely commandeered by the other? Levinas might say that these women suffer from the same delusion as Western philosophy.

> To be without a choice can seem to be violence only to an abusive or hasty and imprudent reflection, for it precedes the freedom non-freedom couple, but thereby sets up a vocation that goes beyond the limited and egoist fate of him who is only for-himself, and washes his hands of the faults and misfortunes that do not begin in his own freedom or in his present. It is the setting up of a being that is not for itself, but is for all, is both being and disinterestedness. . . . Responsibility for the other, this way of answering without prior commitment, is human fraternity itself, and it is prior to freedom.[28]

Feminists have struggled for the rights to make choices, to enjoy freedoms, to be "for-herself" in spite of the compulsion to live for others. Historically, their existence as "responsibility for others" has not been the basis for participation in "human fraternity," but rather exclusion from it. Levinas does not acknowledge that the desire for freedom from the demands of the other is contextualized by different material, historical, and cultural situations.

The best defense for Levinas comes from Lisa Guenther's *The Gift of the Other* and "'Like a Maternal Body': Emmanuel Levinas and the Motherhood of Moses." Guenther argues that Levinas is not trying to dictate women's roles, rights, or behavior; instead, he describes some parallels between the responsibility of mothers and the obligations we all bear. She supports this conclusion through analysis of some of the biblical passages cited by Levinas.

In *Totality and Infinity*, Levinas repeatedly invokes Isaiah 49 where God compares himself to a nursing mother.[29] In this verse, god is addressing Zion who has asked why God has abandoned her (Isaiah 49:14):

Can a mother forget her nursing child,
> Or show no compassion for the child of
> her womb?
Even these may forget,
> Yet I will not forget you.

(ISAIAH 49:15)

In reassuring Zion that he will take even better care of her than a nursing mother, god speaks to her as a daughter who still needs the care of a mother. God is a feminine other to Zion and the care that he gives to her can be passed onto the next generation. The implication is that a mother's care is received from her own mother and is to be paid forward to her children, grandchildren, great grandchildren, and so on; the mother-child relationship extends beyond the present dyad to an indefinite number of generations forward and backward.

Zion is much like the imperfect mother to whom God compares himself. She does not feel compassion for her children, she has forgotten them, and they are like strangers to her.

Then you will say in your heart,
> "Who has borne me these?
I was bereaved and barren,
> Exiled and put away—
> So who has reared these?
I was left all alone—
> Where then have these come from?"

(ISAIAH 49:21).

However, God's extended generosity applies not only to one's own descendents but to strangers as well. Thus God's generosity allows Zion to care for her own children, even if they seem like strangers. Similarly, Zion can care for the stranger as though it were her own child. "In this sense God becomes for Zion like a 'feminine Other' in *Totality and Infinity*; She gives the capacity to welcome strangers whose arrival on the doorstep commands me to give beyond my present resources for hospitality."[30]

Interestingly, when Levinas refers to Isaiah, he is discussing *paternity*, not maternity. To describe the father in *Totality and Infinity*, he draws on the model of a mother—Zion—who relies on the strength and compassion of god the father. For Guenther, this is key to undoing Levinas's seeming rigidity regarding sex and gender roles: "When Levinas cites *Isaiah* 49 in his discussion of paternity, he makes room for a reader to suggest that the 'father' in paternity might also be a mother, that the 'son' might also be a daughter, and that the parent's own parent, God, might be like a mother who inscribes the memory of his child on her hands, and never fails to show 'compassion for the child of her womb.'"[31]

Guenther's claim that Levinas was probably not thinking of maternity in strictly biological terms is further supported by Levinas's references to Moses in *Otherwise Than Being*. The context for this discussion comes from the book of Numbers:

> Moses heard the people weeping throughout their families, all at the entrances of their tents. The Lord became very angry and Moses was displeased. So Moses said to the Lord, "Why have you treated your servant so badly? Why have I not found favor in your sight, that you lay the burden of all this people on me? Did I conceive all these people? Did I give birth to them, that you should say to me, 'Carry them in your bosom, as a nurse carries a suckling child, to the land that you promised on oath to their ancestors'?"
>
> (NUMBERS 11:10–12)

Moses clearly invokes motherhood as the model of responsibility. Like Zion, Moses is alienated from the people he is supposed to care for; though he did not conceive or give birth to these people, he must care for them like a mother for her baby. Guenther indicates that in these passages invoked by Levinas caring for others is not strictly mothers' work; it is only *similar* to it: "In *Otherwise Than Being*, Levinas suggests that responsibility for the Other obligates me to bear her 'like a maternal body' (OB 67; AE109), even though she is a stranger whom I have 'neither conceived nor given birth to' (Num. 11:12, cited in OB 91; AE 145). . . . In this sense, maternity would not refer to a biological or social imperative for women to reproduce, but rather an ethical imperative for each of us to bear the stranger *as if* she were already under my skin, gestating in my own flesh."[32] Guenther argues that Levinas's use of Moses also points to the multiple quasi-mothers that made Moses' own maternity possible. First, there is god, who acts as a mother to Moses. Second, there is the pharaoh's daughter who finds Moses as a baby and raises him like her own son. Most interestingly, even Moses's biological mother, Jochebed, is only able raise him by acting *like* a mother to him. According to the narrative in Exodus, at the time Moses was born, the Israelites were beginning to outnumber their Egyptian captors. So Pharaoh ordered that newborn Israelite boys be killed. Jochebed, unwilling to kill her son, placed him in a basket that gently carried him to the river. After the pharaoh's daughter finds and adopts Moses, she unknowingly hires the child's biological mother as his wet nurse. Just as Ruddick claims, even Moses's biological mother must adopt him. Among these biblical figures who hold the predictable maternal ideal, maternal responsibility is often unbidden, shifting, and unpredictable.

Guenther argues that the appearance of such a wide variety of mothers in these important biblical passages suggests that Levinas's figure of maternity should not be thought of narrowly. She claims that Levinas denies "any strict correlation between women and mothers, or even between motherhood and responsibility."[33] Thus, she concludes,

> The maternity of Moses and of god suggests that one is not born, but rather becomes *like* a mother. The biological fact of incarnation in a female body need not condemn me to a destiny of childbirth, nor does incarnation in a male body free me from the responsibility of bearing the Other "like a maternal body." In this sense, maternity becomes more than a social role or fixed biological destiny, either of which would bind the identity of women to childbirth and child rearing. By understanding maternity *ethically* as the embodied response to an Other whom I may or may not have "conceived and given birth to," we recognize maternity as a locus of responsibility, without expecting women to bear that responsibility alone.[34]

For Guenther, Levinas neither sentences women to maternity and gender-based obligations nor frees men of ethical responsibility.

Another of Guenther's key claims is that since the ethical calling makes one *like* a mother, then this means that the ideal of mothering need not map onto its reality. Indeed, she acknowledges that while Levinas does not characterize motherhood realistically, she considers this is an appropriate gap between *what is* and *what ought to be*:

> Motherhood is not always a patient, generous, compassionate practice of ethical substitution. Maternal generosity can spill over into resentment and anger, even to the point of becoming violent. Women and men who raise children, like anyone else, have moments of impatience, fatigue, distraction, selfishness; these moments do not indicate a failure of particular mothers to reach the ideal of maternal sainthood, but rather a confirmation of the difficulty of ethical life and the vulnerability of human creatures who are both limited and responsible for Others who push their limits. If the human were unfailingly saintly, there would be no need for hagiography nor even for an ethics of responsibility; knowing the good, doing the good, and being good would all neatly coincide. . . . To be *like* a maternal body even when you are one is to admit a gap between mothering as an ethical and political practice, and the mother as an ontological, biological, or social identity. By recognizing that it is possible to be *like* (or also *unlike*) a mother even while one "is" a mother, we recognize a difference between ontology and ethics, between being and the otherwise-than-being.[35]

For Guenther, while we can aspire to ethical sainthood, lapses are not really a failure; they are confirmation of our all-too-human limitations. While Levinas helps us to *know* the good, we remain limited in how good we can actually *be*. Mothers, like other mortals, are imperfect, but the figure of the maternal remains instructive for Guenther. The biological relation to another is not the *cause* of one's responsibility toward that other, but the gift of care that is passed from one generation to the next is the condition for the possibility of ethics. In stating that ethics is similar to the maternal relationship, Guenther argues, Levinas affirms the possibility that even a stranger can be taken in and cared for like family. As in the poignant ending of the *Grapes of Wrath* in which a young mother whose baby has died feeds a starving man from her breast, by making one into a mother, the child calls on a radical generosity that can be applied to the stranger.

While Guenther embraces the fallibility of mothers, nowhere does Levinas acknowledge that a mother might lose patience, act selfishly, be violent toward her children, or be limited in any way in her capacity to give. He never equivocates; the mother's vulnerability, permeability, responsibility, and devotion are complete. In my view, this oversight is even more stark given his invocation of Zion and Moses. Both figures are fallible and unwilling mothers, but Levinas does not mention these limitations in his characterizations of maternity. On the contrary, the mother that Levinas presents is more like the god that supports Zion and Moses when they falter. She is the mother who is always compassionate and always remembers her child.

It might seem that in order to read Levinas as acceptable to feminists our best option is to claim that when he speaks of the feminine, women, and the maternal, he does not intend to invoke or implicate actual female-identified people. In fact, Levinas equivocates a great deal on this point, and arguments on both sides are probably valid. Yet, in some respects, this is beside the point. The deeper concern is that he advocates values that naturalize gendered roles as they have been prescribed by patriarchy and elevates them to an ethical imperative.

As I argued in chapter 3, mothers' feelings toward their children are much more complex than Levinas would have us believe. Although he attempts to illuminate the meaning of maternity in *Otherwise Than Being*, his ignorance of the conflicts between mother and child is striking. Nevertheless, it could be argued that Levinas's use of maternity is only metaphorical: he does not overtly claim to give an accurate description of maternal experience; thus it is inappropriate to critique him on this basis.[36] In contradicting this claim, Jacques Derrida's analysis of philosophical uses of metaphor in "White Mythology: Metaphor in the Text of

Philosophy" is helpful. As Derrida asserts, the philosophical use of metaphor is never neutral; philosophers *actively establish* the meaning of the metaphors they employ.

Derrida argues that, in philosophy, a metaphor "promises more than it gives."[37] And this is clearly the case in *Otherwise Than Being*, where the metaphorical characterization of motherhood obscures its actual complexity in favor of an obfuscating and worn-out straw figure. Derrida argues that such figures are treated as modes of expression of the idea, but in fact they have a history of their own.[38] In fact, the biblical mothers are not, as Levinas treats them, evidence of their lasting truth. They are examples of a *historical* understanding of motherhood, which, in this case, reveals that certain one-sided tropes of maternity are very long-standing indeed. They cannot be relied on to provide the truth of motherhood, but are instead evidence of past attitudes and impressions.

Derrida claims that when philosophers use metaphors they are not used as mere ornaments; they are treated as an *essential*, internal link to the phenomenon they are used to elaborate. [39] This is definitely true in Levinas's case. He practices a circular hermeneutics between his notions of motherhood and ethical subjectivity in which elaboration on one phenomenon is also intended to elucidate the other. In the end, we "know" motherhood differently than we initially did, and, to a great extent, this is overdetermined by Levinas's theory of subjectivity. The *image* he presents of motherhood is really a concealed metaphysics, an essentialist depiction of motherhood. Levinas has not so much unveiled a truth as he has created one.

Especially given his apparent ignorance of the complexities of motherhood, it is disturbing that Levinas appropriates the maternal perspective and attributes it to all ethical beings. Derrida poses this concern in speaking of Levinas's quotation of the Song of Songs, "[the] phrase translated and quoted . . . it is torn from the mouth of a woman, so as to be given to the other. Why doesn't he clarify that in this work?"[40] This question could be directed to the references to Zion as well. Guenther also mentions this worry with regard to the use of Moses: "We could argue that by referring to Moses as an example of maternity—especially in the absence of any female examples of maternity—Levinas appropriates the female capacity to give birth to the male body."[41] This anxiety is put most vehemently by Donna Brody: "It might also be objected that the female capacity for child-bearing is poached, colonized, and substituted from her to him where it figures as a kind of agamic or parthenogenic [sic] reproduction of other-in-the-same. In other words, she may be read as redetermined according to the most eminent meaning—or she may be read as *altogether* obliterated, exiled even from the significance of maternity."[42]

It is a common and tiresome practice of male philosophers, poets, and other meaning makers to borrow the experiences of women via metaphor. In Beauvoir's "Myth" chapter in *The Second Sex*, she gives innumerable examples of how men make woman the other, then identify with that otherness. At least since Plato's *Theaetetus*, maternal experience has been exemplary for philosophy, and yet has been appropriated in a way that excludes women from that which they represent. (Women only give birth to *bodies*, while *men* give birth to *ideas*.) Male philosophers have displayed their womb envy in a manner that denigrates the unique capacities of female bodies. A slightly more authentic response than this reaction formation can be seen in the essay "Yogurt Couvade" by Rob Hardy as he describes the experience of observing his pregnant partner's body:

> She crossed the room, loose-jointed and front-heavy, and lifted the yellow maternity blouse up over her head. She looked like a daffodil gone to seed, the withered corona twisting above a plump ovary bursting with seed. As she dropped her blouse into the laundry basket, the brown line under her belly button reminded me of the rust stain in the bathtub stretching from leaky faucet down to the drain. Her body itself was a living metaphor, a noun curled up inside another noun. It was only by metaphors that I could relate to the experience of pregnancy. As a man, I could never experience the thing itself, from the inside; I could only press my hand against the skin of metaphor.[43]

Hardy claims that it is only through *metaphor* that men may understand the experience of pregnancy, but this is not fully the case. They may also understand it by asking and listening to women themselves. When philosophers make metaphors about pregnancy, childbirth, and mothering, divorced from any serious dialogue with those who have lived through it, they don't come to understand women's bodily experience, they *appropriate* it, and often very poorly.

Ultimately, one should approach Levinas's maternal metaphor with skepticism, but this is not to say that Levinas is of *no* use to feminists and others interested in maternal ethics. As Guenther points out, to be *like* a maternal body is to have dependents that are very hard to shake. The fetus is the vampiric primal parasite—a profound dependency that can suck the nutrients from one's blood—that suggests the grasping and bottomless needs of others. The biblical quotes referenced by Levinas demonstrate the frustration one might feel at the burden of responsibility for others even though Levinas's passages on maternity do not directly thematize this problem. Oddly enough, he is most helpful in understanding mothering when he is either not speaking directly of mothers, women, or the feminine or when they are only implied peripherally. One example is his theory of an ambiguous intersubjectivity that is a more accurate reflection of mothers' lives, as discussed previously in chapter 3.

AMBIGUOUS INTERSUBJECTIVITY IN LEVINAS

Proximity and Subjectivity

In *Otherwise Than Being* Levinas denies the idea that subjectivity is primarily self-coincidence or self-knowledge and posits that "a subject is a hostage."[44] For Levinas, subjectivity is incarnate consciousness; it is exposure and proximity to sensibility and to the other.[45] The other is not just another point of view, but a primordial disturbance in my appropriation and enjoyment of the world. Levinas's subject is radically open, destabilized, and, above all, vulnerable. Even sensibility is a radical disruption of the self: "[Sensibility] is being torn up from oneself, being less than nothing, a rejection into the negative, behind nothingness; it is maternity, a gestation of the other in the same."[46] For Levinas, to be a subject is to be incessantly undermined by one's proximity to the other. While some may find Levinas's language hyperbolic, it has much in common with firsthand accounts of motherhood. As explained in chapter 3, mothers frequently find themselves hostages to their children. A mother sometimes experiences her child as a monstrous *Other* who keeps her captive, threatens her body, eats away at her vitality, upsets her sense of self, invades her home, and commandeers her life. In many respects, the birth of the child is the death of the mother as she has known herself.

According to Levinas, proximity to the other is substitution, giving one's material substance to the other, putting myself in her place not as an alter ego, but as the food in her stomach. And my obligation to feed the other is absolute. If we are to understand Levinas concretely, proximity begins in the intertwining of bodies. In pregnancy and nursing, the mother's bodily boundaries expand to include another. Her body, her blood, and much of her food become sustenance for the other. Yet mothering remains an embodied experience, even beyond these short stages. As argued in chapter 3, older children—adult children as well—get under their mother's skin in both positive and negative ways.

Proximity describes the way the other draws me toward her, to provide for her, to give over myself. Yet, for Levinas, it extends beyond mere physical contact or seeing the other, beyond "handshakes, caresses, struggle, collaboration, commerce, conversation,"[47] beyond consciousness or knowledge. This undermining proximity can even persist in spite of a child's death. Recall the mother in chapter 3 who describes her experience of her adult child's death: "A woman named Elizabeth Stone wrote that having a child is 'to decide forever to have your heart go walking around outside your body,' Suzanne says. 'That's what becoming a parent is like. And now I've lost that piece of myself.'"[48] Like this woman, Levinas describes the other as the pulsing of breath and heartbeat: "the body which makes giving possible makes one other without alienating. For this other is the heart, and the goodness of the same, the inspiration or the very psyche in the soul."[49] This statement seems sentimental enough to be embroidered on a pillow. But in fact it is gruesome and cruel for another to be one's heart, goodness, breathe, psyche, and soul. All that might serve as the center of oneself belongs to another. It is to have one's vital organs outside one's body exposed to all the cruelty and indifference in the world, to be "an open cauldron of blood."[50] To become a mother is to be turned inside out and never to be quite right-side in again. According to Levinas, there is no "right-side in;" there is no subject that exists before vulnerability to others. The self only arises in relation to others; there is no preexistent, pure self to return to. Thus, to revert to oneself, to try to find oneself as autonomous, would be to find no self at all; "to revert to oneself . . . is to be like a stranger."[51]

Alterity, Ethics, and Freedom

While it is as near as any intimacy, proximity occurs across an abyss and cannot overcome the insurmountable alterity of the other. Describing the encounter with radical alterity is a central focus in *Totality and Infinity*. Levinas explains that the face of the other indicates the presence of an unknown infinity. Realized suddenly, it provides an abrupt leap of under-standing. However, this understanding is not *knowledge* of the person, as though one suddenly knows what that person is about. On the contrary, it is an awareness that one does *not* know, that this person is wholly other to oneself, utterly unique. The other's infinity is always more than one comprehends it to be. When one sees the other as a body, a personality, a set of thoughts, symptoms, behaviors, attitudes, or feelings, these are signs of an unreachable world. According to Levinas, to have a proper respect for the other means to recognize that one can never fully know him. The mere presence of the other challenges the free reign of one's spontaneity, because when one moves about the world without regard for the other, one bumps into her. Thus the face tells us that to be impetuous is to be violent. The face *exposes* the other to us. To expose another is to leave him in a dangerous situation; to expose a baby means to leave it outside to die. Thus the other's face reveals him to us, but he is revealed as unprotected. For this reason, Levinas says "the epiphany of the face is ethical."[52] The appearance of infinity in the face is accompanied by the awareness of vul-nerability and thus the call to be ethical.

Mothers provide numerous accounts of the ethical epiphany of the face. In *Down Came the Rain: My Journey Through Postpartum Depression*, Brooke Shields describes the moment when she felt suddenly compelled to protect and care for her daughter:

> At the hospital exit, as expected, we were met by cameras and comments. The photographers asked the baby's name and tried to get a close-up of our five-day-old daughter. I was struck by how much of an intrusion this was. I was accustomed to it, but it felt different where she was concerned. It felt extremely personal and even more invasive. Suddenly I didn't want them to know her name, nor did I want the cameras in her little face. I regretted putting her through this but felt as if I didn't have a choice. A wave of fear washed over me, and I instantly thought something was going to happen to her out there. I sought the refuge of the locked car. Rowan didn't cry once. As I entered the waiting vehicle, a smile frozen on my face, Rowan looked straight up at me as if to say, "Mom, these people are too close." I looked down at her and was taken aback by the directness of her gaze. Once again, she seemed wiser than I felt. Silently I made a promise to protect her.[53]

Shields's daughter is exposed by the cameras. They reveal both the vulnerability and the wisdom that are displayed on her face, and, in Levinas's terms, Rowan's infinity calls Shields to protect her.

Eva Kittay describes a similar experience in "'Not *My* Way Sesha, *Your* Way, Slowly': 'Maternal Thinking' in the Raising of a Child with Profound Intellectual Disabilities." Kittay describes an interaction between her disabled daughter Sesha and Sesha's caregiver Peggy. Peggy had not wanted to take the job, but agreed to a trial week. During this week, Peggy was working on some exhausting physical therapy with Sesha:

> I sat her down in her stroller and sat down on a park bench. I realized I was simply too exhausted from the effort. I thought, how am I going to do this? How can I possibly do this job? When I looked down at Sesha and saw her little head pushed back against her stroller moving first to

one side then to another. I couldn't figure out what she was doing. Until I traced what her eyes were fixed on. She had spotted a leaf falling, and she was following its descent. I said 'Thank you for being my teacher, Sesha. I see now. Not *my* way, *your* way, slowly.' After that I fully gave myself over to Sesha. That forged the bond.[54]

In both these accounts the women feel compelled to care for the child after witnessing the child's vulnerability and uniqueness. As Levinas predicts, the child herself induces the mothering person to care. Their vulnerability has a certain power: "Infinity presents itself as a face in the ethical resistance that paralyzes my powers and from the depths of defenceless eyes rises firm and absolute in its nudity and destitution."[55] George Kunz has named this phenomenon "the paradox of power and weakness."[56] The weak person is powerful because she calls the powerful to respond to her needs. "The child and the ill person calling me to their aid, those suffering poverty inspiring my compassion, even the irresponsibility of an enemy urging me to help them become responsible points to this paradox."[57] In this sense the ethical person is rendered passive by the other. This susceptibility compels protection. Sesha's observance of the leaf and the expression of wisdom in Rowan's eyes are indications of their unique perceptions of the world, suggestions of an inaccessible infinity. For Levinas, to have a proper respect for the other means to recognize that one can never fully know her. In both cases the mothering person witnesses something in the face of the child—wisdom, intentionality, and also vulnerability. This epiphany compels her to give herself over, to promise to protect.

According to Levinas, we are constantly constrained and motivated by others. Yet this does not mean that we are not free. No person is a sovereign subject, and the ability to assert one's will against others is domination, not freedom. Instead he argues that freedom is made possible by ethical responsibility. "Conscience . . . is the revelation of a resistance to my powers that does not counter them as a greater force, but calls in question the naïve right of my powers, my glorious spontaneity as a living being. Morality begins when freedom, instead of being justified by itself, feels itself to be arbitrary and violent."[58] Ethics is freedom called into question, but freedom is also defined by the opportunity to be ethical. Freedom begins when one suspends her rights in favor of another, when he controls his caprices, when she restricts her reign. Freedom is not an exertion of power, but the exercise of restraint. And this possibility for ethical freedom is not recognized until one notices that one has already violated the other. Levinas writes: "The first consciousness of my immorality is not my subordination to facts, but to the Other, to the Infinite."[59] The other causes me to realize my "moral unworthiness,"[60] that I have already harmed her; thus the possibility of restrained freedom becomes possible. It is the reconfiguring of "innocent spontaneity" as arbitrary, violent, and shameful. This is a paradoxical opportunity; one's response to the other is not *enforced*, but it is *coerced* by her vulnerability. In Shields's case, as for many others, she cares for her daughter even when the difficulty of doing so leads her to suicidal and murderous thoughts.

Peggy's choice to become Sesha's caregiver was also freely obligatory. In caring for Sesha, she enters voluntary servitude. Kittay says that Peggy had not wanted to take the job, but that by the end of the one-week trial "it was already nearly too late to quit. Sesha had worked her way into Peggy's heart."[61] As Kittay describes it here, Peggy's commitment to Sesha was not a simple choice. She had not wanted to take the job, and it was not forced on her, yet she felt compelled to take it. Her adoption of Sesha, in Ruddick's terms, had an odd temporality to it. "It was *already nearly* too late too quit." In fact, the time to commit or quit would have been right then, at the end of the one-week trial. While she could point to a moment of commitment—when she witnessed Sesha's infinity—it was also as though the obligation began before any deliberate or reflective choice.

The awkward temporality of adoption, whether by a biological parent, a paid caregiver, or a legally adoptive parent, describes for Levinas the temporal structure of all ethical commitment. He does not think that responsibility arises from commitment, but that commitment already presupposes obligation. "The relationship of proximity . . . [is] anachronously prior to any commitment."[62] Ambiguous intersubjectivity, characterized by both proximity and alterity, is obligation. And obligation is perpetually anachronistic; its time is never the present. Indeed, this could also be said of Shields's commitment to Rowan. When she pledges to care for Rowan outside the hospital, she is already obligated to her. But when did this obligation begin? When she decided to conceive? When she began fertility treatments? When Rowan was conceived? When she was born? There is no clear answer, no clear origin for her obligation. "This is an an-archic plot, for it is neither the underside of a freedom, a free commitment undertaken in a present or a past that could be remembered, nor slave's alienation, despite the gestation of the other in the same, which respon-sibility for the other signifies" (105). Obligation is an-archic; it is without *arché*. An *arché* establishes the beginning of linear time, but we are always already within time. We cannot witness the *arché*.

For Levinas, proximity and alterity form an irresolvable ambivalence, "not a dialectical unity of unity and difference" (83). Proximity cannot overcome alterity; alterity cannot abolish proximity. Dialectical unity is a mere exercise of reason (84), but the relation to the other precedes and defies reason. This ambivalence is "the thorn in the flesh of reason, which is the shudder of subjectivity" (84). Subjectivity seeks unity with itself; it seeks understanding, but self-coherence would eliminate the necessary intrusion of the other. As there is no unity with oneself, there is also no unity to be found with the other; this would imply reciprocity between two equal terms—self and other. But the relationship to the other is al-ways asymmetrical, "going to the other without concerning oneself with his movement toward me" (84). The other and oneself are not two magnets that are mutually drawn to one another. The other is a magnet that draws oneself, an uncharged piece of metal, closer. Yet, despite this attraction, these two never overcome the chasm of alterity. According to Levinas, the allure of ethics is never satiated.

ETHICAL AMBIVALENCE

Levinas thinks that the other appears to be in conflict with the self when one understands the self through enjoyment and self-creation (72–73). From this perspective, alterity is the interruption of self-fulfillment and nourishment. Levinas illustrates this repeatedly with the example of taking the bread from one's own mouth to feed another. To be sure, mothers frequently blame an inability to nurture themselves (both literally and metaphorically) for the loss of their independent selves. Recall Naomi Wolf's lament for "the self that is not food for others,[63] but eats and drinks the world" and Jane Lazarre's "mother knot":

> I turned to that self inside of me, that girlwoman who had once been all I needed to know of myself, whom I had fought to understand, to love, to free—I turned to her now and I banished her. Into a protective shell tied in a knot, she retreated, four, five, six times a day, whenever Benjamin wanted to nurse. Soon, even when I sought her, she would not come, but began to stay out of reach longer and longer, sometimes not reappearing for whole days. For if she was present when the baby needed me, she was of necessity pushed aside, sent to go hungry. She who had been in my life, whom I know I had to nourish daily in order to be fed in return, hid for weeks, hoarding her gentleness and her strength, placing no gifts in my outstretched hands.[64]

The part of one's identity that finds itself in satisfaction of its own needs, in the "singularization" of the ego, encounters the needs of others to be an intrusion.[65] As I demonstrate in chapter 3, mothers frequently set aside self-creation, fulfillment, and expression to respond to their children's needs, and, as Levinas predicts, it is a responsibility that cannot easily be shifted to another. Yet, for Levinas, the self that mourns her lost independence has a mistaken view of freedom; we are only free insofar as we are ethically obligated to others.

Although we may remember a commitment made to the other, the obligation that is its origin is immemorial. This emphasizes the passivity of the ethical "agent," but it also stresses that the obligation arising from the other's face is not *causal*. Causal relationships presuppose a linear temporality, but obligation does not submit to this temporality. Ethical obligation has no present, it has always already happened. So, although we are compelled by it, we are not *determined* by the face of the other.

The opportunity to be ethical establishes freedom, and with this freedom comes the possibility to abandon or even to murder.

In *Totality and Infinity*, Levinas describes murder as a paradoxical power. Murder seeks to annihilate the other, but the other's face "expresses my moral impossibility of annihilating."[66] This "impossibility" is not complete; it contains within it the option to kill. Yet it remains unclear in Levinas's philosophy how murder can actually occur. In "Peace and Proximity" he writes: "By starting with this extreme straightforwardness of the face of the other (*autrui*), we have previously been able to write that the face of the other in its precariousness and defenselessness, is for me at once the temptation to kill and the call to peace, the 'You shall not kill.' The face which already accuses me makes me suspicious but already claims me and demands me."[67] On the one hand, it is because violence would be so easy that the command "thou shalt not kill" makes sense. The other's vulnerability, therefore, is no straightforward call to be ethical. We may want to make way for the passing cyclist and also to push him down. We may want to soothe the crying baby and also toss her out the window. Mothers are often shocked by their desire to do violence to their children, especially when they are small and defenseless, but weakness can inspire malice as well as nurturance. On the other hand, according to Levinas, the impulse to harmonious coexistence is more fundamental: "War presupposes peace, the antecedent and non-allergic presence of the Other; it does not represent the first event of the encounter."[68] He thinks that one does not usually feel hostile toward the other; that existence does not chafe us. Pacifism, not murder, is precedent. To say that war presupposes peace begs the question; it does not explain how violent impulses can be overcome.

In these passages Levinas seems to deny the fact that ethical living is often a *struggle*. Certainly his language is the language of struggle, and it would not be accurate to say that he is dismissive of the devastating impact of the other's demands. Yet his simple assertion that war presupposes peace seems rather weak when juxtaposed with mothers' accounts of murderous rage. Although he understands that maternity involves sacrifice, that it undoes a person at both visceral and metaphysical levels, he is relatively unconcerned with the devastation caused by the demands of the other. In his account the mother is always compassionate, she always remembers and cares for her child. In this respect, Levinas thinks that ethics is not really a struggle at all, that there should be no maternal ambivalence. In his model, then, mothers ought to be rather poor ethical exemplars. At this point, we are compelled to return to the earlier question of whether or not Levinas is describing what *is* or what *ought to be*. Is he describing the way mothers are, even if incompletely? Or is he describing the way that they should be, even if his demands are impossible?

It is a common and justifiable reading of Levinas to consider his work as descriptive phenomenology. In the *Stanford Encyclopedia of Philosophy*, Bettina Bergo begins her discussion of Levinas as follows:

> Levinas's philosophy has been called ethics. If ethics means rationalist self-legislation and freedom (deontology), the calculation of happiness (utilitarianism), or the cultivation of virtues (virtue ethics), then Levinas's philosophy is not an ethics. Levinas claimed, in 1961, that he was developing a "first philosophy." This first philosophy is neither traditional logic nor metaphysics, however. It is an interpretive, phenomenological description of the rise and repetition of the face-to-face encounter, or the intersubjective relation at its precognitive core; viz., being called by another and responding to that other. . . . He proposes phenomenological description and a hermeneutics of lived experience in the world. He lays bare levels of experience described neither by Husserl nor by Heidegger. These layers of experience concern the encounter with the world, with the human other, and a reconstruction of a layered interiority characterized by sensibility and affectivity.[69]

If we are to take Levinas as an existential phenomenologist, as describing intersubjectivity and its implications for ethics, then he does capture the intersubjective ambiguity between mother and child, but he does not recognize that infinite demands actually *deplete* us, making it difficult or impossible to serve the other. His attitude is reminiscent of Melanie Klein, who claims that a girl's desire for a baby, present from early childhood, diminishes the aggressive tendencies she might feel toward her actual baby. Her child's helplessness and vulnerability fulfill her lifelong desire to offer "more love than can be given to any other person."[70]

Perhaps Levinas slips between describing the world as it appears and as it should be. As Lisa Guenther argues, there may be an appropriate gap between *what is* and *what ought to be*.[71] This is also a viable interpretation, as there is much in Levinas that is not verifiable through phenomenological description. Consider the fact that, for Levinas, our responsibility for the other is infinite. Most people hold that there are limits to one's responsibility for others. One can only be responsible for what one is aware of and when one has the power and resources to help; it is fair to weigh one's own well-being against what would be sacrificed for the other; we cannot be responsible for what others choose to do. In short, people generally believe that what we *should* do is limited by what we *can* do. The question of what we *can* do may be addressed empirically. However, for Levinas, the *ought* exceeds the *can* and is therefore outside the purview of descriptive phenomenology.

Yet if Levinas describes an ideal to which mothers can aspire, then he lets us down in this regard as well. Idealizations of mothering only make its practice that much more difficult. When mothers think they should be able to give to their children infinitely and are unable to do so (as no human could), they feel guilty, angry, worthless, ashamed, depressed, and fearful of the judgment of others. These feelings paralyze mind and body, making it difficult to respond to one's child at all, let alone appropriately. As Alice Miller writes in *For Your Own Good: Hidden Cruelty in Childrearing and the Roots of Violence*: "I cannot listen to my child with empathy if I am inwardly preoccupied with being a good mother; I cannot be open to what she is telling me."[72] Levinas's denial of maternal ambivalence, or any substantial ethical conflict, takes him too far from *what is* to help us with *what ought to be*. His idealization of maternal sainthood is out of touch with the struggles of mothers, and this will only be counterproductive. What is more helpful to women is an accurate understanding of their own experiences; for this the maternal icon must be dethroned.

In *Torn in Two: The Experience of Maternal Ambivalence*, Rozsika Parker describes ambivalence as an achievement that can ultimately enhance the mother's responsivity to her child. However, this requires that she let go of the maternal ideal and recognize her own limitations in the face of the tremendous weight of her responsibility. One mother, Selma, attests to this: "Last week when he wouldn't stop crying, I shook him, which I know is a really bad thing to do. Afterwards I thought about it, and found myself admitting, really for the first time, the full weight of his dependence on me—acknowledging that the baby is entirely dependent on me for twenty-four hours a day—and what a huge drain that is. The funny thing is that since then his crying has not got to me in the same way."[73]

As Selma lets go of the maternal ideal and its accompanying guilt, she recognizes her own limitations. This diminishes her hostility toward her son and enables her to respond more appropriately to his needs. Parker states: "I think the conflict between love and hate actually spurs mothers on to struggle to understand and know their [child]. In other words, the suffering of ambivalence can promote thought—and the capacity to think about the baby and child is arguably the single most important aspect of mothering."[74] Thoughtful recognition of one's limitations as a mother is essential to a practical ethical response to one's child. Yet, as I will argue, deliberation is a critical dimension of ethical life that Levinas mistakenly denies in his emphasis on the passivity of ethical responsiveness.

Understanding maternal ambivalence is not only necessary to the psychological well-being of individual women. There is a political dimension to the naturalizing of maternal care as well. By eliminating any sense of conflict that mothers might justifiably feel against their children, Levinas supports a status quo that demonizes women who fail at mothering. In "Monster Stories: Women Charged with Perinatal Endangerment," Anna Lowenhaupt Tsing describes the persecution of women in the courts and the media who may have been responsible for the deaths of their perinatal infants. One example is "Marlene Harris," a twenty-five-year-old maid. She had planned to give her baby up for adoption, but was having second thoughts at the time labor began. She was afraid that the baby would be taken away from her before she got to hold him. Instead of driving to the hospital, she went to a motel where she gave birth alone. Cold and disoriented after giving birth, she got into a warm bath with the baby and fell asleep. The baby drowned. Tsing also describes the case of "Donna

Sloan," a nineteen-year-old college student who gave birth to her baby in her dormitory bathroom. She had not realized she was pregnant and thought that her labor pains were gas. The baby was stillborn. At the heart of the legal cases against each of these women was the assumption that she should have "direct intuitive knowledge gained from her bodily experiences. Within this convention, a woman unaware of her pregnancy or labor must be a physical or psychological anomaly."[75] The courts and media believed that Donna Sloan could not have been unaware of her pregnancy and Marlene Harris had to have known she put her baby at risk by getting into the bath with him. Maternal instinct should have alerted them to the correct course of action. Thus, they wondered: "What kind of a woman could endanger her own offspring at the moment of birth, the moment which should excite her most maternal sentiments? This question generated its own answer: Only a person completely lacking in parental—and human—sensibilities could commit such an act. To those who considered their cases, these women were, as one prosecutor put it, 'unnatural,' 'bizarre,' and 'without basic human emotion.'"[76] The accusation that women like Sloan and Harris are "without basic human emotion" is the flip side of the claim that mothers are, or should be, always able to respond appropriately to their children.

Levinas denies that there are any practical limitations in women's abilities to care for their children. Yet there are innumerable factors that play into this capacity to care for another, including the material, physical, and psychological. Decent caregiving takes skill, thought, emotional intelligence, and resources. Recognition of these necessities is absolutely critical to providing proper support for mothers and children. In many cases the abuse, neglect, and abandonment of children is a failure of the social system that ought to support mothering work, not a failure of mothers themselves. For example, currently in Great Britain decreased social support for families with disabled children has put many families in the tragic position of having to place their disabled children in institutions. Riven Vincent, a mother of a child with severe quadriplegic cerebral palsy and epilepsy, was recently quoted in the *Guardian* as saying: "I have no wish to put my daughter into a home. We want to look after her, all I am asking for is a little more support. Without this we simply cannot cope and nor can families up and down the country just like ours."[77] In order for children to receive proper care in our society, the limitations of mothers absolutely *must* be recognized.

When mothers lack the resources to care for a child, giving that child up may be an important act of ethical mothering. The options available to *some* women (alternatives that Levinas denies) include giving a child up for adoption or having an abortion. In "Abortion Is a Motherhood Issue," Judith Arcana argues that when a woman has an abortion she is not eschewing accountability; she is, in fact, taking responsibility for the life of her child:

> [Women] considered the conditions surrounding the mother, and the probability of her child's life being a strong one, including joy, good work, health, maturity, and usefulness. In their considerations then, as now, women sometimes judged that that probability was too slight, uncertain or simply absent. Their choices, like our own when we abort were never made in a vacuum; even in our time, in this woman-hating, mother-blaming society, there is always the decision made on balance, weighing both the potential years of the child's life and the mother's struggle to nurture it against great odds.[78]

Sometimes it is simply not possible for a mother to provide for a child's well-being. Ending a new life, instead of leaving it to an existence of pain, may be the most ethical choice. Above all, the choice to have an abortion is not a means to escape responsibility; many women find it to be the best way to meet their obligations. In Levinas's universe, we are not allowed to think about our limitations in caring for others, and so these factors never come into play.

Levinas's metaphorical use of the maternal body as a model for ethics is obsolete in the face of some women's abilities to have abortions, use birth control, or give their children up for adoption. He prefers the image of the maternal body since it gives without *willing* to give. We need not dispense with the idea that the obligation to care begins before deliberation, but this is an insufficient account of ethical motivation. The ethical response does not always take the form of an epiphany. The daily drudgery and joys of mothering require all of one's creativity and deliberation. It requires a daily commitment that is usually more mundane than transcendent, but Levinas does not speak to the earthly tedium of breasts leaking milk at inopportune moments, the smells of dirty diapers and sweaty socks, and fights over appropriate clothing and curfews.

It is not getting pregnant that makes one a mother, in this way being *like a maternal body* is not a comprehensive image for ethical responsibility. Being pregnant does not necessarily compel one to take care of a child. It is the daily commitment to take care of a child that makes a woman (broadly defined) into a mother. Importantly, this expands the idea of who can be considered a mother. A woman who gives up her child for adoption or has an abortion can still be regarded as a mother, if she does so with a sense that this is the best way to provide for her child. Adoptive mothers are just as authentic as those who give birth to their children and perhaps provide a better metaphor of ethical responsibility. People seem more willing to understand the adoptive child as initially a stranger toward whom one might have mixed feelings, but for whom one feels drawn to care due to her vulnerability. Adoption asserts that choice is involved in the care of a child; it is not automatic, immediate, or grounded in maternal instinct. As Kittay says, it is a bond, a duty, and a commitment all in one. It is both voluntary and compelled, both reasoned and felt. Of course, Ruddick's solution might not appeal to Levinas, since his vision of a subject as a hostage means that she is "obsessed with responsibilities which did not arise in decisions taken by a subject 'contemplating freely.'"[79] The paradigm of adoption might make it clearer that an epiphany is an insufficient motivation for ongoing commitment to care for another.[80] While Ruddick wants to ally ethical behavior with ethical *thought*, Levinas seems largely indifferent to this. Yet maternal experience with the phenomenon of adoption confirms that a conscious commitment to the other works in concert with the repeated realization of the other's infinity and vulnerability as well as other factors. There is no reason why we must affirm epiphany at the cost of denying the centrality of deliberation and daily commitment to ethical life.

———————

Levinas's account of ambiguous intersubjectivity is, in some aspects, accurate to the experience of mothers. Ethical obligation indicates the limits of self-knowledge and disrupts the complacence within ourselves. It is an interruption of personal projects and aspirations. It shows how we are deeply indebted to others, not just as a baby is indebted to his mother, for providing for our needs, securing our survival, and flourishing. We are also indebted to those who need us, those who interrupt our flourishing, our enjoyment, and compel us to face our responsibility to others. Ultimately, ethics can lead us to a more robust identity, an identity that is not just seeing who we expect to see when we look in the mirror and finding a consistent unity across time. Others force us to recognize that we must continually take up the question Who am I? As Levinas says, "The oneself is a creature, but an orphan by birth or an atheist no doubt ignorant of its Creator, for if it knew it it would again be taking up its commencement."[81] We are all infants in the sense defined by Winnicott, one who "cannot understand what he owes to his mother."[82] True, we cannot fathom what we owe our mothers, but we also cannot comprehend what we owe the other who upsets our self-satisfaction.

While some scholars applaud Levinas's ethics as replacing a tradition of individualism with a relational ontology, as providing a necessary *feminine* counterpoint to the overly masculine history of ethics, the concern remains that it may not be sufficiently *feminist*. In Levinas's account women gain selfhood and ethical status in their roles as housekeepers, lovers to men, and mothers. He has been thoroughly and rightly criticized by feminists for these failures and therefore no simple appropriation of his ideas is possible. If Levinas's hagiography is meant to show us the way to be good mothers, then his efforts are also potentially destructive. It is more helpful to mothers to understand the reality of their situation, and, while Levinas's account of ambiguity does contribute to this aim, his ignorance of maternal ambivalence does not.

Unfortunately, Levinas appropriates the maternal perspective without consideration of the experience for actual women. Careful attention to the phenomenon might have helped him to avoid his easy appropriation of patriarchal values. Instead, he ignores vital aspects of maternity that are part of all of ethical life—the desire to flee from one's obligations, fantasies of murder and suicide, and feelings of rage. Mothers have the intense desire to protect, to even sacrifice themselves for their children, but these same children can become sacrificial victims both in fantasy and on suburban front lawns. Even when a mother loves her child as deeply as Levinas predicts, this does not eliminate the intensity of her conflicted feelings. Mothers do have an individuated sense of self that existed before the birth of the child and that does not exist only to serve, but also to flourish in and of itself. And the flourishing of a woman can sometimes be *at odds* with the raising of children, even when it is also necessary to it. Levinas's philosophy could be amended by taking *adoption* as the paradigm example. This removes the assumption that mothers will be the automatic and natural caregiver. In this view, all children are strangers—orphans in need—and their care is not to be taken for granted by anyone.

Levinas believes that conflicts of interests can be resolved by yielding to the Other; the self has no robust ethical standing. To take this stance is to ignore one of his own best insights, our simultaneous proximity and distance. If we take seriously the intertwining of self and other, it is not possible to simply put the other before oneself. An unbalanced asymmetry renders ethics impossible, especially when there is no broader context of social support. He misses the important insight, articulated by Kittay and other care ethicists, that the caregiver must be provided for. In order to be edible, one must also eat. Levinas is missing several critical components that can be furnished by Merleau-Ponty and Beauvoir: a more careful logic of ambiguous intersubjectivity, an understanding of how asymmetrical relations can nevertheless be balanced, the factor of social context and support, and, finally, a better idea of how ethical failure relates to ethical success.

Five

MATERNITY AS DEHISCENCE IN THE FLESH IN THE PHILOSOPHY OF MAURICE MERLEAU-PONTY

D ehiscence occurs when a body opens and spills its internal contents. It happens naturally when a plant comes to reproductive maturity: an anther opens displaying its pollen to the wind; a fruit splits and sheds its seeds; the operculum of moss, fungi, or algae is discarded to release its spores; the seedpods of milkweed burst releasing their tiny downy parachutes. Dehiscence also means the opening of a wound along a surgical suture that causes fluid to leak. Much like being a mother, dehiscence indicates a breach in one's internal integrity that can be life giving and/ or life threatening.

Maurice Merleau-Ponty appropriates the term *dehiscence* to describe one aspect of our ontological and existential condition.[1] He thinks that each person experiences a prereflective coherence between herself and the world, between himself and others. We do not feel ourselves to be the author of our experiences; they come to us as though written "anonymously" as *real* beyond individual perception. This sense of the world's veracity is supported by our social life. Although we do not share the exact outlook of others, our differing perspectives converge in one and the same world. This means that together we inhabit a sensuous unity, but we also suffer a division. While the other is not hidden from me, locked within interiority, she also is not fully laid out for my examination. These structures, described phenomenologically in the *Phenomenology of Perception*, become ontological in *The Visible and the Invisible*. In his later work, Merleau-Ponty deems the things of the world, including people, to be expressions of one *sensible* flesh. While flesh establishes our continuity, it also involves an inherent dehiscence between the sensing and the sensed and between the self and the other. This is not dualism, but a description of the fundamental ambiguity of our relations.

In this chapter I propose that maternity can be aptly characterized as a case of dehiscence in the flesh. From pregnancy to caring for adopted and older children, the mother-child relation illustrates how human beings coconstitute the world with one another. The mother, in particular, is the child's first environment. Some scholars worry that in taking the maternal as flesh, the mother is equated with nature and her subjectivity is erased. However, this concern is eased if the concept of flesh is properly understood as involving dehiscence, an *écart*, a necessary separation. For Merleau-Ponty, reversibility is never a perfect or harmonious unity. Likewise, the mother's relation to her child, as well as her relation to nature, is necessarily ambiguous.

To elaborate on Merleau-Ponty's notion of ambiguous intersubjectivity, I explicate his use of Hegel's "immanent logic of human existence." This discussion of Hegel also helps to explain how Merleau-Ponty differs from theorists discussed earlier and highlights the implications of his philosophy for our considerations of ethics. The ambiguity of our intersubjective relations, as described both by Merleau-Ponty and in maternal accounts, results in an ambivalent ethical orientation, contingent as it is on negotiating the interrelated yet discrete interests of the self and the other. Although Merleau-Ponty never wrote an ethics, he describes a life world that comprehends intersubjective ambiguity, provokes the question "What should I do?" and indicates that the answer will often be conflicted and founded in ambivalence.

AMBIGUOUS INTERSUBJECTIVITY
AND MATERNAL FLESH

In the *Phenomenology of Perception,* Merleau-Ponty emphasizes our sense of coherence with the world. Prior to reflection, one does not stand out as situated over and against the world and others. We are immersed in a reality whose qualities and meanings appear as both shared and self-evident: "My consciousness . . . is hardly distinguishable from what is offered to it."[2] We inhale the scents of the world, drink its fluids, eat its fruit, we bump into its hard surfaces, absorb its heat, we ache at its beauty and gag at its ugliness, all without a thought of doing so. The sensory is open to me "through a gift of nature, with no effort made on my part" (*Phenomenology* 251). When I put on some music, *there is music.* When someone hits me, *there is pain.* When I eat, *hunger is sated.* There is no immediate distinction between myself and these perceptions. There is no need to imagine an *I* or a *world* over and against one another, in order to perceive the sensory phenomena. "Nothing here is thematized. Neither subject nor object is *posited*" (281). Even when we do abstract ourselves from this world via reflection, our primary engagement with it is already presupposed and carries on in the background. While I entertain abstract thoughts like my own nonexistence or the illusory quality of reality, the ground retains its solidity, the air remains breathable, coffee still tastes bitter. I do not experience myself as the enactor of these facts, 'I' remain *anonymous.* I am the blind spot in my vision that allows me to believe in the world naively, to not see my own seeing.

For Merleau-Ponty, the sense of continuity with the world extends to other people as well. In the natural attitude others are not minds trapped in an inaccessible interiority. We are all *sentient* creatures in a *sensible* world, and we meet in this public world that we both hold in common. Imagine that my gaze shifts from a book on the table to my friend sitting in front of it. She is as apparent to me as the book. As with the rest of the world, I take for granted that she is as she appears to me. This is *not* to say that to perceive another person is the same as perceiving an inanimate object. I recognize hers as another view upon the world. Though we perceive the world differently, it is, nevertheless, a common world we behold. At the Chicago Institute of Art my friend and I stand on opposite ends of a sculpture of Hyacinth. I am examining the girlish curls tied in a knot on the top of his head. He notes how the right toe delicately scratches the left calf. He sees what I do not, yet I never question if the sculpture is one and the same. Together we take for granted that *there is* the sculpture of Hyacinth. We do not "conceive our perspective views as independent from one another; we know that they slip into each other and are brought together finally in the thing" (*Phenomenology* 411). I know my friend by virtue of our inhabiting this same self-evident world. "We are brought together in the one single world in which we all participate as anonymous subjects of perception" (411). When riding our bikes through town, without speaking, my friend and I both stop at an intersection. She observes, as well as I do, that it is a dangerous street to cross. We hear the roar of cars together, feel the breeze they blow in our faces, and smell the exhaust. The street, like the museum, and every other place a human being can go is a public space that we inhabit together. Typically, I experience her in this world, which is common to us both, without needing to conceptualize her as either separate from or similar to me.

Of course, our sharing a world in common does not mean that it always strikes us in the same way. I listen to a new band by myself, but I am eager for my friend to hear it. I try a new dish, and I want her to try it. Why? It is not because her impressions will inevitably be the same as my own. Rather, her differing view adds another dimension to things that they could not have for me alone. Merleau-Ponty explains: "No sooner has my gaze fallen upon a living body in the process of acting than the objects surrounding it immediately take on a fresh layer of significance: they are no longer simply what I myself could make of them, they are what this other pattern of behavior is about to make of them. . . . Already the other body has ceased to be a mere fragment of the world, and become the theater of a certain process of elaboration, and, as it were, a certain 'view' of the world" (*Phenomenology* 411–412).

Without the other, objects have only one "side" at a time, the side that I see of them, but through another's pattern of behavior—the things that she laughs at, her expressions of exclamation, what she prefers and dislikes—things gain an added contour for me. Her gestures speak to me directly, conveying meaning without need for reflection. As Merleau-Ponty notes, the gesture is understood immediately; there is no need for analogy or interpretation. "The gesture does not make me think of anger, it is anger itself" (*Phenomenology* 214). Consider, for example, your earliest childhood memory of a parent getting angry with you. The facial gestures of anger are as immediately understood as a slap in the face.

Merleau-Ponty emphasizes that communication with others introduces us to the world's truth. Indeed, before I met my friend, the world did not have the same meaning. Moreover, he rightly claims that there is no time for me before which others were there. We do not begin as a singular point of view to which others are added. Every human infant is born into a human *community* without which she would not survive. To ask when others' views came to influence my own is like asking when I realized that objects have a third dimension. The gestures of others are not only acts of *communication* but also *establish* a common meaning (*Phenomenology* 215–216). The faces of one's primary caregivers are the original source of significance. We can see this in laboratory experiments when an infant or toddler is introduced to an unfamiliar, potentially scary toy (such as a noisy robot with flashing lights): securely attached children look at their caregivers to see how they ought to react. If a mother reacts positively to the toy, the child will typically respond in the same manner. If she responds with a fearful facial expression, the child will retreat.[3] When left alone in an unfamiliar place, infants will not explore, but spend the majority of the time crying; those who are left in the room with their mothers take an interest in the toys and the room.[4] Young children look to a trusted person to tell them the meaning of objects, people, and situations. Infants with no one to rely upon, such as those who are neglected, abused, or raised in institutions, do not explore their environment.[5] For a human being, there was never a time before others. They contribute to the constitution of the world as I know it before I am aware of it.

The communication of meaning between mother and child is not unidirectional; the child instills the mother's world with renewed significance. One obvious example is the child's cry. It impacts one on a visceral level causing an instant feeling of urgency, compassion, and/or irritation. Although one cannot always tell precisely what a child needs when he cries, nevertheless, one is immediately called to action. A child's smile or even a simple gaze can also suddenly change one's orientation. Daphne de Marnefffe describes this experience when looking at the face of a nursing baby: "I am not in command of my own joy. The delight I feel at being at the receiving end of those eyes is almost overwhelming, like a gush of uncontrollable laughter."[6] The meaning conveyed by a child's gesture can insight more than a momentary shift of mood. Recall the Kate Moses story quoted in chapter 3: "My daughter, now two, has started licking me. The start of a hug, arms around my neck; or I'm bending down, picking up little plastic kitty cats off the floor, and her tongue laps my cheekbone, flicks the crater of my eye. . . . Her licks have the power to completely alter my mood, capture my full attention, put me under her spell, which is no doubt part of the reason she loves to lick me."[7] The lick is a gesture in which the child achieves an over*lapping* of bodies. She conquers the distance of adult preoccupations and brings her mother into the immediacy of the shared moment. Just like an adult, the child reveals her perspective through the gesture. To her daughter, Moses's body is lickable; it is likable and lovable, an opportunity for play. Moses's daughter endows her body with new meaning: "As a young woman, I thought about my body all the time: how to disguise it, to shape it, to present it, to comfort it; what everyone else thought of it. Motherhood taught me to live in it."[8]

Merleau-Ponty argues that babies and young children are fully immersed in the public world, unimpeded by a belief in personal interiority; and that the earlier we look into the child's development the more pervasive is her or his sense of anonymity (*Phenomenology* 413). In *the Child's Relations with Others*, drawing on Jacques Lacan and Jean Piaget, he describes the child as egocentric, meaning that he is not reflectively aware of himself as a unique point of view, that she inhabits a continuous anonymity. The infant is "unaware of himself and the other as different beings . . . egocentricism is not at all the attitude of a me that grasps itself (as the term 'egocentrism' might lead us to believe). Rather it is the attitude of a me which is unaware of itself and lives as easily in others as it does in itself—but which, being unaware of others in their own separateness as well, in truth is no more conscious of them than of itself."[9] The young child experiences a sense of unity with the world, just as when "I contemplate the blue sky . . . I am the sky myself" (*Phenomenology* 249). According to Merleau-Ponty, all of the child's relations have this character, but, with the mother, he experiences total identification: "The maternal relation is (as the psychoanalysts say) a relation of identification, in which the subject projects on his mother what he himself experiences and assimilates the attitudes of the mother."[10] Whether children are fundamentally egocentric and/or completely identified with the mother is a topic for endless debate. However, it is clear that sometimes the horizons of mother and child can vividly overlap. Mothers can even be drawn into the immediacy of the child's perspective, a blissful, temporary self-forgetting free from adult concerns and judgments. If psychologists and philosophers can claim that the child experiences a sense of unity with the world, it is because adults can sometimes share the child's perspective.

As I show in chapter 3, this connection between mother and child is not to be taken for granted; indeed, cases of extreme neglect demonstrate its importance. The infant experiences the world through the expressions of others, and, without sufficient social interaction, her world appears small, dull, and flat. For lonely infants the world is not enticing. It is well documented that when a child is raised in relative solitude her sensory development is delayed or curtailed. For example, in *Blind Infants and Their Mothers: An Examination of the Sign System*, Selma Fraiberg describes a (socially but not physically) neglected infant, Lenny. Lenny had given up any attempts to explore the world visually. Before Fraiburg intervened, caseworkers had assumed that Lenny was blind. Eva Simms provides another example. She describes a neglected infant who showed only very passive sensory engagement. As Simms says,

Moreover, infants who are not cared for show signs of severe sensory and intellectual impairment after only a year. Research in the relatively new field of sensory integration has shown that the development of our sense unfolds in interaction with the world made inviting by caring adults. Children who are kept in non-stimulating, sterile, and isolated environments have difficulty seeing, hearing, touching, and tasting. The infants' sense, if not engaged by caring adults, will restrict their engagement with the world to familiar structures: the minute shadings of the white crib, a distance that spans a few feet, the touch of others that restricts itself to the feeling of a spoon on one's lips or maybe the grasp of a hand under one's arms when placed on a potty chair. . . . The contrast between the development of neglected children and those who receive adequate care shows that feeding a child does not necessarily mean that the child is nourished.[11]

In *The Child's Relations with Others,* Merleau-Ponty also cites studies of the perception of eleven to sixteen year olds that describe how these are influenced by others: "Recent studies have tended to show that even external perception of sense qualities and space—at first glance the most disinterested, least affective of all the functions—is profoundly modified by the personality and by the interpersonal relationships in which the child lives."[12]

Merleau-Ponty does believe that as we mature we come to realize our differentiation from others. Yet he maintains that anonymous intersubjectivity underlies all our interactions: "the unsophisticated thinking of our earliest years remains as an indispensable acquisition underlying that of maturity, if there is to be for the adult one single perspective" (*Phenomenology* 414). Effectively, this means that on the level of prereflective experience I do not extricate my view from others, but this does not mean I have an all-access pass to their thoughts, feelings, and perspectives. I still perceive from my point of view, and they do so from theirs. Merleau-Ponty states that "although I am outrun on all sides by my own acts, submerged in generality, the fact remains that I am the one by whom they are experienced" (*Phenomenology* 417). Each body has its own integrity, and, thanks to its boundaries, perception is possible.[13] The softness of my pillow brushes against my cheek. Flavor travels across the surface of my tongue. While the body's surfaces delimit it, the boundaries of my body are also the point of contact between myself and the sensible world; without them, no world would exist for me. As our commonalities are discovered through the shared world, so one's separation from others becomes apparent. I like cilantro, but my friend thinks it tastes like soap. I like wheat beer, but my friend thinks it smells like medicine. These seemingly small differences are also indications of a fundamental separateness. Although *together* we inhabit a sensuous unity, we also suffer a division. She tastes with her tongue and I with mine. Even the pregnant mother maintains her own bodily integrity in this manner. As the fetus breathes her amniotic fluid, the mother does not taste it. The same bodies that permit us sensory experience dictate that we shall each have this access only via our *own* body. The same bodies that allow us contact keep us from merging. While the other is not hidden from me locked within interiority, she also is not obvious to me.

Merleau-Ponty continues this line of thinking in *The Visible and the Invisible*. There he also argues that perception happens in a public place, a world that is accessible to one and all. In my relations to others, I do not have access to a "hidden realm of interiority." Instead "it is in the world that we rejoin one another."[14] In the *Phenomenology of Perception*, Merleau-Ponty describes anonymity as, first and foremost, a phenomenon of lived experience. However, in *The Visible and the Invisible* this phenomenology becomes ontology. Not only do we *experience* ourselves as "connatural with the world" (252) we *are*. He writes: "It is to experience therefore that the ultimate ontological power belongs, and the essences, the necessities by essence, the internal or logical possibility, solid and incontestable as they may be under the gaze of the mind, have finally their force and their eloquence only because all my thoughts and the thoughts of others are caught up in the fabric of one sole Being" (*The Visible* 110). This ontological continuity between self, other and world is named the *flesh* (123).

The things of the world, including people, are expressions of this one *sensible* flesh. Flesh is sensible in multiple respects: First, it can be perceived via the senses, smelled, touched, seen, and so on. Second, it is also capable of perception. My nose, ears, brain, etc. are all of the flesh; yet they are also articulations through which the world can bend back upon itself, sense itself, and discern itself. "Color that sees itself, surface that touches itself" (*The Visible* 135). To take a mundane example, after a strenuous workout I can smell my own sweat. The flesh which sweats is the same flesh that smells it. The skin and nose are apertures upon a world of which they are also a part. Thus perception is not evidence of our dominion over the sensory; it is a possibility inherent to the flesh itself realized in human beings as a part of the flesh of the world. Vision and the visible, touch and the tactile, hearing and the sonorous, are "flesh offered to flesh" (*The Visible* 131). "He who sees cannot possess the visible unless he is possessed by it, unless he *is of it*" (134).

The concept of flesh describes more than just our immersion in the world. Also inherent to the flesh is a gap, an *écart,* a dehiscence between the sentient and the sensed. In Merleau-Ponty's classic example of reversibility, when the right hand touches the left hand the two do not merge. "I palpate with my left hand only [my right hand's] outer covering. . . . I am always on the same side of my body; it presents itself to me in one invariable perspective" (*The Visible* 148). This noncoincidence, the "hiatus between my right hand touching and my right hand touched," is not a "failure;" it is the distinction without which no relation would be possible (148). When I look at a painting, I may temporarily lose myself, but I do not really *become* the painting. Reversibility between oneself and the world is never wholly complete: "reversibility [is] always imminent and never realized in fact. . . . I never reach coincidence; the coincidence eclipses at the moment of realization" (147). Nevertheless, *écart* does not reestablish classic dualism either; it does not indicate things that are different *in essence.* The smell of my sweat is certainly *mine,* but I can still encounter it as an object or other. I may even be surprised by it. This is neither a contradiction, nor a failure to understand my proper relation to my body and world. I can take my own body as both subject and object at once, without these two perspectives merging and without completely disconnecting them.

Similarly, the ambiguity of togetherness and separation are fundamental to the flesh itself.

In *The Visible and the Invisible*, Merleau-Ponty describes one's relationship with others as parallel to the reversible relationship with the sensible; "we situate ourselves in ourselves *and* in the things, in ourselves *and* in the other, at the point where, by a sort of *chiasm*, we become the others and we become world" (160). This is an ambiguous intersubjectivity in which I overlap with others, and yet remain distinct. It is analogous to the chiasma of the optic nerves intersecting to create one single view out of binocular vision. Our two eyes maintain their separate viewpoints, but their perspectives converge to reveal the world's depth. Similarly, the other's view is set against one's own. As in the example of the statue of Hyacinth, if one person's position differs from another, this does not indicate the existence of two realities. Instead, the world gains added dimension and appears that much more real. While the mother shares her child's perspective, she does not completely lose sight of her own. When my child cries out in the night, I may jump up and go to her feeling full of sympathy, but I may simultaneously resent my own loss of sleep. It is important to recognize that when "we become the others and we become the world" an *écart* still remains: "It is from the lawn before me that I think I catch sight of the impact of the green on the vision of another, it is through the music that I enter into his musical emotion, it is the thing itself that opens unto me the access to the private world of another. But the thing itself, we have seen, is always for me the thing that *I* see" (*The Visible* 11). Without this divergence between self and other, the world would lack the "objectivity" endowed by intersubjectivity (*The Visible* 142).

Merleau-Ponty often uses metaphors of pregnancy and motherhood to illustrate the meaning of the flesh and to explicate his notion of intersubjectivity.[15] For example, in his first mention of the flesh in *The Visible and the Invisible* he states, "Each landscape of my life, because it is not a wondering troop of sensations or a system of ephemeral judgments but a segment of the durable flesh of the world, is qua visible, pregnant with many other visions besides my own" (123). To be pregnant is to nurture another's horizon within oneself. This is paradoxical and yet it is our constant condition. Our fleshly incarnation means that we can both perceive and be perceived, and that everything I see is suffused with the visions of others—my partner's, my child's, a friend's, a stranger's, and so on. Pregnancy and motherhood in general, put this reality into relief. The other, whether one's child or not, is both familiar and strange. She is made from the same flesh as I am. Like me, she displays her feelings and some of her thoughts on her face with smiles, tears and a furrowed brow. We both encounter the world through smell, taste, vision and thoughts. She sleeps, she dreams, and wakes up, just as I do. Yet there is always something of her that I cannot reach.

Merleau-Ponty's imagery of pregnancy and motherhood is precisely parallel to his characterization of ambiguous intersubjectivity: He declares that we are of the same flesh, suffused with one another, even while we remain distinct. This relation is embodied in multiple ways as I encounter the other through my body, through my embodied relation to the world, and as the other impacts the manner in which I experience my body. While it is possible to understand this other, *to some extent*, through analogy with myself, she still remains entirely different from me, both surprising and mysterious.

Merleau-Ponty also briefly considers the relationship between the biological mother and fetus as an excellent *literal* example of the flesh. He describes the connection between the body and the world as two parts of a complete circuit, and claims that the human fetus in the womb has "prepared but unemployed circuits . . . the seer is being premeditated in counter-point in the embryonic development" (*The Visible* 147). According to Merleau-Ponty, the possibility of the child's uniquely human existence and her co-extension with the flesh of the world is already *pre*figured in the fetal body. In this passage, he describes the fetus as *anticipating* her emergence into the world, seeming to neglect that the fetus is already part of a living circuit with a world provided through and by the pregnant woman's body—the sounds of the mother's heartbeat and voice, the muffled voices and white noise of the world outside her body, the taste of amniotic fluid that is breathed in and out, the swaddling sensation of being nestled in the womb, the rocking motions of the mother's walk, and so on. Research confirms that the maternal body is a sensory world that engages the fetus, demonstrating that she can hear, move voluntarily, swallow, taste, and touch—that fetuses respond to pressure and pain and loud or soothing noises.[16] When the baby is born, she is taken out of a complete environment to which he or she has clearly become accustomed. This fact is recognized by contemporary parenting gurus who advise caregivers to think of the newborn as inhabiting a fourth trimester—still a fetus in terms of its needs and expectations.[17] This fact is especially capitalized on by Harvey Karp's *The Happiest Baby on the Block* books and DVDs. He teaches parents to use the "5 Ss"—sshhing (saying sshh in the baby's ear), swaddling, swinging, side or stomach lying, and sucking—to soothe a crying newborn. The first three of these techniques are intended to mimic the womb environment, and my own experience with these methods indicates that they work remarkably well. Indeed, both folk wisdom and scholarly research agree that neonates are most content when nested in and warmed by another's body, where it is not too light or loud, hearing and feeling the rhythms of the other's heartbeat and breath and smelling her familiar smells.

The mother herself is both sensing and sensed in a reversible relation with the fetus who alternately seems to be a part of her own body and to be the body of another. She is the first world with which the infant is in chiasmic relation. In this respect, this quote rings especially true: "we situate ourselves in ourselves *and* in the things, in ourselves *and* in the other, at the point where, by a sort of *chiasm*, we become the others and we become world" (*The Visible* 160). However, in this case a greater passivity is at work than this statement implies. The fetus does not situate herself; she *is situated* in the gestational mother who, at least initially, *is* all things, all others, and the entire world to the fetus. Thinking the birth mother as flesh suggests that intersubjectivity extends beyond sharing perspectives on a common world, beyond our filtering, highlighting, and obscuring the world for one another. It suggests that, from the start, we *are* this common world for one another. More specifically, the gestational mother (not just *any* other) is the first landscape within which we find ourselves.

Upon birth, the infant is exposed to a much wider world than before, but if cared for she continues to be nestled close to the bodies of her caregivers; they continue to constitute the world for her. For example, as I describe it in chapter 3, mother and child share one physiological process in breast-feeding. Eva Simms also describes this "primal housedness and well-being" drawing on Bachelard, Merleau-Ponty, and her own experience.[18] Simms reflects on how she was her daughter's first environment: "I was her house, but more than that I was the field that nourished her, the rain that quenched her thirst, the sun that warmed her skin . . . milk is the visible sign of the invisible, the in-between body, the *chiasm*, mother-infant flesh."[19] Breast-feeding is a symbiotic relationship as, for example, the rooting reflex already suggests the existence, location, and shape of the breast and as the amount of milk produced meets the baby's demand for it. "Implicit in the first cry, the first turning of the head toward the (m)other's voice, the first search for the breast is intentionally a directedness that presupposes that there is something to turn to."[20] Simms illustrates how the maternal can indeed be thought as first flesh: "In the beginning, the maternal world and thing-world are the same."[21]

In the case of mother and child, shared flesh is deeply ambiguous. Simms describes the aspect of breast-feeding in which the perspectives and bodies of mother and child are aligned. Of course, as I have explained in chapter 3, women also feel that breast-feeding and other aspects of childcare threaten to consume their vitality. They liken these same beloved children to parasites and cannibals. Clearly there is a divergence of perspectives as well—the *écart* that Merleau-Ponty describes as integral to intersubjectivity on the levels of experience and ontology.

Merleau-Ponty may have planned to consider the maternal body an instantiation of the flesh, as his working notes for *The Visible and the Invisible* seem to imply: "Do a psychoanalysis of Nature: it is the flesh, the mother" (267). However, there is some concern among feminist scholars that drawing a parallel between the mother and flesh erases the subjectivity of the mother and conflates her with nature. In the next section of this chapter, I will review these concerns. Then in the following segment I will address this concern by further clarifying the logic of his theory of ambiguity intersubjectivity. There is textual evidence that Merleau-Ponty employs principles from Hegel's logic; investigating these principles will help us to better understand his notion of ambiguous intersubjectivity and address feminist concerns.

FEMINIST READINGS OF MAURICE MERLEAU-PONTY

In "Only Nature is Mother to the Child" Dorothea Olkowski critiques Merleau-Ponty for denying the sociality of human origins. According to Olkowski, Merleau-Ponty denies maternal subjectivity, placing our origins in a wild nature. "All signs of the female, the woman who gives birth, who cradles, caresses, nurses, and cares for the infant, are erased. As such, in place of the personal, intimate relation with this fully human woman, the infant comes to itself from out of the prepersonal and anonymous realm of nature."[22] In Olkowski's view, Merleau-Ponty conflates the maternal with nature, reinstating women's traditional exclusion from culture.

A similar objection is made by Luce Irigaray in "The Invisible of the Flesh: A Reading of Merleau-Ponty, *The Visible and the Invisible*, 'The Intertwining—the Chiasm.'" She criticizes Merleau-Ponty for failing to consider that only the maternal-feminine gestates and gives birth. As a result, she claims, he misunderstands perception, sexual difference, and the flesh. Irigaray argues for the radically passive origin of perception: the formation of the eyes, optic nerve, and brain in "this mystery of the prenatal night where he was palpated without seeing";[23] vision developing within the obscurity of intrauterine life, "the infant's nocturnal abode" (152) where nothing can be seen and the sense of touch (and perhaps hearing) is primary. One's origin necessarily remains in darkness, an obstacle between the passive and active dimensions of perception, an interruption in one's continuity with the world. In opposition to this, Irigaray says that Merleau-Ponty denies the obscurity of our beginnings, reducing the (m)other to the same, and therefore "nothing new happens, only this permanent weaving between the world and the subject which presupposes that the subject sees the whole" (170). Within his "closed system" (161), this "solipsistic relation" (180), it is as though Merleau-Ponty's seer has never been born, because he remains in a prenatal continuity with the world (173). "It has no spacing or interval for the freedom of questioning between two" (183). Irigaray claims that to overcome his "labyrinthine solipsism" a radical other is needed—the other of sexual difference, the maternal-feminine, an other who cannot be seen (as the fetus cannot see the mother; 157).

According to Irigaray, the maternal reveals a fundamental *ir*reversibility at the source of the reversibility. The child is unequal to the mother, since the mother gives birth to the child and never the reverse. The child (especially the male child) can never appreciate her perspective; he can never witness the same landscape. But Merleau-Ponty, she claims, mistakenly assumes a persistent mutuality, eliminating alterity, and thus never escapes solipsism. For Irigaray, fecundation is not mutual; we do not diverge from a common flesh. The child comes from the mother's flesh, and this indicates the source of all difference—sexual difference.

Scholars agree that Merleau-Ponty does not have any explicit theory of sexual difference, and he has been thoroughly critiqued for this neglect.[24] For example, Judith Butler worries that while Merleau-Ponty wants to describe concrete, existential structures, at times "he offers a description of bodily experience clearly abstracted from the concrete diversity that exists."[25] In "Through the Wild Region: An Essay in Phenomenological Feminism," Jeffner Allen also claims that Merleau-Ponty ignores the uniqueness of women's embodied experience. She believes that this omission does not simply create a lack in Merleau-Ponty's philosophy; it reaffirms the masculinist assumption that men's experiences can serve as the model for all: "Women are the concealed term that is purportedly included in the term 'human beings.' In androcentric culture, where women's situation is that of the other, 'human being' is not a term that pertains directly to women, for we are unlike human beings in general, i.e. men. . . . Neuter neutral inquiry, including the claim that 'I am my body,' is not harmless. It acts, rather, to further conceal women's experiences of our embodiment."[26] Shannon Sullivan also critiques Merleau-Ponty along these lines in *Liv-*

ing Across and Through Skins and "Domination and Dialogue in Merleau-Ponty's *Phenomenology of Perception.*" She agrees with Allen that Merleau-Ponty assumes a gender neutral body unmarked by race, class, or sexuality. She specifically targets the concept of the anonymous body arguing that it is, in fact, the masculine body posing as "body for all." Sullivan says that Merleau-Ponty is guilty of "ethical solipsism," because he merely generalizes his own experiences.[27]

A related but different criticism is that Merleau-Ponty may be dependent on an implicit theory of sexual difference for his notion of the flesh (as Irigaray implies). Elizabeth Grosz raises this concern in "Merleau-Ponty and Irigaray in the Flesh":

> Merleau-Ponty does not explicitly address the question of sexual difference in *The Visible and the Invisible*, yet, if Irigaray's reading is appropriate, it is clear that his work derives much from a kind of implicit sexualization of ontology, the utilization of a whole series of metaphors embedded within and derived from relations between the sexes. The metaphors are the condition of the possibility of his understanding of the flesh, which is itself the condition of the possibility of the division and interaction of subjects and objects. In this sense, the feminine may be said to be the unspoken, disembodied underside of the flesh: the flesh as a point-for-point convergence with the attributes of femininity.[28]

This denial of sexual difference connects to the concern that Merleau-Ponty is in denial of alterity more broadly speaking. In "From the Body Proper to Flesh: Merleau-Ponty on Intersubjectivity," Beata Stawarska, claims that Merleau-Ponty fails to preserve the other's "free subjectivity and autonomy" and collapses bodily relations into a single universal.[29] She considers this move as emblematic of the way that "the masculine frame of mind continuously misrepresents the structures of intersubjectivity (and not only gender), in its tendency to reduce the other to the same."[30] In particular, she objects to his classic example of reversibility— one's hands touching each other. "Merleau-Ponty takes a specific, intrasubjective experience of the body, as in my right hand touching my other hand, to be a paradigm for relations to other embodied subjects, as in my right hand touching the hand of the other when we greet each other by shaking hands."[31] Stawarska argues that a relationship to one's own body should not be used as the exemplar for relations with others.[32] In doing so, she thinks that Merleau-Ponty forgets the particularity of perspectives and that "this basic distinction between self and other is disregarded or regarded as a secondary phenomenon."[33]

The scholars discussed raise a number of important concerns, which I will address in the next few pages. First, Merleau-Ponty has no theory of sexual difference. This is undeniably true. Yet the fact that he does not explicitly deal with sexual difference does not mean that he considers all bodies to be the same. Butler, Sullivan, and Allen mistake anonymity for universality. Merleau-Ponty is defended against this view by Silvia Stoller in "Reflections on Feminist Merleau-Ponty Skepticism" and Gail Weiss in "The Anonymous Intentions of Transactional Bodies." Stoller argues that anonymous corporeality is not neutral: "In equating 'anonymous body' and 'neutral body' [Sullivan] confuses anonymity with neutrality; anonymous does not mean that subjects face each other 'neutrally,' nor does it mean that their bodily identity is completely 'unknown,' or even one of 'anyone and thus of everyone' (5). Given the fact that for Merleau-Ponty the human subject is always a situated subject—and this applies also to its anonymous mode of being—such a conclusion is unfounded."[34] Similarly, Weiss asserts:

> To say that an experience operates anonymously, then, is not equivalent to saying that it is universal or that it is trans-historical. It is worth noting that the examples of anonymity provided by Merleau-Ponty are always grounded in the experience of a particular body in its concrete engagement with the world. . . . To say that these transactions tend to be anonymous does not mean that we are not, at the same time, two particular bodies, marked by our race, class, gender, etc., engaged in a social relationship. The point is that this very social relationship is predicated on its anonymity.[35]

My view of anonymity supports that of Weiss and Stoller. For Merleau-Ponty the body is always situated within a biological, social, and historical context, even in its anonymous mode. This means that sex and gender will *necessarily* be a factor in embodied experience.

Although Merleau-Ponty did not directly address sexual difference, this is not grounds for dismissing his feminist potential. His fascination with unique experiences of embodiment is demonstrated throughout *The Structure of Behavior* and *The Phenomenology of Perception*. His insightful remarks on pregnancy in his lectures on child psychology and pedagogy (which I will present further on in this chapter) are good evidence for a specific interest in female embodiment. Furthermore, his metaphorical treatment of maternity is not the "unspoken, disembodied underside of the flesh";[36] to employ images of a phenomenon is not to ignore it. Rather, these depictions of motherhood demonstrate an unusually subtle understanding of maternity, especially when compared to Levinas's attempt. Although Merleau-Ponty did not complete the work for us, many feminists have found that he contributes invaluable resources for thinking about embodied sexual difference.[37] Their excellent work demonstrates that, while he does not address sexual difference himself, Merleau-Ponty provides some helpful theoretical groundwork for feminists to think about women's embodied experience in its particularity.

The second major concern of Merleau-Ponty's feminist detractors is that he eliminates alterity. Unlike Irigaray, Merleau-Ponty does not found all difference in *sexual* difference. For this reason, Merleau-Ponty's philosophy could never satisfy her. However, reading Merleau-Ponty on his own terms, I think it is clear that Irigaray and his other critics underestimate the importance of alterity to his philosophy. As I have explained, Merleau-Ponty's notion of intersubjectivity is ambiguous: I overlap with others and yet remain distinct. It is precisely because the two (or more) views that come together are *different* that they add greater depth to the world; the solitary individual, were such a creature even possible, would perceive a flattened world in which objects have no backside. Although there is a prereflective sense of unity with others and the world, an *écart* between perceiver and perceived and between self and other remains a necessary aspect of these relations. The world's depth is a consequence of there always being an inaccessible aspect to people and things that can be perceived by others while remaining (at least temporarily) invisible to me.

Irigaray claims that for Merleau-Ponty the subject sees the whole, but this is not true to his account. The prereflective experience of continuity does not deny the fact of alienation. He writes: "Reversibility between oneself and the world is never wholly complete: "reversibility [is] always imminent and never realized in fact. . . . I never reach coincidence; the coincidence eclipses at the moment of realization" (*The Visible* 147). Even as we are in and of the world, the world still escapes us, and for this reason he would agree with her claim that there is *ir*reversibility at the heart of reversibility. Reversibility never achieves complete or harmonious unity.

In "Vision, Mirror, and Expression: The Genesis of the Ethical Body in Merleau-Ponty's Later Works," Alia Al-Saji makes a similar claim about reversibility. She explains that a difference remains between hands when one touches another. This is true whether or not it is my two hands touching each other or my hand touching another person's hand. "In Merleau-Ponty's account, there is some slight difference (*écart*) between two bodies that resists the cycle of totalizing vision, a singularity that cannot be incorporated into it. For my hand and that of the other remain distinct, as do my two hands that touch. [38] Al-Saji would agree with Stawarska that the relationship to one's own body is distinct from that of the relationship to another's body. However, Al-Saji thinks that Merleau-Ponty also agrees with them that an *écart* exists in both cases, but that one relationship is not reducible to the other. I would argue, and I think Al-Saji would agree, that the case of my hand touching my other hand is not meant to be *paradigmatic* of all relations of reversibility. Rather, my self-touching is *analogous* to my touching another. To say that they are analogous is to say that there is both similarity *and* difference between these two cases.

There is more noteworthy support in secondary literature for my claim that alterity is a vital element of the Merleau-Pontian universe. In "*Écart*: The Space of Corporeal Difference," Gail Weiss describes *écart* as "a space of noncoincidence that resists articulation"—at the heart of our relations.[39] She agrees that Irigaray does not realize how foundational *écart* is for Merleau-Ponty. Weiss describes its role in his philosophy as follows: "*Écart*, as the moment of disincorporation that makes all forms of corporeal differentiation possible, is also precisely what allows us to establish boundaries between bodies, boundaries that must be respected in order to respect the agencies that flow from them. From a Merleau-Pontian perspective, these boundaries can best be respected by not artificially viewing bodies as isolated from one another but by acknowledging the reversible relationships that are exhibited within and across them."[40] Interestingly, Weiss turns Irigaray's criticism back upon itself and says that one could accuse her of ignoring nonreversible difference between the mother and fetus: "It is also possible to take Irigaray to task for offering an idealized account of intrauterine existence characterized by fluid interactions between mother and fetus, in which each resonates, aggressively as well as lovingly, to the movements and demands of the other (the same could be said of her depiction of female sexuality)."[41] According to Weiss, it is Irigaray who presents us with a closed system, not Merleau-Ponty, leaving no central role for others in the mother-child relationship. Weiss insists that it is always mediated by others. I will make this case more strongly in chapter 6, but for now I will say that social support, or its lack, can make a dramatic difference in the woman's attitude toward the fetus.

In "Grounding Agency in Depth: The Implications of Merleau-Ponty's Thought for the Politics of Feminism," Helen Fielding also insists that *écart* is critical to Merleau-Ponty: "In my contact with others there is a coming close, a contact with the more determinate qualities, but this is accompanied by a spreading and a fading away of our backgrounds, our pasts and our futures. Others always remain distant from me in their own depth."[42] She reaffirms this view again in "Envisioning the Other: Lacan and Merleau-Ponty on Subjectivity" and adds that the *écart* between people parallels the *écart* between different senses.

> In Merleau-Ponty's understanding of reversibility, there could never be a fusing together of sensibilities but nor is there an absolute isolation from others. Rather, our relations with others involves a reciprocity and mirroring that demand not a possession of the other but a dispossession (Merleau-Ponty 1968, 266). Although there is a "surface of separation" between self and the other, this is also the place where people come together—it is the "geometrical locus of the projections and introjections."

The negativity to which they both refer is, then, for Merleau-Ponty, the hinge or the *écart* that separates the senses, that allows our lives to "rock into one another" while remaining distinct (Merleau-Ponty, 1968, 234).[43]

Fielding argues that for Merleau-Ponty, in regards to both the senses and other human beings, there is neither fusion with nor isolation from the other. In both perception and human interactions, there is a "surface of separation" that makes both distance and proximity possible. Indeed, the depth of the other is witnessed precisely in her distance, just as the thickness of things only becomes apparent when held at a distance from the eyes.

Although there are significant disparities of interpretation in the secondary literature on Merleau-Ponty, on the issue of alterity there is primarily a difference in *emphasis*. That is, while some scholars concentrate on Merleau-Ponty's overcoming of dichotomy and theory of connection between self and other, others focus on the *écart* between self and other. Merleau-Ponty's philosophy demonstrates that *both* these aspects are vital; both alterity and interconnection are characteristic of self-other relations. Understanding this requires a speculative moment in the Hegelian sense. That is, both alterity and interconnection describe a way of relating one term to another, but we need to understand the relationship between these two relationships—the relationship between alterity and interconnection. It is important to look at the logic at work in Merleau-Ponty's philosophy in order then to address how the mother can be understood as flesh in a nonreductive manner.

THE LOGIC OF THE FLESH

Merleau-Ponty presents us with a view of human relations that may seem paradoxical.[44] On one hand, the other appears to me as a pattern of behavior, publicly observable in a world that we share. Yet, she also remains inaccessible to me, perceiving the world in unique and surprising ways. This seeming contradiction begins with his early work. For example, in the *Phenomenology of Perception*, he declares, "But *this alien life, like mine* with which it is in communication, is an *open life*" (412). How can an *alien* life be *like mine*? How can another be both *open to me* and *alien*? How can one *communicate* with an alien? To this, Merleau-Ponty answers, "Solitude and communication cannot be the two horns of a dilemma, but two 'moments' of one phenomenon, since in fact other people do exist for me" (418). In these passages Merleau-Ponty's thinking and language are distinctly Hegelian. He asks us not only to take opposing terms together: intimacy and alienation, similarity and difference, community and individuality, and so on, but he also asks us to think about the relationship between these "moments." For Merleau-Ponty such oppositions reveal the immanent logic of human experience. In this section I will show the textual evidence that Merleau-Ponty employs Hegel's logic in his thinking of ambiguity. Clarifying how these principles work will help address feminist concerns and further illuminate the ambiguous intersubjectivity of mother and child.

According to Merleau-Ponty's essay "Hegel's Existentialism," in the *Phenomenology of Spirit*, Hegel proposes "to reveal the immanent logic of human experience in all its sectors. . . . Experience here no longer simply means our entirely contemplative contact with the world as it did in Kant; the word reassumes the tragic resonance it has in ordinary language when a man speaks of what he has lived through. It is no longer a laboratory test but is a trial of life."[45] According to Merleau-Ponty, Hegelian logic is not arbitrary or abstract, but comprehends the challenges of human existence: "We will not admit a preconstituted world, a logic, except for having seen them arise from our experience of brute being, which is as it were the umbilical cord of our knowledge and the source of meaning for us" (*The Visible* 157).

Merleau-Ponty judges as *bad dialectic* a logic that imposes its own laws upon the ineluctable (*The Visible* 94). Here Merleau-Ponty may be referring to "the late Hegel, who treated history as the visible development of a logical system. . . . But if the Hegel of 1827 may be criticized for his idealism, the same cannot be said of the Hegel of 1807."[46] He might also be referring to that flimsy oversimplification of Hegel's logic which describes it as a process of thesis, antithesis, synthesis (terms that Hegel does not use), assumed to be applicable to any dichotomy.[47] As I will indicate, he could be describing Sartre's appropriation of the master-slave dialectic. To better understand what Merleau-Ponty means by good and bad dialectic, we will look to the mature (though abbreviated) formulation of Hegel's logic, *The Encyclopedia Logic*.

In the *Logic*, Hegel declares that thinking is not subject to a preconceived set of formal laws but its own self-given laws and determinations, the preconstituted logic that Merleau-Ponty also eschews. Hegel does not believe that one can make whatever connections they see fit between one thought and another and call it logic. For Hegel, such a thinker takes the reins from thought itself. He believes that the thinker must humbly follow where thought leads; conducting what is essentially a phenomenology of thinking. As we will see in more detail, these determinations and laws— the *Logic*—arise as thought reflects upon itself; the *Logic* is conceived by thinking as thinking conceives of itself. The three moments of the logical are the side of abstraction or of the understanding, the dialectical or negatively rational side, and the speculative or positively rational one.[48] Note that these are the actual terms used by Hegel in the *Logic,* not the shorthand terms of thesis, antithesis, and synthesis critiqued by Merleau-Ponty.

Understanding helps one make the straightforward determination between what a thing *is* and what it *is not*. This moment of thinking is necessary and helpful to the practical sphere and includes such particular realizations as "This is a chair, not a table." It allows us to form universal categories, as in "All chairs are objects that are made for sitting upon." The understanding also enables us to make distinctions and to identify, for example, elements of a theory—matter, color, magnitude, etc. Hegel also affirms that ordinary understanding has many useful functions: it allows us to focus our interests, to choose a profession, to make judgments (as in jurisprudence), to distinguish between the duties of a government's branches, to make decisions, to stay on topic, and to think in a linear fashion. Without the understanding we could not distinguish one thing from another, determine a preference, devise a theory, or carry on practical business of all sorts. In short, the understanding is what enables us to be reasonable in the everyday sense of the word. "It should not be absent, and . . . to the degree that it is absent, its absence must be considered a defect" (127).

Nevertheless, Hegel insists that thinking must go further. This is not meant as a moral imperative for the thinker. Rather, this means that the understanding is thinking in its most stilted form and quickly reveals itself as such. Ordinary understanding is merely one-sided; it is not the whole truth, but only one moment of it. Since the understanding is only one-sided, the abstractions of the understanding will turn into their opposite. This is when we encounter the dialectical moment—"the self-sublation of these finite determinations on their own part, and their passing into their opposites" (128).

The dialectical moment is when we find that the one-sided determination of the understanding is insufficient. In this moment it becomes apparent that while a thing *is what it is*, it also *is what it is not*. Consider this classic example: the oracle at Delphi stated that Socrates was the wisest man in Athens. According to Plato, Socrates stated that he did not understand how this could be, since he knew nothing at all. After some dialogue and thought, Socrates believed that the oracle must have considered him wise because Socrates was aware of his own ignorance. Ordinary understanding would indicate that either Socrates is wise or he is not. However, this rigid way of thinking does little to reveal the true nature of Socrates' wisdom. In fact, and as the dialectical moment would have it, Socrates is both wise and ignorant at the same time. Furthermore, *Socrates could not be wise were he not also ignorant*. Here we see that wisdom also includes ignorance and vice versa; the two cannot be considered mutually exclusive.

One might say that, according to the dialectical moment, one thing can never be distinguished from another. Hegel anticipates this unfortunate interpretation: "The dialectical moment, taken separately on its own by the understanding, constitutes *skepticism* [simply that one doubts what others take to be true]. . . . Dialectic is usually considered as an external art, which arbitrarily produces a confusion and a mere *semblance* of *contradictions* in determinate concepts" (128). In ordinary understanding one thing is often explained in opposition to what it is not—its negative. But for Hegel, negation is the movement when one thing *becomes* its opposite. Nevertheless, the two do not collapse into one another. In the dialectical moment, both difference and sameness must be admitted. In this sameness the two do not become equivalent, rather their intimate relationship is revealed. We can already see here much in common with Merleau-Ponty's characterization of intersubjectivity.

The dialectical is not superior, or opposed, to the understanding. Rather the two are meant to be taken together. "The dialectic is the genuine nature that properly belongs to the determinations of the understanding, to things, and to the finite in general" (128). Thus the dialectical moment does not raze the understanding. Rather there is an ambivalent toggling back and forth between one thought (Socrates is wise) and its negation (Socrates is ignorant) in order to have a better understanding of both (wisdom embraces ignorance, ignorance can indicate wisdom). Clearly this is an unsteady state, and the *Logic* does not rest in the dialectical moment. However, in order to better understand the impetus to move beyond the dialectical we must consider one of the *Logic*'s actual thought determinations.

Hegel's *Logic* begins with *pure being*. "Pure being makes the beginning, because it is pure thought as well as the undetermined" (136). Without presupposing too much, the most that can be said about thought in the beginning is that it *is*. To comprehend what we mean when we say that *thought is*, we must know what is meant by the *is* itself. In order to understand thought, therefore, we must understand *being*. Since we are concerned with thought itself, pure being must not be considered a representation of anything else. In other words, pure being must not refer to *what* is, but to the *is* itself. This is why, at this moment, we speak of being as *pure* being. *Pure* being exists only in the moment of understanding. As Hegel states above, it is totally undetermined—it has, as yet, no other, no relation to any dialectical opposite. For these same reasons, pure being is the most abstract thought in the *Logic*. It is being in its initial one-sided determination.

In trying to understand pure being, it quickly becomes apparent that pure being is so abstract that it is, in fact, nothing at all. Since pure being has no actual content, when one thinks of pure being one thinks of nothing. "The true situation is that being as such is not firm and ultimate, but rather something that overturns dialectically into its opposite—which, taken in the same immediate way, is *nothing*. . . . This pure being is the *pure abstraction*, and hence it is the *absolutely negative*, which when taken immediately is *nothing*" (139). Nevertheless, thinking of nothing is still *not* not-thinking. Nothing *is* that of which one thinks. The being of nothing is indicated in the thought of nothing. Thus, when we think of nothing, we have continued to think of pure being. At this point, we are left moving between the two thoughts "*pure being is nothing*," and "*nothing is pure being*."

We seem to be left in limbo—unable to proceed and unable to go back. Still, one can strain too much in trying to distinguish pure being from nothing. Hegel predicts our inclination to move beyond these abstractions and explains that this is a force behind the progression of the logic: "All that really matters here is consciousness about these beginnings: that they are nothing but these empty abstractions, and that each of them is as empty as the other; the drive to find in being and in both [being and nothing] a stable meaning is this very necessity, which leads being and nothing further along and endows them with a true, i.e., concrete meaning" (140). The fact that being and nothing are difficult to distinguish is precisely that which we ought to observe. We are not meant to simply think "being and nothing," but to reflect upon the process of thinking them. Each one vanishes into its opposite. As we think being, it becomes nothing. As we think nothing, it becomes being. It is the particular relation between being and nothing that is now worthy of note—this is a relationship of *becoming*. "As their unity, *becoming* is the truest expression of the result of being and nothing; it is not just the unity of being and nothing, but its inward *unrest*—a unity which in its self-relation is not simply motionless, but which, in virtue of the diversity of being and nothing which it contains, is inwardly turned against itself" (143). The moment in which becoming is discovered is the speculative moment. As Hegel explains, the nature of the speculative moment is a sustained unrest. It is neither anxious, like the ambivalence of the understanding and the dialectic, nor is it static, like remaining in either ordinary understanding or the skeptical. "The *specu-latively* or *positively rational* apprehends the unity of the determinations in their opposition, the affirmative that is contained in their dissolution and in their transition" (131). In the speculative moment, the opposition between the understanding and the dialectical becomes a totality.

We can see why this moment is called speculative, because it is the moment when we take a step back from thinking and reflect upon it. We cannot just think it *through*, but must also think it *over*. This is how movement is gained in the *Logic*. It is how we come to understand how thought proceeds and it is the most truly philosophical moment of the *Logic*: "But it is one thing to have feelings and representations that are *determined* and *permeated* by *thinking*, and another to have *thoughts about them*. The thoughts *about* these modes of consciousness—generated by *thinking them over*—are what reflection, argumentation, and the like, as well as philosophy are comprehended under" (25). In the *Logic*, thought is its own nourishment. "But what we have here is the free act of thinking putting itself at the standpoint where it is for its own self, *producing its own object for itself* thereby, and *giving it to itself*. . . . Philosophy shows itself as a circle that goes back into itself" (141). For Hegel, speculative philosophy does not simply mean to contemplate one's reflection, but to catch one's reflection contemplating itself. In philosophy, for Hegel, thought comes to self-knowledge simultaneously as it comes into being (becomes).

Bad dialectic, for both Merleau-Ponty and Hegel, rests in the negative moment; it "ends up at cynicism at formalism, for having eluded its own double meaning" (*The Visible* 94). The cynic or skeptic as described in the *Phenomenology of Spirit* experiences a false sense of freedom which arises from a sense of division from the object: "What skepticism causes to vanish is not only objective reality as such, but its own relationship to it."[49] The skeptic actively negates the possibility of objective reality; she is in control of what qualifies as truth, and the only truth she recognizes is the power of her own negation. Thus the skeptical is merely the negative dialectical moment. The speculative moment in Hegel's logic goes beyond this to what Merleau-Ponty refers to as *good* or *hyper*dialectic. He writes: "The bad dialectic begins almost with the dialectic, and there is no good dialectic but that which criticizes itself and surpasses itself as a separate statement; the only good dialectic is the hyperdialectic. . . . What we call hyperdialecitc is a thought that on the contrary is capable of reaching truth because it envisages without restriction the plurality of the relationships and what has been called ambiguity" (*The Visible* 94). Ironically, bad dialectic is a moment within good dialectic. It is a one-sided negation, a short-sighted ambivalence. Hyperdialectic observes this ambivalence and sees the truth in the relation between terms—neither being nor nothingness, but becoming. The result is an ambiguous and complex manifold; a relation that should not be reified.

The association of Merleau-Ponty with Hegel will not be sufficient for most readers to overcome the charge that Merleau-Ponty eliminates alterity; Hegel has been frequently and famously critiqued on this point. Gilles Deleuze, for instance, argues that Hegel subsumes difference to identity.[50] Similarly, William Desmond claims that Hegel subsumes the other within the greater whole.[51] However, other scholars defend Hegel on the grounds that speculative logic is about the relationship between opposites, which makes no sense if there is no real difference between them.[52] For example, in "Identity, Difference, and the Logic of Otherness," William Maker writes that the "view of Hegel's system as an intolerant omnivore . . . suffers from one defect. It is wrong."[53] As I have argued, my reading of Hegel is consistent with this more recent scholarship that "not the elimination but the proliferation of difference is the heart of Hegel's system."[54] In my view, Merleau-Ponty and Hegel privilege neither identity nor difference. Both *Aufhebung* and Merleau-Ponty's philosophy of ambiguity highlight the relation between opposites, a relation that disappears if they are merely synthesized.

Like Hegel, Merleau-Ponty fetishizes neither identity nor difference. For the purposes of this book, it is most relevant to see how speculative logic is at work in his account of intersubjectivity. This also provides the opportunity to review some of the characterizations of intersubjectivity presented in the previous chapters of this book and their relation to Merleau-Ponty's notion.

The first movement of the logic, the understanding, dictates that *the self = the self*. Antonio Damasio's principle of the singularity of self ("one body goes with one self") exemplifies this type of thinking.[55] Recall, from chapter 3, in *The Feeling of What Happens*, Damasio argues that "things are [either] in or out of you" and that for each body there is no more than one person.[56] Of course, Damasio is not entirely wrong. This understanding is true, necessary, and practical. It is important that one not continually confuse oneself with others, not to live in a diffuse fusion with the world as Merleau-Ponty claims the infant does. If one goes to the doctor, one needn't bring one's entire family. But this characterization of the self is incomplete. It raises problems of egoism, solipsism, and narcissism. It invites the question: why be ethical? It does not recognize the contributions of others to my own existence or how integral they are to who I am. As Irigaray and Kristeva have argued, it is also a forgetting of the maternal and of nature.

The second moment is the dialectical, when the first determination is revealed as insufficient. In chapter 3 maternal experience was shown to contradict Damasio's first principle. In pregnancy, breast-feeding, and beyond to relationships with older and adopted children, maternal subjectivity is not simply singular. Care ethicists also argue that individualist notions of the self stand in stark denial of the mother-child relationship, of the fact that our existence is dependent on others before we can even entertain the possibility of individuality. In this moment it becomes apparent that while a mother *is who she is*, she also *is who she is not; the self = the other*.

There is truth to this view, as Levinas's characterization of epiphenomenal subjectivity demonstrates. The maternal metaphor helps him clarify how subjectivity can be understood as "an irreplaceable hostage"; how as ethical beings we are captivated by the needs of others.[57] In his respect, Levinas accurately (though inadvertently) characterizes the experience of maternal ambivalence: the way a mother often experiences her child as a monstrous *Other* who keeps her captive, threatens her body, eats away at her vitality, upsets her sense of self, invades her home, and commandeers her life. Levinas explains how when subjectivity seeks internal self-coherence it seeks the understanding that *the self = the self*, but this attempted self-satisfaction will inevitably be foiled (except perhaps in the case of a sociopath) by the intrusion of the Other. As there is no unity with oneself, there is also no union to be found with the other. For Levinas, our relations are fundamentally asymmetrical, the Other is held high above the self. Thus, in his account, proximity and alterity form an irresolvable ambivalence, "not a dialectical unity of unity and difference."[58] Though Levinas seeks to provide the conditions for the possibility of ethics, he effectively demonstrates why one would vacillate between wanting to destroy or nurture the other.

Levinas is an example of how one can become stuck in the dialectical by failing to take the speculative view. Unfortunately, he understands the third movement of Hegel's *Logic* in its simplified form, as synthesis, and claims that "dialectical unity" is a mere exercise of reason.[59] Unlike Merleau-Ponty, who sees the immanent logic of human experience at work in (early) Hegel, Levinas believes that the relation to the Other precedes and defies reason. In elevating the Other above the self, Levinas institutes a perverse and tormenting infinite responsibility that devastates women's actual abilities to care for their children, undermining the very ethics he would establish.

The dialectical movement is an overcorrection; "the philosophy of the negative bypasses the goal" (*The Visible* 88). No mere synthesis would correct this course. This is evidenced in Sartre's partial appropriation of Hegel in *Being and Nothingness*. When Sartre attempts to bring self and other together, intersubjectivity becomes an eternal conflict. In the encounter with the other, I am objectified. Without the other's existence I could never conceive myself from an outside perspective. Yet the other's look leaves me feeling judged, defenseless, enslaved, endangered, fixed, and irredeemable. "Fear is . . . the discovery of my being-as-object on the occasion of the appearance of another in my perceptive field."[60] Thus, with the other's look, a world that was once mine now escapes me and I must instead take responsibility for the stranger that I have become to myself. Sartre then adds that in order to cope with this situation and free myself from being objectified, I objectify the other in response. For, by objectifying or negating the other, her negation of me is no longer central to my experience. In *Being and Nothingness* intersubjectivity is reciprocal negation. Adding the negation of the other to one's own negation becomes an eternal power struggle. Sartre provides no way of moving forward from this difficulty. Like Levinas, Sartre neglects the speculative moment in *Being and Nothingness*.[61]

Merleau-Ponty critiques this "philosophy of negativity" in the chapter "Interrogation and Dialectic" from *The Visible and the Invisible*. He addresses Sartre directly in this passage:

> Whence comes this uneasiness that a philosophy of the negative leaves: it described our factual situation with more penetration than had ever before been done—and yet one retains the impression that this situation is one that is being surveyed from above, and indeed it is: the more one describes experience as a compound of being and nothingness, the more their absolute distinction is confirmed; the more the thought adheres to experience, the more it keeps it at a distance. Such is the sorcery of the thought of the negative.
>
> (187)

Philosophy of negativity is ambivalent, unable to integrate multiple meanings (*The Visible* 91), ignorant of "where the two moments cross, there where 'there is' something" (95). In contrast, Merleau-Ponty's (and Hegel's) logic demonstrates that two seemingly contradictory aspects of human relations can be taken together; both alterity and interconnection are characteristic of self-other relations. Solitude and communication are two moments of *one* phenomenon—ambiguous intersubjectivity. As in perception, a mother can temporarily lose herself in visceral and ecstatic relation to her child. Yet, even as "we become the others," irreversibility remains (*The Visible* 160). Every intimacy is also a slipping away.

We can see this "immanent logic of human existence" in the lives of mothers. Mothers are strikingly aware of their distinction from their children; this is the point of view of the understanding. The mother has her own needs for sleep, food, work, and play, which are frequently interrupted by her child. In some cases women are able to find time for themselves and negotiate healthy boundaries between themselves and their children.

Nevertheless, women recognize that meeting their own needs is more complex than simply seeking space from their children. This is the dialectical moment. Just as Socrates is both ignorant and wise, the mother is both more and less than one. If she feels an investment in her child's well-being, then her own desires often feel directed against herself when they are in opposition to her child's needs and wishes. At these moments a woman can feel most displaced by motherhood, as she simultaneously loses and finds herself in relation to her child. This is the negative moment, the bad dialectic, when one can become trapped in ambivalence, torn between one's own needs and the needs of a beloved child. It can persist in the form of Sartrean-style struggle for dominance or Levinasian-style maternal self-sacrifice.

But this is not the end of it. Mothers too entertain a speculative moment, a stepping back to reflect on the contradictions inherent to the relationship. In chapter 3 we saw examples of the speculative moment in art, poetry, and philosophy. Mierle Laderman Ukele's performance piece "Some Kinds of Maintenance Cancel Others Out, Keep Your Head Together—1,000 Times, or Babysitter Hangup—Incantation Ritual," is an excellent example. As a part of this performance Ukele calls the babysitter a total of one thousand times to ask if her children are OK. Ukele's piece is not just a synthesis of her art and mothering, it is a simultaneous reflection on and enactment of the tensions in the ambiguity of her relationship with her children and her own ambivalent *Befindlichkeit*. Kristeva's "Stabat Mater" is another brilliant example, where the author's poetic description of motherhood continually interrupts her scholarly writing on the topic. Creative work by mothers on motherhood enacts the simultaneous immersion within the mothering relation and the reflective distance needed from it.

The speculative moment is at once a preservation of contradictions and a transformation of them into something more useful and true. Indeed, this reflective distance can help to realize the creative force of maternal ambivalence. The ability to think through ambivalence and ambiguity seem to make all the difference in whether or not a mother's rage can be checked. Indeed, Merleau-Ponty argues that we must have an understanding and acceptance of ambiguity in order to deal with emotional ambivalence. In "The Child's Relations with Others," Merleau-Ponty writes:

> In sum, the subjects who carry within themselves extremely strong con-
> flicts are precisely those who reject, in their views of external things, the
> admission that there are particular situations that are ambiguous, full of
> conflicts, and mixed in value. This occurs in such a way that one can say
> that a very strong emotional ambivalence shows up, at the level of un-
> derstanding or perception, as a very weak ambiguity in the things and in
> his view of things. Emotional ambivalence is what demands the denial of
> intellectual ambiguity. In subjects whose intellectual ambiguity is strong
> it often happens that the emotional foundation is much more stable than
> in other subjects.[62]

An understanding of ambiguity is necessary to emotional maturity and entertaining the speculative moment can be one method of coming to this realization and dealing with maternal ambivalence. This reinforces my earlier claim that when reflection is possible a woman can better understand herself and her *actual* child; a purely emotive response will be insufficient. Maternal thinking is the vehicle through which mothers can negotiate the contradictions of their relationship, recognition of both union and radical divergence. Hegel's logic helps to clarify how the ambivalence engendered by the dialectic between mother and child is not overcome through a synthesis that would be an ossification. Its tension cannot be resolved, but it can become productive insofar as it reveals our fundamental ambiguity.

Accusations that Merleau-Ponty denies maternal subjectivity are based on one-sided readings that overemphasize continuity over alterity. The concept of the flesh neither eliminates individual subjectivity nor declares an easy unity with the world and with others. A key dialectic of the body is the dehiscence between subject and object, the outcome of which is not an either/or but a both/and. Yet the "constitutive paradox" remains (*The Visible* 136). "The body is a being of two leaves" (*The Visible* 137). This "double reference" informs us "that each one calls for the other" (137). As the subject and object call for one another, likewise the baby calls for the breast and the breast calls for the baby. These two aspects do not dissolve into one another; they work in concert. The body, both sensed and sentient, is "two segments of one sole circular course which goes above from left to right and below from right to left, but which has one sole movement in two phases" (138). Merleau-Ponty points to this circularity of dialectical relations between organism and environment as early as *The Structure of Behavior*.[63]

This dialectic of dehiscence is especially evident in the embodied and intersubjective lives of mothers, where the child is both a subject and object to the mother. There is no reason to think that even in prenatal life there is pure unity. Every cell is created through its own division. Likewise, the human being comes to exist through splitting and dividing. Childbirth is itself a form of dehiscence. The body is "born of segregation" from the flesh of the world and from the flesh of a woman (*The Visible* 136). This ambiguity, complementarity, and divergence persists: "Eight years in, I can't always tell the difference between my children's needs and my own. . . . The needs of our children and our world and our selves merge and divide and merge again, until sometimes you can't tell one strand from another."[64] Even for the mother whose child has died, the dialectic is not resolved. She loses a piece of herself, one of her own vital organs.[65] Contrary to critics such as Irigaray, the dehiscence of motherhood is consistent with the orientation of Merleau-Ponty's philosophy.

Merleau-Ponty's logic also addresses the criticism that he equates the mother with nature. He argues that all human beings are natural beings. We are embodied creatures who cannot escape the needs for clean air, water, and food. We were gestated within another, feeding, breathing, and excreting through her body. These bodies will someday return to inert matter; they will become food for other creatures or be burned to ashes and smoke. Merleau-Ponty describes this aspect of our relation to nature as anonymous because it is not the result of my own volition or reflection. Yet this prereflective life describes only half of our relation to nature; we are also alienated from it. This alienation is evidenced in our ignorance of our intimacy with it. We do not always recognize that which is personal, unique, and deliberate, founded in a prereflective nonvolitional body. We pollute our soil, water, and air. We struggle through science and philosophy to understand nature as though it were a stranger. Indeed, we are never completely able to thematize nature or our relation to it; it is irreducible to our attempts to know it. Our relation to nature is ambiguous because it exceeds us, yet it *is* us.

The mother's place in nature, like all human beings, is also ambiguous. Yet her ties to embodied existence are especially difficult to ignore. As one mother said regarding her pregnancy and delivery: "It was the most intensely physical experience I had ever gone through. For a long time I was totally reduced to my 'body.'"[66] In the case of a biological mother, her immersion in bodily nature becomes acutely obvious because of a combination of bodily changes and social context. Consider breast-feeding. When a woman breast-feeds, she experiences an additional bodily process, one that is not shared by the majority, considered disgusting by many people, and inadequately accommodated by society.[67] The production of breast milk depends on its expression, either by the baby, by hand, or by a breast pump. If the milk is not expressed at regular intervals, not only does its supply diminish, but it causes leaking, painful engorgement of the breasts, and mastitis (breast infection). The expression of milk, including direct breast-feeding, cannot be done just anywhere. It is unsanitary to express milk or breast-feed in a restroom (you would not consider eating your lunch there), and women who breast-feed in the open risk exclamations of outrage, looks of disgust, and charges of indecency.[68] Unless a woman can afford the four-hundred-dollar-hand-free breast pump, expressing her milk necessarily entails an interruption of whatever else she is doing for at least twenty minutes, approximately every three hours (depending on the age and needs of the child). The breast-feeding mother may rightfully find her personal existence overwhelmed by the demands of nature and the limitations of society.

If you have never breast-fed it may be difficult to identify with this example. Compare it to an imaginary scenario in which you are one of only a few people who needs to urinate. It is a bodily process that you must attend to periodically or suffer embarrassing leaks, pain, and risks to your health. Since the majority of people do not urinate, most public places have no place for you to do it. Obviously, you cannot just urinate anywhere or you risk arrest and the revulsion of others. Now imagine that it takes at least twenty minutes for you to urinate, and it can take a total of approximately eight hours per day (as breast-feeding a newborn can). Anyone suffering these conditions would find himself newly "submerged in nature" and isolated in the home. Not only would one be spending a considerable amount of time attending to one's body, it would limit one's ability to engage in activities outside the home or a few urinating-friendly locations. Since it takes up so much time and can only be done in certain locations, it would interrupt one's usual activities, work, and social life. One could come to feel that one's life was devoted to merely caring for the body, in the private realm, not participating in public meaning-making activities.

Of course, we need not refer to this imaginary scenario to understand the situation of the breast-feeding woman. Consider the person in a wheelchair trying to get into a building that has stairs at every access point. Think of the person with a mental disability whose only access to income requires filling out complicated forms. In each of these cases, society neglects to consider the brute facts of an individual's life. This lack of accommodation means that the individual's difference becomes a grave disability. A person in such a situation may feel herself trapped in an unforgiving body, punished by nature, but in fact human beings built the stairs and designed the bureaucratic forms. Societal practices impinge on the body and are at least partially responsible for disabling many people.

It is not only the breast-feeding or pregnant mother who finds herself subject to her body/nature. The mother of older children may also be acutely aware of her embodiment. Her ability to meet her own needs for sleep, nourishment, and exercise can greatly impact her ability to interact with her children positively.[69] This, of course, is not always a negative change. As Kate Moses describes it in chapter 3, having children can *retrieve* one's living relation to the body, transforming it from one of domination to cooperation.[70]

Even to the extent that motherhood is "natural," this does not exclude it from human significance, reflection, and resistance to "biological destiny." As the above examples illustrate, mothers can justifiably find themselves at odds with their bodies, especially when societal practices exacerbate their physical needs and limitations. This is a key factor in maternal ambivalence. Merleau-Ponty himself acknowledges this difficulty in his lectures on child psychology and pedagogy. In the lecture titled "The Adult's View of the Child," Merleau-Ponty describes ambivalence in pregnancy:

> [The pregnant woman] feels her own body to be alienated from her; it is no longer the simple extension of her own activity. Her body ceases to be entirely hers; it is systematically inhabited by another being. Her body will shortly bring another consciousness to the world. Her own pregnancy is not an act like others she accomplishes with her body. Pregnancy is more an anonymous process which happens through her and of which she is only the seat. . . . In addition, pregnancy is accompanied by all sorts of anxieties, worries, and ambivalent feelings. The woman's sentiments regarding her pregnancy are always mixed sentiments, since there is always a latent conflict between her personal life and the invasion of what could well be called the species-life.[71]

In this passage Merleau-Ponty acknowledges the bodily burden of the pregnant woman, but does not equate her with nature. On the contrary, her sense of alienation is heightened by the "invasion of . . . species-life." Even while she is the "seat" of a process that she cannot control (short of having an abortion), she remains an individual who can reflect on and object to her own role in nature or "species-life." Yet Merleau-Ponty argues that human interrogations of nature are another instance of nature's dehiscence, that nature is necessarily divided within and against itself. Thus even this resistance to species life does not sever the mother from nature.

To say that the maternal is a place of fleshly dehiscence is not to turn the female reproductive role into an ontological principle. The maternal body is *one* place where the physical and metaphysical, and the human and nature, immanence and transcendence intersect. It is true that the maternal body and mothering person is the first world of the fetus and the infant. And it may also be true that the fetus, infant, and young child live in a sense of union with the mother or other primary caregivers. But this does *not* mean that the mother *is* or *experiences herself* as undifferentiated flesh. Merleau-Ponty directly denies any simple fusion between pregnant mother and embryo in *The Visible and the Invisible*: "The vortex of the embryogenesis suddenly centers itself upon the interior hollow it was preparing—a certain fundamental divergence, a certain constitutive dissonance emerges" (233–234).[72] If the maternal body is to be thought of as flesh, then the child comes to be through a process of self-othering, a radical divergence in which the terms *self* and *other* are not, themselves, mutually exclusive. This relation overcomes the bad dialectic of self versus other and of being and nothingness. As there is no simple unity here, there also is no harmony without "constitutive dissonance."

MERLEAU-PONTY'S ETHICS (IMPLIED OR INFERRED)

Some Merleau-Ponty scholars have inferred an ethics from his philosophy and believe that, although he does not directly prescribe rules of behavior, he makes ethics philosophically possible and psychologically explicable. In secondary literature we can again see the difference in emphasis between those who see alterity as most critical and those who stress commonality.

Numerous scholars agree that by upsetting the distinction between self and other Merleau-Ponty undercuts the egoism/altruism dichotomy and opens new possibilities for thinking about ethics. In "Vision, Violence, and the Other: A Merleau-Pontian Ethics," Jorella Andrews makes this case: "First, then, a truly ethical situation for Merleau-Ponty can only emerge when participants understand that they are internally related to each other in ways that are as yet indeterminate, and that they are profoundly *together* in their respective differences."[73] Similarly, in "The Foundations of Merleau-Ponty's Ethical Theory," Douglas Low declares that connection makes ethics possible, "[Ethics] involves recognizing the other as a being like oneself, who can experience and suffer like oneself. There is here an empathy, and identification with the other, an overlapping of ego boundaries to include others."[74] In "Sociobiological and Social Constructionist Accounts of Altruism: A Phenomenological Critique,"

Edwin Gantt and Jeffrey Reber claim that in describing human beings as fundamentally interconnected, "always already being-for-the-other,"[75] Merleau-Ponty undermines the assumption of humans beings as disparate egos that are at base selfishly motivated—an assumption that renders ethics impossible.

In "Responsivity of the Body: Traces of the Other in Merleau-Ponty's Theory of Body and Flesh," Bernhard Waldenfels makes a similar but more subtle argument that there is a proto-ethics in the human's responsiveness to and primordial unity with the world. He writes: "Stretching throughout the work of Merleau-Ponty like a red thread is what I call the motif of responsivity (or answerability) . . . between the organism and its world."[76] According to Waldenfels, since Merleau-Ponty's "subject" is constituted in terms of its responsiveness to its environment, the "alien" is thus fundamentally constitutive of the "self." Waldenfels claims that this responsiveness goes beyond that notion of a subject seeking knowledge; it has a distinctly ethical flavor. Responsiveness is "consenting to the offers (*Angebote*) and demands (*Ansprüche*) of the other. In this expanded sense, demands have to be understood in the double sense of an 'appeal to someone' (*Anspruch an*) and a claim to something (*Anspruch auf*)."[77] Waldenfels claims that our relationship to the natural world and our relationships with other human beings are parallel. As our perceptual responses make us who we are, so do our responses to other people. He thinks that responsiveness eliminates the need to posit egoism and altruism as the only alternatives, by upsetting the radical distinction between oneself and the alien. The other's demands are "intertwined with my own being . . . otherness penetrates into the heart of self-presence."[78] "Bad ambiguity" is when otherness is subsumed to a totalizing whole, but he thinks the notions of flesh and reversibility overcome this. For Waldenfels it might be said that perceptual responsiveness is necessary but not sufficient for ethical responsibility.

These accounts prioritize connection for a viable theory of ethics. As Waldenfels notes, even if sympathy with and responsiveness to others is necessary for ethics, it is not *sufficient*. The phenomenon of maternal ambivalence demonstrates that the desire to commit violence can occur even when there is a feeling of sympathy and connection with the other. In fact, intense intimacy can lead to feelings of claustrophobia and thus *instigate* violence. Misappropriations of Merleau-Ponty that base ethics solely in a sympathetic response, do not explain why it is often a *struggle* to respond to others, why our actions and desires can conflict, and why we can respond to others' needs even when we don't *want* to do so.

In contrast, Alia Al-Saji claims that the possibility of a Merleau-Pontian ethics would be found in his theory of alterity:

> There is no longer a mere difference of number between my body and that of the other, but a differentiation that spans the dimension of the flesh. This new dimensionality, this multiplicity of dimensions of the flesh, represents for us the concrete possibility of an ethics. It opens up between myself and the other, beyond the numerical distinction of our bodies or our two looks, all the possible differentiations that can be generated between us, and that express the singularity of each. Hence, voice, gesture and speech, as well as thoughts, are inserted between us.[79]

According to Al-Saji, our differences are discovered through our expressions. The immediacy of the other's anger, for example, does not simply unite us to one another; it demonstrates a division. It makes the other before me a *particular* other. If we inhabited an undifferentiated group life, I would necessarily be angry as well, and the anger of one would be the same as the anger of another. But my responses to an expression of anger will vary; I can be sad, reasonable, indifferent or terrified, and this will depend on the particular person who is angry with me. This communication between us is also a divergence. This recognition of difference means that our vision is not hegemonic "that vision can become part of ethics."[80]

Similarly, in "'All Things Considered': Sensibility and Ethics in the Later Merleau-Ponty and Derrida," Ann Murphy says that Merleau-Ponty's account of sensibility provides an *opening* for ethics—"it is an elaboration of embodiment that provokes the question of response but no definitive or prescriptive answer. Hence the structure of sensibility begs the question of ethics and the problem of response but can provide nothing by way of a normative ethics."[81] Murphy acknowledges that both violence and hospitality are possible under Merleau-Ponty's philosophy; the opening to responsibility provides the opportunity and the compulsion to *both* of these options.[82]

For each of these scholars Merleau-Ponty's characterizations of sensibility and intersubjectivity already imply a latent Merleau-Pontian ethics. Andrews, Low, Gantt, and Reber think that he explains why human beings are not just selfishly motivated, why we can be generous. They believe that to be ethical means to be connected and to have empathy. Unfortunately, these four do not rigorously observe the is/ought distinction. They read Merleau-Ponty as describing humans in communion and then claim that we ought to be in harmony with one another. Waldenfels, Al-Saji, and Murphy are more cautious in their conclusions. They do not think Merleau-Ponty ordains specific attitudes or behaviors, but rather that he opens up the possibility of ethical theory. There are some indications Merleau-Ponty intended to provide such a foundation. At the end of his posthumously published prospectus for *The Visible and the Invisible*, he states that to establish "good ambiguity . . . a spontaneity which gathers together the plurality of monads . . . would be metaphysics itself and would at the same time give us a principle of an ethics."[83] What principle would this be? What ethics would it establish? He did not elaborate.

The overarching question of Merleau-Ponty's work is our place in the world and our responsiveness to it. Any responsibility we do take up necessitates the ability to respond, which in Merleau-Ponty is revealed through consideration of the sensible. But does being able to *respond* necessarily mean that we are *responsible*? Merleau-Ponty's philosophy describes our social and physical embeddedness. With this intertwining comes a vulnerability to one another. We are dependent on others for our very perception of reality. The character of our fleshly ontological condition means that we are capable of responding to others both as we interconnect and as we differ. This means that the other can be disruptive. Consider the false friend. Given that I depend on others for my sense of "objectivity" and the solidity of the world, finding out that I have been lied to by a trusted friend undermines the very reality that we have coconstituted. "The relations with the other are always complicated,"[84] and ethical life is thus necessarily conflicted. We cannot take others' or our own positive ethical response for granted. Even when our intentions are good, we may not know how to get the best result. In short, it is a fact of ethical life that we will sometimes fail to help the other and that she may fail us. Recognizing this inevitability (overlooked by Levinas) is paramount.

In his Sorbonne lectures on child development, Merleau-Ponty claims that ambivalence undergirds our conscious experience. He advocates replacing Freud's notion of the unconscious with ambivalence: "We should prefer this notion of ambivalence, which paints perfectly all that is equivocal in certain behaviors, 'resistances' to treatment, in which the subject is partially complicit, attitudes of hate that are at the same time love, desires that express themselves as agony, and so forth" (73). Emotional ambivalence is the prereflective underside to intellectual ambiguity. Thus to the extent that that intersubjectivity is togetherness, this mutuality will involve love as well as hate.

Merleau-Ponty describes the mother-child relationship as a paramount instance of this ambivalence. He writes:

> Evidently major troubles will arise from the manner in which [the mother] envisages her connection with the child. This connection is essentially ambivalence: the infant belongs to her, but she also belongs to him. A variety of positive and negative feelings are activated by this connection. . . . Pregnancy returns the mother with another being to the current of common life in communion. At the same time, in a negative sense, it becomes necessary to renounce many personal projects, to endure exhaustion and fear of deformation. She feels that this mysterious operation which is occurring in her puts her in danger (i.e., the symmetry between birth and death). Moreover, in this difficult situation, a situation over which she has no control, she must passively await its development. She is accompanied by all sorts of fantasies. The child is sometimes imagined to be a hero, sometimes a monster. . . . Hence, Hegel [states], "the birth of the child is the death of the parents." The birth of the child is at the same time the fulfillment of their union as well as its transformation.

(79)

Merleau-Ponty realizes that the mother's relationship to her child will be among the most conflicted. And it is clear that Merleau-Ponty sees a combination of natural-physical factors and cultural factors conspiring to amplify maternal ambivalence: the shared embodiment of mother and child, the physical dangers of pregnancy, the uncertainty of the child's future, and the interruption of the mother's personal aspirations all seem to be inevitable facts. Merleau-Ponty does not take for granted that a mother will bond to her infant once it is born. He writes: "At the same time, we must give the mother flexible time, long enough to take possession of her child, to identify with the infant, and to love him as her own. The relation between mother and child is partly a weak instinctual relation and also a human relation" (80). The woman's socially imposed role is another critical factor: "The father's attitude toward his children is as ambivalent as the mother's. He identifies with the child and oscillates between domination and sacrifice. . . . However, the father's problems with the child are much less acute than those of the mother for several reasons . . . our customs give the man a greater serenity in his conflicts with the child from the fact that he is separated from the child most of the day" (82).

Merleau-Ponty recognizes that the maternal-child relation is even more ambiguous than most relations and that the mother will be highly ambivalent in her relationship to her child. Because of her physical and psychic ties to a dependent other, her embodied existence is more difficult to ignore than average and she is more likely to feel at odds with it. Even in pregnancy, when mother and child seem most closely joined, there is "constitutive dissonance" between them. Though the mother finds herself to be a place of fleshly dehiscence, and while this can serve to undermine her personal life, it can never erase her subjectivity or her humanity. It is the flesh that makes possible both individual and social life. And maternal experience demonstrates that the ambivalence incited by our ambiguous social life can be a productive tension.

Thus far in this book we have explored different moments that characterize the phenomenon of intersubjectivity. According to the more straightforward understanding of intersubjectivity, I am me and you are you; *self ≠ other*. It is important to be able to distinguish oneself from others in this way. Yet maternal experience demonstrates that this understanding is only a half-truth; maternal subjectivity is not merely singular. The other side of this coin is the dialectical move made by Levinas; *the self = the other*. This is no simple equation, but it does mean that to the extent that there is subjectivity it is attributable to the other's ethical appeal. This position illustrates our fundamental interconnection with others and makes our ethical being more comprehensible. For Levinas, this view affirms an infinite responsibility of the self for the other, which I argue is ultimately detrimental. Such a self-sacrificing take on ethical obligation has been especially damaging to women. The negative dialectical approach to intersubjectivity sets up an irresolvable ambivalence between self and other for either dominance (as in Sartre) or submission (as in Levinas). The negative dialectical position merely reinstates a dualism between self and other. Through taking the speculative or hyperdialectical view, Merleau-Ponty helps us to think how these apparently opposing truths can be taken as two sides of the same phenomenon. Merleau-Ponty's logic "envisages without restriction the plurality of the relationships and what has been called ambiguity" (*The Invisible* 94).

It is Merleau-Ponty who best characterizes the ambiguity of our intersubjective relations. He enables us to see how we can communicate with one another across the abyss between us. He renders moot the question "Why be ethical?" by demonstrating that we are already intertwined with others, hence already immersed in ethical relations of some kind. What remains is to better understand one's place in the world. This view of the human condition is precisely what Merleau-Ponty believes he has in common with Hegel. He writes, "Hegel's thought is existentialist in that it views man not as being from the start a consciousness in full possession of its own clear thoughts but as a life which is its own responsibility and which tries to understand itself."[85] The meaning of our ethical life must follow from our orientation to our existence and to others, and this is what Merleau-Ponty helps us to understand more clearly.

Of course, being in ethical relations does not mean that we will necessarily care for one another. And it does not indicate the best course of action. Since ambivalence undergirds our relations with one another, these relations are always complicated and conflicted. Merleau-Ponty demonstrates the possibilities for both responsibility and irresponsibility. As Mauro Carbone says in "FLESH: Towards the History of a Misunderstanding": "The stranger, as flesh of my flesh, is just because of that my brother. But my brother could well be Cain. I myself could be such. As a condition for *all* these possibilities, as a condition of 'a reversibility always imminent and never realised in fact, flesh founds *every* possible ethics and *every* possible politics, that is, does not found *any* particular ethics or politics."[86] In "The Ineradicable Danger of Ambiguity at Ch[i]asm's Edge," Phillip E. Young even demonstrates how Merleau-Ponty's philosophy could be co-opted by totalitarians. All this is to say that Merleau-Ponty's philosophy does not inevitably dictate a moral scheme that we would embrace. He invites us to ask the question "What should I do?" but does not answer it for us. To ask this question for oneself is to begin to take responsibility.

Merleau-Ponty writes: "The very productivity or freedom of human life, far from denying our situation, utilizes it and turns it into a means of expression."[87] One's situation provides her with the means to expression, thus one's own guilt and responsibility cannot be merely individual. Still, one's freedom is an indication of personal accountability. "There is equal weakness in blaming ourselves alone and in believing only in external causes."[88] This ambiguity between our immanence and transcendence in our ethical life invites us to ask different kinds of questions with regards to our treatment of one another. For example, instead of just asking why an individual man raped an individual woman (What makes *him* do something so horrible?), we need to look at the bigger picture, a society in which such acts are not only common, but both subtly and bluntly condoned. What was the situation that enabled or encouraged this act? Clearly, ethics are not *only* a matter of individual virtue. Even Aristotle, the original virtue ethicist, insisted that a certain amount of *luck* is required to enable one to live the good life. If we take luck to mean the situation that surrounds a person, her influences, opportunities, and resources, then it is not something to be left to the fates alone.

Merleau-Ponty shows that ethical discourse is relevant to creatures such as us, beings who are knitted within their context, who are points of convergence and divergence in the flesh of the world, who are situated within relations that are individual, societal, and historical. One's situation will undoubtedly impact one's answers to the ethical questions posed by life. Merleau-Ponty says "A moral imperative only emerges in contact with a situation."[89] This principle certainly applies to mothers.

In this book I argue that maternal ambivalence is both predictable and understandable. However, I take it for granted that harming a child is not. Indeed, it seems that a great number of women experience maternal ambivalence without acting out their aggressions. How does a woman's situation influence this outcome? It is never easy to draw a cause-and-effect relationship between a certain situation and a particular action. Since the individual person is a variable factor in this equation, it would be imprecise to claim that *Situation A* causes *Behavior B*. How then are we to consider the situation of mothers with respect to their (inter)subjectivity, ambivalence, and ethical orientations?

The way in which our ethical response is situated is considered more robustly by Simone de Beauvoir. In the next chapter we will consider how Beauvoir helps to further develop Merleau-Ponty's emphasis on situation and makes it more concrete. She articulates how immanence and transcendence converge in our ethical relations and specifically considers the conditions for maternal responsibility: "The mother's relation with her children is defined within the overall context of her life; it depends on her relations with her husband, her past, her occupations, herself; it is a fatal and absurd error to claim to see a child as a panacea. . . . The young woman must be in a psychological, moral, and material situation that allows her to bear the responsibility; if not, the consequences will be disastrous."[90] Given our interdependence, Beauvoir articulates how the burden of ethical life should not rest solely on the shoulders of the individual. Yet she also asserts that the individual is strictly responsible for the way in which she *takes up* her situation.

Six

MATERNITY AS NEGOTIATING MUTUAL TRANSCENDENCE IN THE PHILOSOPHY OF SIMONE DE BEAUVOIR

Without failure, no ethics. For a being who, from the outset, is an exact coincidence with himself, a perfect plenitude, the notion "ought to be" [devoir être] would not make sense. One does not propose ethics to a god. It is impossible to propose one to man if he is defined as nature, as given. . . . This means that there can be an "ought to be" [devoir être] only for a being who, according to the existentialist definition, questions himself within his being.

—SIMONE DE BEAUVOIR, "INTRODUCTION TO AN ETHICS OF AMBIGUITY"

Beauvoir finds that our ethical life is inherently tragic and full of insoluble contradictions. Neither the meaning of our existence nor our ethical standing is assured at any moment. The liberation of others from mechanisms of oppression is the precondition for their freedom, and the freedom of others is the precondition for ours. But these same freedoms are in conflict with one another. We depend on others, but we cannot count on their generosity or collaboration. Beauvoir finds that it is precisely *because* of our inability to achieve self-coincidence that it makes sense to have an ethics. This lack is *vulnerability* to others and to a future that always remains unknown. Each time we struggle to overcome who we have been and what we have accomplished, we create a new position to be surpassed. Though many of our strivings are ultimately futile, they are also precisely the manner in which we become present to our existence.[1] Our efforts on behalf of ourselves and others are the thrust of ethical life; and the alternative to acknowledging their potential failure is inauthenticity—the denial of my own and/or the other's freedom and/or limitations.

The failure to coincide with oneself is more than an inability to achieve one's self-serving goals—to acquire wealth, academic degrees, fame, and so on. It also indicates the impossibility of caring for others and liberating them completely—to answer every time they call, to be present to all of their hopes and pains, to rescue them from every crisis. More than any other person, this is what a mother is expected to do for her children; thus ethical failure is a constant threat to her. Beauvoir richly describes the ways in which motherhood amplifies the painful tensions of ethical life and leads to an attitude of ambivalence toward one's children. Indeed, we find that maternal ambivalence is an ethical "failure" in the positive sense that it has for Beauvoir. It is a failure to deny the openness of the future, to ignore the needs and values of others, to plow through to one's ends without regard for their full consequences, and to adhere to abstract principles that may be inappropriate to the circumstances at hand. Maternal ambivalence is a robust exemplar of the contradictions of our ethical life.

Maternity is a unique ethical condition, but it brings into sharp relief the pattern of interdependence that is relevant to all human relationships. It highlights how tragic ethical failure can be. It is not always possible to work for the good of all; even mothers must sometimes sacrifice the freedom or care of one for another. The acknowledgment that someone will be (even temporarily) neglected or abandoned requires that we continue to question the validity of our projects and the costs of achieving them.

INTERSUBJECTIVE AMBIGUITY
AND EXISTENTIAL MORALITY

Our freedoms support each other like the stones in an arch . . .

—BEAUVOIR, "PYRRHUS AND CINEAS"

Beauvoir's philosophical ethical project, including "Pyrrhus and Cineas" (1944), "Moral Idealism and Political Realism" (1945),"Introduction to an Ethics of Ambiguity" (1946), *The Ethics of Ambiguity* (1948) and *The Second Sex* (1949), calls for us to "assume our fundamental ambiguity. It is in the knowledge of our genuine conditions that we must draw our strength to live and our reason for acting."[2] She indicates the many contradictions at the heart of human existence, acknowledges the conflicts both within ourselves and in our relationships, and demands that we act from out of the knowledge of this ambiguity rather than its denial. While it may be possible to willfully ignore the human condition, Beauvoir demonstrates that if one exercises her freedom then she will continually confront ambiguity. For Beauvoir the realization of freedom is transcendence—exceeding who one is in the present and who one was in the past through engaging in projects that change the future in a direction she values. The desire for transcendence prevents our complacency, our contentment with past achievements.[3] A project completed becomes a past to surpass. Yet the exercise of freedom is not just the glorious, uninhibited expression of free will. In taking action one is faced with disruptive questions about the boundaries between oneself and others and the implications of one's actions for them.[4] Works of transcendence bring to light the highly constrained nature of human freedom; it arises within a context of interdependence. "Man can find a justification of his own existence only in the existence of other men. . . . I concern others and they concern me. There we have an irreducible truth."[5]

There are a number of ways that the exercise of one's freedom depends on others. For one, we require others to give our projects (and thus ourselves) validity and solidity. According to Beauvoir, we are like children who rush to their parents for approval of our every creation.[6] It is not enough that our works please us individually; we want them to have an intersubjective importance. What is the point of a great painting or poem that no one sees? Even the works of Vincent van Gogh, who was relatively solitary in his lifetime, are incomplete until others engaged with them. Still, we need more than just appreciators of our works, we also need collaborators. Everything from creating a more efficient bureaucracy to liberating Paris from the Nazis involves cooperation with others. Where would van Gogh be without the financial and emotional support of his brother Theo? What is more, if the full realization of our projects is in their impact on the future, then we rely on others to continue them beyond our lifetimes. The continuation of Beauvoir scholarship and the offering of courses in feminist phenomenology mean that the realization of Beauvoir's transcendence continues to our present day. Of course, there is no guarantee, even if others take up our project, that it will continue in the spirit we intend: case in point, Parshley's infamous translation of *The Second Sex*. As Beauvoir writes: "An action thrown into the world is not propagated infinitely like the wave in classical physics. . . . The action does not stop the instant we accomplish it. It escapes us toward a future, where it is immediately grasped again by foreign consciousness. It is never a blind constraint for the other but a given to be surpassed, and the other surpasses it, not I."[7] Although we cannot control or predict the continued impact of our works, without the investments of others, our efforts would not even make a ripple.[8] "Thus, we see that no existence can be validly fulfilled if it is limited to itself. It appeals to the existence of others."[9]

The investment of others in my projects requires that they voluntarily share the values that I wish to assert. Others can be enslaved to build a pyramid, but, once the whip stops cracking, what is to prevent them from robbing the tomb? The long-standing value of my projects requires that others not be compelled by force or necessity to join my cause. They must have adequate health care, food, shelter, and security so that their lives are not consumed with bare survival.[10] This is one reason why we have an interest in the well-being of others. To oppress others would be to fundamentally misunderstand the nature of our own freedom. If others are not free, I have no colleagues, comrades, or allies and my projects will lead a short life.[11] For that reason she states: "To will oneself moral and to will oneself free are one and the same decision."[12] Our own freedom depends on the welfare of others.

If this concern for the other seems egoistic, it's important to remember that for Beauvoir the self is not pregiven. Our transcendent projects are the essence of our existence. Since we depend on others for their realization, we have a most fundamental need for other people. "It is because my subjectivity is not inertia, folding in on itself, separation, but, on the contrary, movement toward the other that the difference between me and the other is abolished, and I can call the other mine."[13] It would be a solipsistic error to think that any project, from constructing a house to building a fortune, is merely the distinction of an individual. It is also an attachment with the others who are involved. Paradoxically, any individuality is founded through intertwining with others, and as the other becomes *mine*, I have responsibility for her. "Is this kind of ethics individualistic or not? Yes, if one means by that it accords to the individual an absolute value and that it recognizes in him alone the power of laying the foundations of his own existence. . . . But it is not solipsistic, since the individual is defined only by his relationship to the world and to other individuals; he exists by transcending himself, and his freedom can be achieved only through the freedom of others."[14]

For Beauvoir, each person's entanglement in the web of human relations is an existential *fact*, preexisting the willing of one's freedom. Others are necessary to one's ethical freedom, but they are also integral to one's natural freedom. Natural freedom—the possibility for transcendence initiated by others' objectification of oneself and one's rebellion against this objectification—is the kind of freedom we cannot escape. This is the idea of freedom shared by Sartre in *Being and Nothingness* that "every man is free, that there is no way of his not being free."[15] For example, Beauvoir claims that the victim of torture is free in the natural sense; she may still assume an attitude of compliance, forgiveness, or rebellion. Clearly, this notion of freedom attends less to the constraining power of situation than ethical freedom does, even though it acknowledges the importance of the existence of others. For Beauvoir, without the other's objectifying viewpoint, one would be trapped in immanence: "It is the existence of other men that wrests each man from his immanence and enables him to accomplish himself as transcendence, as flight toward the object, as a project."[16] For Beauvoir, this objectification precedes our morally free acts.

Beauvoir believes that natural freedom is consistent with ethical freedom, even though it sets up a conflict in which subjects try to assert themselves over and against each other: "But this foreign freedom, which confirms my freedom, also enters into conflict with it: this is the tragedy of the unhappy consciousness; each consciousness seeks to posit itself alone as sovereign subject. Each one tries to accomplish itself by reducing the other to slavery."[17] The existences of others, who attempt to overpower me, judge me, or treat me as a means to their ends, places my identity continually under threat. The struggle against this reification is an original impetus to realize my freedom. In the context of this ongoing challenge, I seek to reestablish myself by realizing my perspective and values through my actions. For that reason, Beauvoir believes that natural freedom does not suffice for an ethical life; it ought to drive one toward greater accomplishments.

> What meaning can there be *to will oneself free* [ethical freedom], since at the beginning we *are* free? . . . This objection would mean something only if freedom were a thing or a quality naturally attached to a thing. Then, in effect, one would either have it or not have it. But the fact is that it merges with the very movement of this ambiguous reality which is called existence and which *is* only by making itself be; to such an extent that it is precisely only by having to be conquered that it gives itself. To will oneself free is to effect the transition from nature to morality by establishing a genuine freedom on the original upsurge of existence.[18]

The torture victim's attitude of forgiveness or rebellion is an incomplete response. It is her concrete efforts to eradicate torture, to liberate other victims, or perhaps to take revenge on its perpetrators that fully realize her freedom. Of course, one can be too broken, lazy, cowardly, defeated, or passive to will her freedom and thus fail to recognize the importance of others. However, the existence of our natural freedom means that we will always be confronted by others and the denial of their significance will be a hard-won delusion.

Conflict with others is also inevitable at the practical level for the simple reason that peoples' desires and interests clash: "I am not dealing with one freedom but with several freedoms. And precisely because they are free, they do not agree among themselves."[19] Since transcendent projects extend beyond oneself, they can impinge on other people. A project that benefits some may devastate others. The dam built on a river provides electricity, but might also ruin fishing downstream. "What is good for different men differs. Working for some often means working against the others. One cannot stop at this tranquil solution: wanting *the* good of *all* men. We must define *our* own good. . . . The respect of the human person in general cannot suffice to guide us because we are dealing with separate and opposed individuals."[20]

In spite of the fact that some toes will inevitably be stepped on, Beauvoir declares it a moral error to assert oneself without concern for others, bulldozing through to one's ends or soaking up the privileges of the oppressor class without regard for the impact on others.[21] This is because one's actions create the circumstances within which others will be either impeded or enabled to act. "What concerns me is the other's situation, as something founded by me. . . . I am the facticity of his situation."[22] This worry is a central basis for Beauvoir's "existential morality," which is given its most mature expression in *The Second Sex*.[23]

Every subject posits itself as a transcendence concretely, through projects; it accomplishes its freedom only by perpetual surpassing toward other freedoms; there is no other justification for present existence than its expansion toward an indefinitely open future. Every time transcendence lapses into immanence, there is degradation of existence into "in-itself," of freedom into facticity; this fall is a moral fault if the subject consents to it; if this fall is inflicted on the subject, it takes the form of frustration and oppression; in both cases it is an absolute evil.[24]

The key existential good is an ever-reaching freedom upon an open future of possibilities. The existential ethic, the realization of one's freedom, consists in striving to exceed that which one currently is, to achieve transcendence through engaging in projects—meaningful work that affirms one's own perspective, values, and creativity. The individual who surrenders to her objectification and immanence, who quits striving toward the creative possibilities available to her, has failed morally. In addition, a moral society, institution, or person creates greater opportunities for human beings' ingenuity, expansiveness, and potential. When restrictions are imposed on the individual that foreclose her opportunities, she is "frustrated and oppressed." And Beauvoir maintains that it is unqualifiedly immoral to destroy another's ability to live toward her own ends: "Whatever the problems raised for [man], the setbacks that he will have to assume, and the difficulties with which he will have to struggle, he must reject oppression at any cost."[25]

Ultimately, this means that we owe others more than a policy of noninterference; we owe them our vigorous effort toward their liberation. Beauvoir maintains that it is insufficient to grant that the other has ontological freedom. The enslaved, impoverished or colonized person is severely limited by his situation; opportunities for the practical realization of freedom differ tremendously for the child born in an American suburb and one raised in a Brazilian *favela*. The concept of ontological freedom is largely blind to these differences. To remain ignorant of such inequalities is disingenuous, to deny the importance of situation and leave the marginalized to their own struggle is to remain complicit with their oppressors. Often, any tool with which an oppressed person might have attacked the civilization that subjugates him has been confiscated: "having been kept in a state of servitude and ignorance, they have no means of breaking the ceiling which is stretched over their heads."[26] To be politically detached is simply another way of siding with whomever is strongest at the time.[27] Beauvoir insists that caring for the oppressed should not merely be a form of detached paternalistic charity. Since the other's freedom is integral to one's own, it is everyone's cause. "It is this interdependence which explains why oppression is possible and why it is hateful."[28]

Although at first it may seem to contradict her emphasis on interpersonal strife and individual freedom, Beauvoir holds generosity as the highest human achievement: "The conflict can be overcome by the free recognition of each individual in the other, each one positing both itself and the other as object and as subject in a reciprocal movement. But friendship and generosity, which accomplish this recognition of freedoms concretely, are not easy virtues; they are undoubtedly man's highest accomplishment; this is where he is in truth: but this truth is a struggle endlessly begun, endlessly abolished; it demands that man surpass himself at each instant."[29] This notion of generosity involves an enlightened recognition of the others' and one's own simultaneous objectivity and subjectivity, which one must continually labor to maintain. This generosity is not at odds with personal liberty; it is precisely the recognition of the other's freedom. Thus the greatest generosity would be to advocate for the other's concrete freedom, to be a platform for her transcendence: "A lucid generosity is what should guide our actions. We will assume our own choices and posit as our ends the situations that will be new points of departure for others. But we must not delude ourselves with the hope that we can do anything *for* others."[30] The best we can do for another is to put him in a position of being capable of striving in the direction he wills.

Recent Beauvoir scholarship agrees that, for Beauvoir, human relations are marked by mutual affirmation and reciprocity; freedom is always relational.[31] For example, Barbara Andrew claims that "recognition of the others' freedom is the only acceptable moral attitude or attunement towards the world."[32] She aligns this view with care ethics: "recognition of the other's freedom is a response to the ethical needs of those others as well as one's own ethical needs, and thus is a form of care."[33] Andrew minimizes the importance of interpersonal conflict to Beauvoir's philosophy: "[Beauvoir] does not see a necessary struggle or a need to destroy the other to establish one's own subjectivity. . . . Transcendence occurs only through reaching out to others."[34]

Numerous scholars agree that Beauvoir's work has been interpreted falsely as an elaboration of Jean-Paul Sartre's *Being and Nothingness*. When her work is considered on its own merits, they think, it becomes

clear that for Beauvoir human relationships are not primarily characterized by struggle, that negation of the other is not fundamental for her as it
is for Sartre. Ursula Tidd argues this point: "In terms of the Sartrean account of the structure of consciousness—that it entails a double negation:
the Self negates itself as not the Other, and negates the Other as object to
be transcended—Beauvoir accepts the first negation but not the second.
In her account of consciousness, the Other cannot be a mere object of
consciousness to be transcended; the Other is already incorporated within
the Self's transcendental movement."[35] Fedrika Scarth also attributes the
conflictual model to Sartre. She states that "[Beauvoir's ethics] is driven
by her insistence, contra Sartre, that ethical relationships with others are
possible and that relating to others ethically will require the acceptance
of our ambiguity as situated and embodied subjects."[36] Julie Ward draws
the same conclusion from Beauvoir's autobiographical work. Ward thinks
that harmonious relationships between female friends are Beauvoir's ideal
model:

> Among female friends, Beauvoir feels recognized and importantly, *pre-
> served*, whereas with her male love-objects, she experiences a loss of self.
> So, the early diary not only shows that Beauvoir possesses a positive no-
> tion of being seen by the other but also that the model of this positive
> relation to another is evident in some of Beauvoir's female friendships.
> For Beauvoir, it is precisely with Zaza and Hélène that being with the
> other is a comfort, not a conflict, and provides continuity, not disruption,
> to being a subject.[37]

In "Teaching Sartre About Freedom," Sonia Kruks argues that these
ideas align Beauvoir more with Merleau-Ponty than Sartre: "There is for
Merleau-Ponty, unlike Sartre, an undifferentiated or 'general' being, a 'primordial layer at which both things and ideas come into being,' which is
'anterior to the ideas of subject and object' and in which each of us par-
ticipates as embodied existence. It is through this common participation
that we escape the solipsism implied in the Cartesian cogito—a solipsism
still lurking in *Being and Nothingness*."[38]

As it should be obvious by now, contemporary Beauvoir scholarship is strongly motivated to distinguish Beauvoir as a philosopher in her own right, apart from Sartre. Kate and Edward Fullbrook's *Simone de Beauvoir and Jean-Paul Sartre: The Remaking of a Twentieth-Century Legend* is often credited with spearheading this effort. The Fullbrooks argue that many of Sartre's insights from *Being and Nothingness* originate in his reading of Beauvoir's *She Came to Stay*. Margaret Simons also makes this claim and supports it with research on Beauvoir's diaries that reveal the variety and chronology of her intellectual influences and origination of her ideas.[39]

In many cases Beauvoir scholars are attempting to retrieve her from critics of her pessimism toward maternity. These detractors believe that Beauvoir describes maternity in negative terms because she appropriates a Sartrean repulsion toward the female body and a one-sidedly conflict-ridden (Sartrean and Hegelian) account of consciousness.[40] For example, Genevieve Lloyd critiques Beauvoir's account of the female body as "an intrinsic obstacle to transcendence. . . . Underlying de Beauvoir's descriptions of female biology is the original Hegelian opposition between the individuality of self-consciousness and the inchoate generality of life."[41] Lloyd believes that, for Beauvoir, the female body and its accompanying role must be transcended to achieve authenticity and freedom.[42] Similarly, regarding Beauvoir's decision to write books instead of have children, Alice Jardin claims: "Beauvoir's decision not to have children in the world might be seen as but an acting out of her complete denial of the maternal, of her refusal of the maternal body's most intimate influences upon her own body and body of work."[43]

In response to this critique of Beauvoir, some supporters "creatively reinterpret" her views deemphasizing the importance of conflict.[44] According to Scarth, Beauvoir's highly conflictual picture of pregnancy is a "rhetorical strategy" designed to overturn the patriarchal myths of pregnant women as passive vessels.[45] For Scarth, Beauvoir's talk of alien invaders and parasites illuminates the transgression of boundaries in pregnancy as "an intense experience of otherness within."[46] Scarth further states: "Beauvoir's language *is* excessive, in the sense that many women probably would not recognize themselves and their experience of maternity in it; it is unfamiliar, strange, and disturbing."[47]

In *The Philosophy of Simone de Beauvoir: Gendered Phenomenologies, Erotic Generosities*, Debra Bergoffen tries to rescue Beauvoir in a similar manner. She claims that Beauvoir and Irigaray have similar ends in mind, although they go about it differently: "Where Beauvoir turns to the model of the generous man and the generous mother and to the phenomenon of the gift to explore the possibilities of immanence, subjective ambiguity/undecidability, and the couple, Irigaray turns to the pregnant body."[48] Along with Irigaray, Bergoffen thinks that the pregnant woman is engaged in an ethical relation originating in the body's response, that the pregnant body recognizes the fetus as a "gift of generosity, abundance and plenitude to which nothing is owed,"[49] and that this bodily response is also the source of the intentional generosity of the mother. "[Beauvoir] does not seem to realize that the maternal body has already expressed [the desire for the happiness of the other]."[50] According to Bergoffen, Beauvoir overlooks the inherent generosity of the maternal body and thereby fails to realize the potential in her own work: "Whether Beauvoir has been taken in by a patriarchal imagery which divests pregnancy of its activity or is overreacting to patriarchy's distorting 'religion of maternity,' the effect is the same, she misses the radical implications of her affirmations of the erotic body."[51]

Bergoffen implies that there is a unidirectional causality between the pregnant mind and body—that the pregnant body's generosity inclines the mother herself toward generosity, but that the body's response is unaffected by the mother's existent feelings. However, as I discuss in chapter 4, on Levinas, I am skeptical of the idea that maternal munificence originates in the responses of the maternal body. Too little is known about the relationship between the pregnant body and mind. It could be that the body's reaction to pregnancy is already affected by the mother's attitude toward it. For example, in "Being Torn: Toward a Phenomenology of Unwanted Pregnancy," Caroline Lundquist notes that in denied pregnancies the "normal symptoms" of pregnancy, such as weight gain and morning sickness, are suppressed or reduced. This seems to imply that the mother's conscious acknowledgment of her pregnancy is necessary in order for it to take its typical course. In addition, denied fetuses are frequently underweight. This is an extraordinary finding since, as Lundquist also notes, the human female is unique in that when resources are limited, her body will direct them toward the fetus first. This means an unwanted fetus cannot be deliberately starved; the mother's body will be deprived first. Yet in denied pregnancy the fetus often *will* be deprived of vital nutrients, even when there are enough for both. While no simple conclusions can be drawn from these facts, I think it is safe to say that they complicate any easy assumptions about the generosity of the maternal body.

Even if reciprocity and generosity are paramount to Beauvoir's ethics, this is insufficient cause to eliminate the strong emphasis she also places on conflict. In *The Second Sex*, for example, Beauvoir often gives voice to the importance of interpersonal struggles: "Once the subject attempts to assert himself, the other, who limits and denies him, is nonetheless necessary for him: he attains himself only through the reality that he is not. That is why man's life is never plenitude and rest, it is lack and movement, it is *combat*."[52] While initially recognizing the ambiguity of our human relations, many scholars ultimately side with only one aspect; the calling to be ethical is affirmed, but the central importance of conflict is denied. However, for Beauvoir, the reason why generosity is so laudable is not because it is necessarily common or prudent, but because it also works against one's own interests: "To will oneself free is also to will others free. This will is not an abstract formula. It points out to each person the concrete action to be achieved. But others are separate even opposed, and the man of good will sees concrete and difficult problems arising in relations with them."[53] The contradictory nature of this dilemma should not to be diminished.

It is especially troubling that Beauvoir scholars take recourse to the mother-child relationship to deny the importance of interpersonal conflict. Beauvoir's descriptions of pregnancy, childbirth, and motherhood are not a mere rhetorical strategy. On the contrary, she considers the real threat to women's freedom that childbearing and rearing presents and considers motherhood as a concrete illustration of her theory. Scarth's assertion that Beauvoir's account of maternity is excessive, that most women would not recognize themselves in it, is simply untrue. While *some* women may not feel this way, many *do* feel as though they are "at war" with their children and have used similarly strong language to describe their experiences. In attempting to make Beauvoir's characterization of motherhood more palatable, Beauvoir's supporters reject her great insights into the intersubjective and ethical lives of mothers.

As I will demonstrate in the next section, this oversight is a serious error. Beauvoir's characterization of the mother-child relationship is a vivid, and at times raw, example of her philosophy of intersubjective ambiguity. Beauvoir realizes mothers often find themselves in violent opposition to their children, whose well-being is also essential to them. Contrary to scholars such as Scarth and Bergoffen, I argue that Beauvoir offers an accurate depiction of the conflicts central to the maternal condition. Mothers who strive simultaneously for their own freedom and the liberation of their children often face tragic choices. As such, it is clearly an ethical situation, possibly even paradigmatic within an ethics of ambiguity. To minimize the importance of conflict in her account of motherhood is not just to misunderstand Beauvoir on this one count but to iron out the paradoxical nature of her ethics of ambiguity.

THE EXISTENTIAL AND ETHICAL SIGNIFICANCE OF MOTHERHOOD

Beauvoir's ethics is very useful to considering the complexities of motherhood. As described in chapter 3, mothers often experience dramatic losses of self, a newfound passivity and vulnerability, and clashes between their freedom and the needs of their children. Considering Beauvoir's account of maternity in light of her philosophy, we find that she provides a means of understanding these difficulties in a positive light. Beauvoir's supposed antinatalism highlights an existentially significant paradox in motherhood—motherhood can simultaneously hold a woman back due to its demands and physical impairments as well as open her to her own authentic becoming. Ultimately, the mother's ethical "failure"—her ongoing struggle to meet the conflicting, yet interdependent, needs for care and freedom of both self and other—can contribute to both their flourishing. Nevertheless there is a tragic element to ethics, that sometimes the needs of everyone cannot be met. No amount of generosity or good intention can overcome this fact. And mothers, because they are typically responsible for the life and death of their children, *especially* cannot escape this reality.

The ambiguity of our intersubjective existence comes into sharp relief in the experiences of pregnancy and mothering. As Iris Young famously notes in "Pregnant Embodiment," to share one's body is to share one's self.[54] Many mothers and pregnant women report that their sense of self is no longer simply singular. They oscillate between defining themselves as an individual person to experiencing a sense of coconstitutionality with their child or fetus. According to Beauvoir, this ambiguity and the ambivalent feelings it gives rise to are not even escaped by the woman who has an abortion: "This intervention she demands is one she often rejects in her own heart. She is divided inside herself. It might appear that her spontaneous desire is to keep this child whose birth she is preventing; even if she does not positively want this motherhood, she feels ill at ease with the ambiguity of the act she is about to perform. . . . In addition to women who think they tried to kill a living thing, there are women many who feel they have mutilated a part of themselves."[55] In fact, women's experiences of abortions vary, and this is no doubt deeply influenced by their situation. Nevertheless, the fact that many women experience their abortions with these mixed feelings indicates that it is not easy to escape a sense of coconstitutionality with one's fetus or child.

In *The Second Sex*, speaking against a tradition that romanticizes the mother-child relationship, Beauvoir emphasizes the negative aspects of this ambiguity. She describes motherhood as immersing women into immanence and characterizes the fetus as a hostile invader who threatens the mother's life and freedom. She claims that the nausea, dizziness, diarrhea, constipation, and other common problems associated with pregnancy are largely psychosomatic—expressing the conflict between woman's own interests and those of the fetus.[56] She writes:

But pregnancy is above all a drama playing itself out in the woman between her and herself. She experiences it both as an enrichment and a mutilation; the fetus is part of her body, and it is a parasite exploiting her; she possesses it, and she is possessed by it; it encapsulates the whole future, and in carrying it, she feels as vast as the world; but this very richness annihilates her, she has the impression of not being anything else. A new existence is going to manifest itself and justify her own existence, she is proud of it; but she also feels like the plaything of obscure forces, she is tossed about, assaulted. What is unique about the pregnant woman is that at the very moment her body transcends itself, it is grasped as immanent: it withdraws into itself in nausea and discomfort; it no longer exists for itself alone and then becomes bigger than it has ever been. The transcendence of an artisan or a man of action is driven by subjectivity, but for the future mother the opposition between subject and object disappears; she and this child who swells in her form an ambivalent couple that life submerges; snared by nature, she is plant and animal, a collection of colloids, an incubator, an egg.[57]

According to Beauvoir, motherhood, and especially pregnancy, sap a woman's energy, often forcing her to give up her independent projects in order to serve another's needs. The mother feels the tremendous weight of responsibility for another, the force of another making itself through her in ways she cannot control, and alienation from her body and former life. In pregnancy the mother and child are immersed together in processes of nature, and the woman does not necessarily welcome her newfound vulnerability. Many of the ways in which the child is made, and the mother remade, cannot be willed. This is not to say that they are merely passive instruments of nature, but that the pains, illnesses, and dangers of pregnancy, plus the surprising changes in her body, make a new dimension of the passivity that we all experience especially evident. Although some find Beauvoir's views to be harsh, they do resonate with other women's accounts, as I explain in chapter 3. Beauvoir understands a pregnant woman or mother's negative feelings toward her fetus or child is not merely the emotional reaction of a woman under increased pressures and strains; it is an insightful comprehension of her existential condition.

Nevertheless, in an interview with Margaret Simons, when asked if she thought motherhood was a negative activity, Beauvoir stated:

> No, I didn't say that exactly. I said that there could be a human relation, even a completely interesting and privileged relation between mother and child but that, in many cases, it was on the order of narcissism or tyranny or something like that. But I didn't say that motherhood in itself was always something to be condemned, no, I didn't say that. No, something that has dangers, but obviously, any human adventure has its dangers, such as love or anything. I didn't say that motherhood was something negative.[58]

It is true that Beauvoir did not fully denigrate maternity. In this passage family life is described as a possible venue for transcendence: "[Some people] have been able to realize their freedom; they have given it a content without disavowing it. They have engaged themselves, without losing themselves, in political action, in intellectual or artistic research, in family or social life."[59] For Beauvoir, it is not the specific content of one's projects that mark them as works of freedom, but the manner of going about them. Even those who undertake great political or artistic projects may be surrendering to a false seriousness and immanence if they consider the values toward which they work to be absolute: "By virtue of the fact that he refuses to recognize that he is freely establishing the value of the end he sets up, the serious man makes himself the slave of that end. He forgets that every goal is at the same time a point of departure and that human freedom is the ultimate, the unique end which man should destine himself."[60] If one works toward the "unique end" of freedom, regardless of the setting, one affirms transcendence.

In fact, at times Beauvoir seems positively optimistic about the prospects of motherhood. In *The Second Sex* she says: "These examples all prove that there is no such thing as maternal 'instinct': the word does not in any case apply to the human species. The mother's attitude is defined by her total situation and by the way she accepts it. It is, as we have seen, extremely variable. But the fact is that if circumstances are not positively unfavorable, the mother will find herself enriched by a child."[61] Yet it is important to note Beauvoir's insistence that a mother's attitude is a response to her *situation*. This can account, in part, for some of her negative evaluations of motherhood's impact on women. Throughout *The Second Sex*, Beauvoir places great emphasis on the oppressive circumstances in which women find themselves. For example, Beauvoir discusses the hypocrisy around abortion in France in the 1940s. The subject was taboo, even though, she claims, "in France every year there are as many abortions as births."[62] It was made illegal because it was considered dangerous, though when conducted by a knowledgeable specialist it was much safer than back-alley abortions. In addition, Beauvoir notes that "the same society so determined to defend the rights of the fetus shows no interest in children after they are born."[63] Once born, children were considered the sole responsibility and property of their parents, regardless of the abuses and neglect suffered as a result.[64]

The situation of mothers today remains very difficult to navigate. According to Sharon Lerner's *The War on Moms: On Life in a Family-Unfriendly nation*, 16 percent of families with the lowest incomes get less than two weeks paid vacation and sick leave, and only 59 percent of those in the highest income bracket get that much time paid time off; 71 percent of the poorest working adults cannot take off sick leave for sick children; 34 percent of those in the highest income bracket have the same problem. Families below the poverty line spend a quarter of their income on childcare.[65] And the birth of a baby is the primary cause of a poverty spell for American families.[66]

Conditions such as these place women in the position of making impossible decisions. Consider one example described by Lerner. Gina St. Aubin is a married mother of three and formerly worked as a victim's advocate. After her oldest son was diagnosed with cerebral palsy, childcare became an issue. Her first sitter quit and the second was fired after admitting to frequently leaving the baby out of earshot when he cried. A qualified caregiver would cost as much as her own salary, so St Aubin quit her job. The increasing costs of medical care, gas, food, and clothing caused further financial strain. Lerner writes:

> Gina started to panic. She had already cut back on almost everything she could. The family dressed in secondhand clothes. They hadn't renewed their zoo pass and didn't buy any birthday presents or cards. Rather than making a plate for herself at mealtimes and risking the possibility of wasting food, she usually ate the children's leftovers. [Her son] even stopped participating in the Special Olympics because St. Aubin felt they couldn't afford his entry fee. Finally she decided to cut back on her son's therapies, several of which were not covered by insurance. Although she fears that his prospects will dwindle as a result, it had come to those out-of-pocket costs or the mortgage. . . . Facing the bleakest economy in decades, many families are grappling with similarly unimaginable choices: childcare or food? Tuition or nursing home payment? Rent or medicine? The collapse of the housing market, combined with widespread job loss and the skyrocketing costs of food, gas, and other such essentials, has made the reality of many American families that much harsher.[67]

Facing choices as stark as these, a woman's concerns for her own flourishing are pushed beyond the back burner right off the stove entirely.

Beauvoir asserts that the mother's own well-being is, in fact, important, but, insofar as her welfare is intertwined with her children's, discerning *the good* requires a complex calculus. Moreover, sometimes the decision regards not only the good of the mother versus the good of the child but between multiple children. This was the case for one mother featured on MTV's recent documentary *No Easy Decision*. Markai, the teenage mother of an infant under one, finds herself pregnant after misunderstanding the proper use of her birth control. Believing that she could not follow through with giving her child up for adoption, she faces the decision of having an abortion or raising the new baby. Markai and the baby's father, James, have just reached a level of financial stability that allows them to have their own apartment. Having both suffered poverty while growing up, their key concern is that, if they keep the second pregnancy, the daughter they already have will suffer. They decide that having an abortion is the responsible solution. However, this decision is made with regret. The day after the abortion they struggle with what to call the terminated pregnancy. They find it upsetting to call it a baby, but the solution offered by the counselor at the abortion clinic—calling it "a little bunch of cells"—feels painfully inadequate. Pointing tearfully to their daughter, Markai says "Nothing but a bunch of cells can turn out just like her." This example shows that the good of mother, child, and the rest of the family cannot be divorced from one another. What would be the ethical failure here? To keep the pregnancy or to abort it? In either case, the family suffers. Both Markai and Gina St. Aubin confront the tragic face of ethical failure. They recognize that, whatever their decision, someone *will* suffer. They are left with figuring out who will be neglected and how much, facing their inability to be infinitely responsible for others.

According to Levinas' philosophy, an abortion could never be ethically justified, because one's responsibility for the other is infinite. But infinite responsibility is an unsupportable fantasy. To deny that, in some cases, someone's well-being *will* be sacrificed is just bad faith. It denies both the realities of human limitation *and* freedom. As the existentialism truism affirms: choosing not to choose is still a choice. In Markai's case, choosing not to choose would mean opting for a financially intolerable situation. In Gina's situation it would mean losing her house. In fact, in order to care for their children, mothers *must* recognize their limitations. This is why it is not paradoxical for a woman to claim (as many do) that having an abortion is a *mothering* decision, not shirking their responsibility. In chapter 3 we saw that Judith Arcana argues for this view in her essay "Abortion Is a Motherhood Issue." This perspective is also affirmed in *No Easy Decision*. Following the documentary portion of the show, there is an interview with Markai and two other young women (who do not have children) who have had abortions. They each claim that having an abortion is acknowledging, not evading, their responsibilities. One of the women states: "The decision to terminate my pregnancy was a parenting decision. It was a parenting choice and I feel like that dialogue is not out there at all. People assume that if you have an abortion it's because you are denying the fact that you are a parent, but it's not. It's not at all."[68] These women agreed that in their circumstances, having an abortion was the most responsible option. Beauvoir agrees that making an ethical choice sometimes, unfortunately, involves leaving one person's needs aside. To deny this fact, as Levinas does, is to evade the true gravity of our choices.

If Beauvoir seems ambivalent about motherhood's potential, I maintain that this is the appropriate attitude, given its potentials to initiate both growth and devastation. Beauvoir is apparently aware of the contradictions of her own position: "As the meaning of pregnancy is thus ambiguous, it is natural for the woman's attitude to be ambivalent as well";[69] "pregnancy and motherhood are experienced in different ways depending on whether they take place in revolt, resignation, satisfaction or enthusiasm."[70] It is not that some mothers are satisfied and some are resigned, that some revolt and some are enthusiastic. As we read on, we find that Beauvoir appreciates that an individual woman may experience motherhood in most or all of these manners. She may feel fulfilled at times and revolt at others:

> One must keep in mind that the decisions and feelings the young mother expresses do not always correspond to her deep desires. An unwed mother can be overwhelmed in material terms by the burden suddenly imposed on her, be openly distressed by it, and yet find in the child the satisfaction of secretly harbored dreams; inversely, a young married woman who joyfully and proudly welcomes her pregnancy can fear it in silence, hate it with obsessions, fantasies, and infantile memories that she refuses to recognize.[71]

The mother expresses her ambivalence in contradictory fantasies about the child's future. He may be a hero, a monster, or a little bit of each.

For mothers, as for anyone, Beauvoir arguees that the recognition of her ambiguous condition is the measure of her authenticity. In parenting, the alternatives to this honest assessment are inauthentic denial of one's own independent needs or an oppressive attitude toward one's child.

Devotion is one form of this self-delusion and seriousness that Beauvoir finds especially odious:

> Let's suppose the other needed me and that his existence had an absolute value. Then my being is justified since I am for a being whose existence is justified. I am released from both the risk and the anguish. By positing an absolute end before me, I have abdicated my freedom; questions are no longer posed; I no longer want to be anything but a response to that appeal which requires me. The master is hungry and thirsty; the devoted slave desires only to be the dish that he prepares and the glass of water that he brings to appease the hunger and thirst; he makes himself into a docile instrument. . . . Many men, and even more women, wish for such a rest: let us devote ourselves.[72]

The utter dependency of children combined with the cultural belief that women are naturally responsible for them conspire to yoke mothers to their children. Indeed, maternal devotion is the most culturally glorified escape from freedom for women. It provides a false release from the risks of having one's own projects and facing their potential failure and futility. For a mother to surrender her transcendence to the care of a child is immoral, in Beauvoir's terms, even if the mother thinks she is doing it for the good of her child. Taking up an attitude of devotion exacerbates mothers' resentment toward their children, clouding their ability to parent effectively. Recall from chapter 3 that Freud proposed that an excess of devotion was actually repressed ambivalence:

> Every psychoanalyst knows how infallibly this anxious excess of tenderness can be resolved even under the most improbable circumstances, as for instance, when it appears between mother and child, or in the case of affectionate married people. Applied to the treatment of privileged persons this theory of an ambivalent feeling would reveal that their veneration, their very deification, is opposed in the unconscious by an intense hostile tendency, so that, as we had expected, the situation of an ambivalent feeling is here realized.[73]

Freud believes that mothers who display a disproportionate amount of fondness for their children do so as a reaction formation to conceal their hatred. Repressed hostility will still find its expression, even if the person who experiences it does not recognize it as such. Beauvoir noticed the conjoined attitudes of self-abnegation and bitterness in her own mother, the only cure for which was being on her deathbed. Beauvoir writes: "No question of renunciation or sacrifice any more: her first duty was to get better and so to look after herself; giving herself up to her own wishes and her own pleasures with no holding back, she was at last freed from resentment."[74]

On this point as well, Beauvoir's attitude is rightly in opposition to Levinas, who thinks that bowing to the other is the solution to ethical conflicts. Levinas proposes that the other should always win out, no matter the cost to oneself, but, as Beauvoir points out, there is a moral cost to this solution. Even when a mother loves her child as deeply as Levinas predicts, this does not mediate the validity of conflicting interests. Mothers do have a more or less individuated sense of self that existed before the birth of the child and that exists not only to serve but also to flourish in and of itself. The person who is denied such opportunities becomes unable to help others thrive. Beauvoir safeguards the importance of caring for both the self and the other and shows how complex this effort really is. When the needs of self and other are intertwined as well as in conflict, to propose Levinas's solution—infinite responsibility for the other—is overly simplistic.

Beauvoir categorically refuses the idealization of maternal self-immolation, revealing its sinister potential. This argument is illustrated in "Throwing the Book," Sara Levine's essay about her mother-in-law's devotion to her son. As Beauvoir predicts, the devoted mother clings to her child's dependence as the source of her own meaning. As a result, she cannot see her son beyond his babyhood: "The woman holds a storehouse of anecdotes about the man I love, anecdotes I longed to hear until I realized all the stories took place before he turned three. Not a single nickname has been allowed to grow stale, though on my first visit to the Cotwold cottage, I observed that 'our best boy,' our 'Small,' routinely bumped his head on the bedroom ceiling, having grown to six-foot-two."[75] In spite of having moved several times, Levine's mother-in-law kept her son's baby dishes in the cabinet and his first Wellies on the doormat. Levine describes a turn in her husband's baby book in which her mother-in-law begins to write from the baby's point of view. "Right after she acknowledges the challenges of raising a baby, almost as if it were too difficult to negotiate the tensions between *I* and *he*, she throws over the vexed I and begins to write the book as if she were the baby herself. . . . Reading this was like watching a woman get swallowed alive."[76] Later in the essay Levine discusses the oppressive tone of the baby book received as a gift for her own daughter. It encouraged her to give easy meaning to the "welter of feelings and sensations" she experienced, from her "big honking mother love" to "the very information (ambivalence, conflict, the seeds of a storyteller's art) that, my mother-in-law instinctively understood, a baby book is obliged to purge."[77] Levine finds that even a seemingly harmless artifact, such as a baby book, encourages women to repress the realities of motherhood and deny their own perspective. "Unfortunately, as I saw my handwriting loop across that paper, a part of me that I liked—the independent thinker part—seemed to sicken and die."[78] Mothers are surrounded by propaganda—from diaper commercials to childcare manuals—that encourages them to focus on trivialities and vague sentimentalities, to cling to their children's dependence as their source of meaning, and ultimately to lose themselves in maternal devotion.

Beauvoir claims that maternal devotion does not end well for mother *or* child. The mother's surrender and despotism go hand in hand: "many so called devotions . . . are in truth tyrannies."[79] If the mother loses her sense of herself as an individual, then she will develop a need for the child to depend on her in order to maintain her identity. To Beauvoir, the self-sacrificing mother becomes like a nurse who resents the patient that gets well.[80] She may work to keep the child dependent; denying him what is needed to realize his potential and to respond to a future that remains unknown. "And in practice raising a child as one cultivates a plant which one does not consult about its needs is very different from considering it as a freedom to whom the future must be opened. Thus we can set up point number one: the good of an individual or group of individuals requires that it be taken as an absolute end of our action; but we are not authorized to decide upon this end *a priori*."[81] A plant strives toward light and water, and the way a particular plant will strive can be known in advance, but a child's ends cannot be known in advance. "The mother can have *her* reasons for wanting *a* child, but she cannot give to *this* other—who tomorrow is going to be—his own *raisons d'être*; she engenders him in the generality of his body, not in the specificity of his existence."[82]

On this topic, her views seem to be in agreement with Sartre's *Notebooks for an Ethics*. He states that, in order to be an authentic parent, one must "consider . . . everyday emancipation as the real end . . . as freedom, [the child] ought to be recognized for himself."[83] The authentic parent gives the child a concrete sense of her freedom and eventually makes herself, as caretaker, obsolete. This does not mean that the authentic parent overlooks the child's need for protection and nurturance. In "Sartre, Embodied Minds, Authenticity, and Childhood," Adrian Mirvish provides a helpful illustration of how parents negotiate between protecting the child in her fragility and encouraging the free pursuit of her own projects. When the parent teaches the child to ride a bicycle, at first he hangs onto it while she gets the feeling of it. Eventually, however, when the child seems ready, the parent must let go.[84] As Beauvoir insists, a parent cannot control who a child becomes: "To bring a child into the world is not to found him."[85] "I bring a child into the world; if he becomes a criminal, I am not an evildoer."[86] Though one may be deeply invested in another's freedom and well-being, another person's life cannot justifiably be one's own project.

Ideally, the mother gives the child a concrete sense of her freedom. As a healthy child develops, every milestone achieved is a step toward a more independent existence. According to Beauvoir, one can only be a point of departure for another, a platform for her transcendence. "I never create anything for the other except points of departure. . . . I am not the one who founds the other; I am only the instrument upon which the other founds himself. He alone makes himself be by transcending my gifts."[87] "And that is exactly what makes for the touching character of maternal love, properly understood."[88] This moving maternal love requires the maintenance of the mother's own individuality, provision for her needs, and meaningful work beyond the care of her children:

> In a properly organized society where the child would in great part be taken care of by the group, where the mother would be cared for and helped, motherhood would absolutely not be incompatible with women's work. . . . It is the woman who has the richest personal life who will give the most to her child and who will ask for the least, she who acquires real human values through effort and struggle will be the most fit to bring up children. If too often today a woman has a hard time reconciling the interests of her children with a profession that demands long hours away from home and all her strength, it is because, on the one hand, woman's work is still too often a kind of slavery; on the other hand, no effort has been made to ensure children's health, care, and education outside the home. This is social neglect: but it is solipsism to justify it by pretending that a law was written in heaven or in the bowels of the earth that requires that the mother and child belong to each other exclusively; this mutual belonging in reality only constitutes a double and harmful oppression.[89]

Beauvoir argues that given proper support women can have both satisfying family life and careers, but the social neglect of mothers continues. For example, in the United States, women do twice as much housework as men, many women are forced by their employers to choose between working more than full time and quitting their jobs entirely, and single women with children earn fifty-six cents of every dollar that married men make.[90] Only one in seven of the fifteen million children who qualified for federally funded subsidized childcare in 2000 received it.[91] Women who are attempting to do it all, in spite of these conditions, are simply worn out. There is what Lerner calls "an epidemic of exhaustion" among mothers "sweeping through cubicle, cluttered kitchens, and child-care centers around the country. Call these women the maxed-out generation, if you like; victims of a family-unfriendly nation; or simply 'hosed.'"[92] For most mothers, a "rich personal life" is but a flight of the imagination. Thus, if

Beauvoir infrequently addresses the elevating potential of motherhood, this is in keeping with her emphasis on the importance of social, political, and material context. She rightly points out that, with conditions as they are, having children threatens a woman's well-being in all respects.

Beauvoir's emphasis on a *situated* ethics is a critical improvement, especially over Levinas. As mentioned in chapter 5, Merleau-Ponty briefly notes the importance of a mother's context in her responses to her child. For Levinas, however, one's responsibility for the other is infinite regardless of social location. In contrast, Beauvoir considers our ethical responses as they are positioned in larger circumstances, especially with regard to maternal responsibility: "The mother's relation with her children is defined within the overall context of her life; it depends on her relations with her husband, her past, her occupations, herself; it is a fatal and absurd error to claim to see a child as a panacea. . . . The young woman must be in a psychological, moral, and material situation that allows her to bear the responsibility; if not, the consequences will be disastrous."[93] Given our interdependence, Beauvoir articulates how the burden of ethical life should not rest solely on the shoulders of the individual. As she demonstrates, the inherently conflicted nature of the mother-child relationship is exacerbated by insufficient social support. Given the contemporary constraints faced by mothers, they need a way to understand the feelings and impulses they are most ashamed of beyond the discourse of individual moral failure or success.

The double binds of mothering can lead to homicidal and/or suicidal depression and acts of violent retribution or neglect. Maternal aggression, a phenomenon that is much more common than recognized, is often a sign that the mother is in need of physical and psychological distance. The desire to pull back, to reclaim one's bodily boundaries, can be an appropriate and productive move toward separation on the mother's part.[94] Her need for independence guards against a potentially consuming intimacy. As Adrienne Rich writes, mothers find the need to "struggle from that one-to-one intensity into new realization, or reaffirmation, of her being-unto-herself. . . . The mother has to wean herself from the infant and the infant from herself. In psychologies of child-rearing the emphasis is placed on 'letting the child go' for the child's sake. But the mother needs to let it go as much or more for her own . . . it is not enough to let our children go; we need selves of our own to return to."[95]

Beauvoir rightly thinks that whether or not a mother is ethical in the existential sense depends both on her situation and how she takes it up. In a society that alternately romanticizes and condemns mothers, it is a brave overcoming of cultural denial to recognize the duality of maternal experience. For this reason, maternal ambivalence, though painful, is a psychological and ethical *achievement*. As Rozsika Parker writes: "the mother's achievement of ambivalence—the awareness of her co-existing love and hate for the [child]—can promote a sense of concern and responsibility towards, and differentiation of self from, the [child]. Maternal ambivalence signifies the mother's capacity to know herself and to tolerate traits in herself she may consider less than admirable—and to hold a more complete image of her baby. Accordingly, idealization and/or denigration of self and, by extension, her baby, diminish."[96]

The potential of motherhood to enrich comes from the fact that others can keep us from "hardening in the absurdity of facticity."[97] A mother's identity may have been based primarily on her own achievements, actions, and qualities before she had children, but, to the extent that she cares for her child's well-being, this is no longer true. For a loving mother, her sense of self, groundedness, and well-being are, at least in part, dependent on meeting the needs of her child. In such cases, one who obstructs her self-determination is also integral to her. Though one is never fully transparent to oneself, self-alienation is dramatic when one is in symbiotic relation to one's saboteur. Beauvoir believes in the transformative power of disturbances to one's self-concept. And, indeed, there is an abundance of recent motherhood memoirs describing how the experience of motherhood changed a woman for the better. In a recent review of a number of these autobiographies, Kristin Kovacic writes: "In each book, it takes a lot of time, a lot of therapy, and a baby, to get to full maturity."[98] Mothering inspires many women to take charge of their own lives for the first time. In two examples, *From Beer to Maternity* by Maggie Lamond Simone and *Lit* by May Karr, motherhood helps the mother, a chronic drunk, to get sober. But as Kovacic notes, it is not mothering alone that does the trick. Motherhood inspires these women to find meaningful projects of their own.

The other invites one to see oneself from an outside perspective, from the point of view of *their* needs and desires. Mothers inhabit a powerful tension between their self-identities and the force of the child's and society's views of her. At many turns women are invited to instrumentalize themselves for the care of others. Should she resist that pull, she will acquire an identity that exists in authentic ambiguity. Where women expect to have an independent identity and yet, as mothers, are fundamentally intertwined with their children, there may be no way to avoid feeling torn.

"WITHOUT FAILURE, NO ETHICS"

—SIMONE DE BEAUVOIR, *THE ETHICS OF AMBIGUITY*

For Beauvoir, a successful ethical life means that one strives toward one's own transcendence and contributes to the opportunities of others.[99] She believes that we are meant to reach beyond our limitations and thus we will often fall short of what we want to be. We require the liberation of others to succeed, but this is far from guaranteed. Caring for other people will often drain us of the energy to pursue our own projects, and when we do manage to help them we may fail to fully liberate them. Those who have opportunities for free action will often not support my own projects, but rather assert their values and desires in opposition to mine. Likewise, since everyone's interests are not the same, those projects of mine that *do* reach fruition are likely to impede some people, even if they aid others. To top it off, these conflicts with others are both fundamental to and frustrate my own freedom. As Beauvoir sees it, failure is entwined in the braid of ethical life.

Beauvoir makes clear the importance of acknowledging our limitations in "Moral Idealism and Political Realism." In this essay she describes the problems with political action, which she conceives as one kind of transcendent action. Political action is tricky because in changing the world to benefit some, others are likely to get hurt. The moral idealist and political realist wish to deny the significance of these facts; both make an absolute object of their ends, which allows them to deny the sacrifices of their causes. This recognition of the possibility for misjudgment in one's ethical and political life is paramount. We must acknowledge our actions entail risks that no absolute authority can safely justify: "This means that the political man cannot avoid making decisions or choices; things will not give him ready-made answers, neither on the level of being nor on the level of values. In each new situation he must question himself anew about his ends, and he must choose and justify them without assistance. But it is precisely in this free engagement that morality resides."[100] Beauvoir requires that we continue to question the validity of our projects and the costs of achieving them. The likelihood of ethical failure does not mean that our existence is absurd and meaningless, but it does indicate that life's significance is not pregiven. "Ethics is not the ensemble of constituted values and principles; it is the constituting movement through which values and principles are posited; it is the movement that an authentically moral man must reproduce himself."[101] The meaning of life must be striven toward and asserted, but also interrogated and justified. To this end, a certain amount of self-doubt is essential.

The fact that we do not achieve moral perfection means that we must continue to strive, and for an existential ethics this is certainly a good thing. Beauvoir rejoices at the tension between failure and success in "Introduction to an Ethics of Ambiguity" as bringing one in touch with a central truth of the human experience. She merrily declares, "I delight in this very effort toward an impossible possession."[102] In this case she focuses on the impossibility of complete self-determination as "delicious torment, cruel happiness, blessed torture."[103] Nevertheless, a bit of self-deception accompanies her happiness in this early work. As she later finds, the disappointment of failing oneself and others cannot be salved. She writes more intimately of the failure to be completely there for a beloved other in *A Very Easy Death*—the chronicle of her mother's last days. In this work the nettles sting cruelly, not sweetly. She writes: "When someone you love dies you pay for the sin of outliving her with a thousand piercing regrets . . . you feel that she should have had more room in your life—all the room, if need be. You snatch yourself away from this wildness: she was only one among many. But since you never do all you might for anyone—not even within the arguable limits that you have set yourself— you have plenty of room left for self-reproach."[104]

Our moral obligations to others are weighty, sometimes to the point of becoming oppressive. For numerous reasons this is even more strongly the case in a mother's relationship to her children—the economic situation of mothers is often so bleak, their responsibility is nearly complete (as the obligation to care for children is insufficiently shared), and the consequences of their actions can make the difference between the life and death of another person. The interconnection between the interests of the self and other is typically a core feature of the mother-child relationship. Yet, because the neediness of children can be so overwhelming, conflicts of interest are even more prominent and inevitable than in any other kind of relationship. Thus the possibility of grave moral failure is a real and terrifying prospect to mothers. The unique features of this relationship mean opportunities for regret are perhaps more numerous than in any other kind. She finds herself continually under question. Perhaps this is why Adrienne Rich once said that "guilt, guilt, guilt" is the mother's real G-spot.

The denial of pre-established ideals requires that one attend to the particular situation. For example, some think that a mother should always attend her child's needs before her own, but life is rarely that simple. Many women who think that they would never have an abortion find themselves in circumstances in which they can not sustain a child's life or provide for her flourishing. Sometimes it is necessary to secure one's own oxygen mask before others. And sometimes "saving" one child might mean aborting the life of another. Assuming we can know the right thing to do in advance is a denial of the unpredictable nature of the future and the needs and desires of other individuals. That is why parents often find unsolicited childcare advice from friends, relatives, and strangers to be so obnoxious. What works for one baby and family does not always work for another. When left to cry himself to sleep, one baby learns to self-soothe while another cries until he vomits. For this reason, Beauvoir refuses to give her readers advice: "It will be said that these considerations remain quite abstract. What must be done practically? Which action is good? Which is bad? To ask such a question is also to fall into naïve abstraction. We don't ask the physicist, 'Which hypotheses are true?' Nor the artist, 'By what procedures does one produce a work whose beauty is guaranteed?' Ethics does not furnish recipes any more than do science and art. One can merely propose methods."[105]

Beauvoir helps to make clear that even the most generous mother will rightfully feel a conflict between her child's needs and desires and her own. Since there is no guarantee that children will recognize their mothers as independent of them and having needs of their own, it may be necessary and appropriate for the mother to assert her interests against those of the child. While a sense of *mutuality* may motivate the desire to nurture, *dispute* forces recognition of interpersonal divergence. One's child, no matter how beloved, is also radically Other, with discrepant goals, experiences, and sometimes even values. A mother's self-coincidence is unsettled by unclear boundaries between herself and her child. Yet the inability to gain full self-certainty is a *good* failure insofar as it opens a gap for ethical self-questioning. Phenomenologically the conflict between mother and child is there. Recognizing this clash is the beginning of negotiating *mutual* transcendence—the only kind of transcendence that is really possible.

CONCLUSION

The Stranger of My Flesh—
an Existential Phenomenological Ethics

An existential-phenomenological ethics is written from the perspective of an incarnate consciousness that is born in proximity to others *and* radical distinction from them. From this point of view, we find that intersubjective existence is a living contradiction. Our connections to others are profound and visceral; we share intimate space, intersect in embodiment, and coestablish the world's meaning, dimensions, and veracity. Our freedom and our life's unique meaning are dependent on our responsiveness to others. We need each other's generosity and collaboration; we are their facticity, and they are ours. Nevertheless, we suffer the abyss of our divergent bodies and perspectives. Although our bodies overlap and interpenetrate, we still remain within our own skin. Even though the other is integral to who I am, she also exceeds my comprehension. We can be drawn into the outlook of another, but we are never in her place. Her alterity is insurmountable. Even the child born of one's own body is estranged flesh.

The other threatens any enjoyment of self-sameness that I might experience; she undermines the complacent familiarity I may temporarily have with myself. And it is this interruption that is the opening for ethics. It is motivated by the needs of others, by their vulnerability, and thus it originates with them, not me. Since I am entangled with others before I have the opportunity to will or deny it, I am drawn to care for them before I can consider whether or not it is in my own interests. In this respect my ethical involvement is passive. Yet full responsivity also requires an active concern and effort. This becomes apparent because the neediness of others can also invite aggression or neglect. The phenomenon of maternal ambivalence vividly demonstrates that the desire to commit violence can occur even when there is a feeling of sympathy and connection with the other. In fact, intense intimacy can lead to feelings of claustrophobia and an oppressive level of responsibility and thus *instigate* hostility. Acting on impulse alone can harm as well as hurt. Passive responsiveness is insufficient; intelligence, strategy, and resourcefulness are needed to navigate these difficulties.

In all cases there are practical limitations on what one can do for another. Caring for others threatens one's own well-being, even as it is absolutely integral to it, because their needs and desires sometimes clash with one's own. There is no easy way out of this problem; devotion, detachment, and self-centeredness are all flawed orientations. The ambiguous nature of our intersubjective life undermines the purity of either egoism or altruism. Such an either/or attitude disregards the ways in which we are integral to one another—that one's own well-being and freedom depends on that of others. Yet the preservation of independence is also integral to ethical responsiveness.

Conducting a phenomenology of ethics, I aim to describe ethical life as it is experienced. Ethics involves an orientation toward others and oneself, and, with its careful attention to lived experience, phenomenology can reveal the structure of these relations. Yet this orientation cannot simply be assumed; there are many obstacles to fulfilling one's duties to oneself and others. To be ethical is something toward which we must strive. And we may often find that ethical success and failure are intertwined.

Like everyone else, mothers are capable of the basest crimes—murder, rape, criminal neglect, and so on. Yet when a mother commits such crimes against her child our horror is exponentially greater. It is not just anyone who is expected to care for a child, to be the person who makes their basic trust in the world possible. Of course, other people can care for a child and help that child to thrive, but the fact of our current situation is that, if a mother is ignorant, insane, overwhelmed, indifferent, or malicious, that child's chances of flourishing (or even surviving) are dramatically reduced. Ultimately, it should come as no surprise that we romanticize this relationship; we do not want to dwell on the gruesome acts committed against the most vulnerable and innocent. Nevertheless, filicide may simply be one extreme result of a fairly normal state.

Conflicts of interest are an unavoidable fact of human existence exacerbated by living in a society that privileges some and exploits others. Thus an active ethical response requires the deliberation of someone who can, with limited resources, balance other-care with self-care. Not every mother is capable of this. And, even in the best of circumstances, and in spite of our best efforts, the needs of everyone cannot always be met; every life may not be sustainable. Love, even maternal love, does not conquer all. But this failure should invite both outrage and action. We must struggle against inequalities and fight for the liberation and care of every human being for our own sake as well as theirs. Of course, it is beyond the ability of a single individual to redress this alone; individual moral responsibility can only be *part* of the solution. The fight for justice must be a collective human effort.

Consider the case of Angela McAnulty. On February 24, 2011, McAnulty, a mother from Eugene, Oregon was sentenced to death by a jury for murdering her fifteen-year-old daughter, Jeanette Maples. McAnulty admitted to having tortured the girl for several years. Testimony revealed that the mother denied her daughter food (placing locks on the cupboards) and water (so that she had to drink water from the toilet in order to survive). The girl had been starved to such an extent that she weighed only fifty pounds when she collapsed from cardiac arrest. Her brain was bleeding from massive head injuries, she had flesh torn from her body with belts and sticks, and suffered hundreds of other injuries, some of them infected all the way to the bone.[1] According to McAnulty's husband, the mother would turn up the television in the living room or the vacuum cleaner to cover the sounds of her daughter's screaming and then she would strip the girl naked and whip her. In his opening statement, Lane County Deputy District Attorney Erik Hasselman stated: "The one woman who could have saved her was the very person who was responsible for her torture, her mother."[2]

Clearly, in the eyes of the judge and jury, McAnulty did something unforgivable and irredeemable; she is the first woman to be sentenced to execution since the death penalty was reinstated in Oregon in 1984 and she will be only the second woman to be executed by the state in history. McAnulty's abuse of her daughter is undeniably horrific, and she should be held responsible for what she did. However, when we remove the assumption that mothers *alone* are responsible for the well-being of their children, we must challenge the prosecutor's argument that only her mother could have saved her. Many other people could have saved Jeanette Maples: her father, her stepfather, her step-grandmother, state officials in Oregon and California, teachers and peers at Jeanette's school. Every one of these people had some indication that the girl could be in trouble. Anthony Maples, Jeanette's father, hadn't seen or talked to his daughter in nearly a decade.[3] McAnulty and Maples's two sons had been removed from their care and placed in foster care by the state of California, yet Jeanette was left with McAnulty.[4] Lynn McAnulty, the girl's step-grandmother, said that she anonymously called Oregon state child welfare officials several times because she suspected that the girl was being abused.[5] The *Seattle Weekly* reported that "friends and administrators at Cascade Middle School in Eugene remember seeing Maples coming to school in torn clothes—sometimes they'd catch glimpses of terrible bruises."[6] Worst of all, Richard McAnulty, the condemned woman's husband, was fully aware that Jeanette was being severely beaten and starved. He also pleaded guilty to murder by abuse for his role in the girl's death, but was sentenced to twenty-five years' imprisonment (instead of receiving the death penalty), though the prosecutor stated that Mr. McAnulty was just as responsible for the girl's death as her mother. All these people could have done more to help Jeanette. Indeed, it takes a village to raise a child, but it also takes a village to allow one to be so severely abused. To merely blame the mother, to pass her off as pathological, is grossly insufficient. It is not enough to ask the question "Why did she do it?" We must also ask: how did *we* let this happen in our community (this community of Eugene, Oregon where I myself was a graduate student at the time)? What might have been done to McAnulty herself that might have contributed to the rage she vented on her daughter? As Meyer and Oberman state: "these cases often leave one with the sense that there is blood on more than one pair of hands."[7]

We need to take collective responsibility for the lives of children, not rely on the resources of a single individual, often largely on her own, because our cultural *myths* say that she is naturally suited to the job. It is urgent that we overcome our denial and realize that the impulses moving women to kill their children are surprisingly commonplace. Our society constantly proclaims the importance of caring for children, and yet we can find children without food, proper clothing, education, health care, and basic safety everywhere. We need to channel our outrage and blame into something more productive, into finding, protecting, and caring for those children who are, right now, suffering.

Philosophers can make a unique contribution to clarifying the complexities of the maternal situation, but in order to do so they must listen carefully to the experiences of mothers to understand their material and social conditions. Generally speaking, the philosophical canon is guilty of either ignoring or mistreating mothers. If philosophy is to have concrete relevance, then it must go beyond the metaphorical and romanticized perspective. The metaphors we use are not neutral; they advocate an interpretation of the phenomenon in question. Thus it is only right to check these metaphorical understandings against the lives they intend to invoke. When we take seriously the true complexity of motherhood, we find that the mother-child relationship is philosophically rich indeed.

At the beginning of this book I said that I would demonstrate that it is *because of*, not in spite of, the tensions inherent to mothering that it is an instructive case for ethics. And, indeed, these discoveries extend beyond the mother-child relationship. We have found that caring for others, though it is something that one sometimes feels compelled to do, does not come naturally. Romanticizing any type of relationship or setting up impossible ideals is counterproductive. Mothers dealing with their ambivalence demonstrate how important it is to recognize one's limitations. The acknowledgment of hostility toward someone in need is central to being able to respond more appropriately to her call. Emotion can be thought provoking, but it is also thoughtful and reflective in itself; it reveals its own understanding of a situation before it is fully reflected upon.

Conflicted mothers teach us that deliberative agency is part of what enables one to resist violence and to nurture another. Empathy and connection are a minute aspect of what is necessary for ethical responsiveness. It is usually more tedious than transcendent. Thus there must be a continually renewed commitment or adoption; one must *repeatedly* choose to care for another. Even in genuine mutuality the insurmountable alterity of the other cannot be overcome. While a sense of *unanimity* with someone may motivate an ethical response, *dispute* forces recognition of interpersonal divergence. When taken together, these attitudes entreat us to expand and practice self-knowledge, sound judgment, and problem-solving abilities in order to respond fittingly to one another.

The ethical successes and failures of mothers demonstrate that although our circumstances do not dictate our behaviors, they highly constrain what is possible. Ethical responsiveness requires skills, intelligence, resources, and emotional support. If an ethical response is asymmetrical (as it typically is in the mother-child relation), then this must be balanced by other factors in a person's life. This is why meeting our responsibilities depends on the familial, political, cultural, and material context. An individualistic model of ethical responsibility is both inaccurate and destructive. It has enabled and encouraged the denial of the need for care and thereby made care work needlessly exploitative.

Acknowledging both our dependence and dependents is critical to becoming ethical and fully realizing our capacities. Children are the primal parasites that make the necessity of caregiving undeniably visible. Yet their dependency has something even greater to offer. They invite a fuller expression of our freedom. This view of freedom is not just the ability to do whatever we want. Rather, by making use of our freedom (in order to write a book, for instance) we become entangled in the lives and needs of others. This freedom is articulated not only in overt acts but also in restraint, in permitting the interruption of our enjoyment and self-possession. This generosity is not at odds with personal liberty; it is precisely the recognition of our mutual value and freedom.

Maternal experience also demonstrates that the likelihood of failure must be a part of any ethical theory. Being generous is not always prudent, beautiful, or fun. The coercive vulnerability of others can incite hostility, resentment, and even violence. But acknowledging this can lead us to consider how to reasonably meet competing demands. Recognizing the prevalence of ethical ambivalence means we cannot so easily dismiss, pathologize, or demonize those who fail. The necessity of adoption means that no one is absolved of responsibility if someone is neglected, abused, or murdered. Nietzsche wrote: "All evil do I accredit to thee: therefore do I desire of thee the good."[8] Mothers have opportunity for great crimes and great heroism. Maternal ethics are illustrative precisely because both these options are possible; we are capable of being both better and worse than we typically imagine.

NOTES

1. MAD MOTHERS, BAD MOTHERS, AND WHAT A GOOD MOTHER WOULD DO

1. http://news.yahoo.com/s/ap/20110416/ap_on_he_me/us_when_mothers_kill.
2. Meyer and Oberman, *Mothers Who Kill Their Children*, 93.
3. Ibid., 89.
4. http://www.latimes.com/news/nationworld/nation/la-na-mother-drowns -kids-20110414,0,221941.story.
5. Ibid.
6. Ibid.
7. http://news.yahoo.com/s/ap/20110416/ap_on_he_me/us_when_mothers_kill.
8. Ibid.
9. Ibid.
10. For examples see LaChance Adams and Lundquist "Introduction: The Philo-sophical Significance of Pregnancy, Childbirth, and Mothering," 3–5.
11. For further examples of feminist phenomenologists see ibid., 13–15.
12. Merleau-Ponty, *Phenomenology*, vii.
13. Ruddick, *Maternal Thinking*, 62.
14. Fisher, "Phenomenology and Feminism," 33.
15. For more details on this approach and its philosophical background see ibid., 6–13.
16. At this point we may begin to ask whether ethical ambivalence and intersubjec-tive ambiguity exist beyond the Western context. I argue that these structures

will exist wherever there is the attempt to negotiate intimacy and separation. Is there a culture on earth or in history in which this was not at issue? This is a question to answer in dialogue with anthropologists and historians. Yet even at this point there is some evidence that these findings will be relevant across cultures. According to some writings by post–World War II Japanese feminists, concerns of maternal ambivalence and intersubjective ambiguity do extend to their context. Some scholars argue that pregnancy, childbirth, and child rearing have given Japanese women experiences of ambiguity and intense self-alienation such as those I have described here, which they describe as akin to the Zen realization of no-self. Sakiko, "Living as a Woman and Thinking as a Mother in Japan." They have also claimed, as I have, that this alienation possesses a positive transformative power. Yusa, "Women Rocking the Boat." Clearly more research would be required to fully consider the applicability of these terms to additional contexts.

17. Some will already note that I differ from scholars who claim that Levinas does not address *actual* mothers. I will give my full reasons for this in the chapter on Levinas.

18. I'm thinking here of care ethics, but of others as well, such as Tuana's *Women and the History of Philosophy* and Pateman's *The Sexual Contract*.

19. Although I don't think that she fully agrees with me on this point, this inspiration came during a presentation by Claire Katz at the *Psychology for the Other* symposium at Seattle University in November 2012.

20. The idea of the "primal parasite" came to me during a reading of a paper by David Alexander Craig on primal parricide at the International Association for Environmental Philosophy, October 2012.

21. Oliver, *Womanizing Nietzsche*, 189.

2. THE MOTHER AS ETHICAL EXEMPLAR IN CARE ETHICS

1. Jagger, "Feminist Ethics," 81.

2. Gilligan, *In a Different Voice*, 30.

3. Gilligan found that both men and women apply both ethical models. Although differences between the groups were not absolute, there were significant recognizable patterns of disparity.

4. Tronto, "Women and Caring," 103.

5. Noddings is one exception to this. She believes that feminine caretaking arises from women's "deep feminine psychological structure" and that women should "retain their natural orientation." Meanwhile, men should not adopt women's relational patterns but instead "bring their best human and masculine qualities to the experience of parenting." Noddings, *Caring*, 129.

6. Bartky, "Feeding Egos and Tending Wounds"; Card, "Gender and Moral Luck"; MacKinnon, *Feminism Unmodified*; Puka, "The Liberation of Caring."

7. See especially Kittay, *Love's Labor.*

8. Puka, "The Liberation of Caring," 65.

9. Ruddick, *Maternal Thinking*, 25.

10. I find it curious that most care ethicists give very little consideration to this radical aspect of Gilligan's work or to abortion at all.

11. Ruddick, *Maternal Thinking*, 210.

12. Ibid., 39.

13. Ibid., 218.

14. Wolff, "Secret Thoughts of an Adoptive Mother."

15. I'll elaborate on the manner in which reason and passion work in concert further on in this chapter.

16. Kittay, *Love's Labor*, 69.

17. Held, *Feminist Morality*, 196.

18. I am thinking especially of Held's essay "Care and Justice in the Global Context" where she brings the perspective of care to provide more balanced and sensible solutions to global issues such as those considered in international relations.

19. Ruddick is one exception to this. I will explain this aspect of her account in the next chapter.

20. Held, *Feminist Morality*, 198.

21. As an example, consider Manninen's "The Pro-Choice Pro-Lifer."

22. Grimshaw, *Philosophy and Feminist Thinking*, 250–251.

23. As Ruddick states: "Any idealized figure of the Good Mother casts a long shadow on many actual mothers' lives. Our days include few if any perfect moments, perfect children perfectly cared for. . . . Many mothers who live in the Good Mother's shadow, knowing that they have been angry and resentful and remembering episodes of violence and neglect, come to feel that their lives are riddled with shameful secrets that even the closest friends can't share." Ruddick, *Maternal Thinking*, 31.

3. MOTHERHOOD'S JANUS HEAD

1. Rich, *Of Woman Born*, 15 and 21.

2. Quoted in Oakley, *Becoming a Mother*, 142.

3. Jones, "Love with Teeth," 40–41.

4. Lazarre, *The Mother Knot*, 46.

5. Ibid., xxii.

6. De Marneffe, *Maternal Desire*, 120.

7. Dally, *Mothers*, 186.

8. Rich, *Of Woman Born*, 24.

9. Oakley, "Normal Motherhood," 99.

10. Oakley, *Becoming a Mother*, 12.

11. Badinter, *Mother Love*, 4.

12. Hrdy, *Mother Nature*, 290.

13. "Consider early-twentieth century admission records for Broadmoor, Britain's state asylum for the criminally insane. Forty-eight percent of the women hospitalized between 1902 and 1927 were women who had committed infanticide." Ibid., 280. "As in much of Catholic Europe, a *ruota*, or rotating barrel [in which babies could be left], was installed in 1660 to replace the old marble basin at Florence's main foundling home, the Innocenti. By 1699, however, it was necessary to place a grill across the opening to prevent parents from shoving in older children as well." Ibid., 304.

14. Ibid., 303.

15. Parker, *Torn in Two*, 5.

16. Ibid., 1.

17. Ibid., 103.

18. Winnicott, "Transitional Objects," 202.

19. Winnicott, "Hate in Countertransference," 201.

20. Ibid., 202.

21. Freud, *Totem and Taboo*, 66.

22. Klein, "Love, Guilt and Reparation," 322.

23. Ibid., 318.

24. Both Beauvoir and Merleau-Ponty rely a great deal on Deutsch's work in their characterizations of maternal ambivalence.

25. Deutsch, *The Psychology of Women*, 294.

26. Freud, "A Case of Obsessional Neurosis," 240.

27. Freud, "Thoughts for the Times on War and Death," 299.

28. Freud writes: "The emotional life of man is in general made up of pairs of contraries such as these. Indeed, if it were not so, repression and neurosis would perhaps never come about." Freud, "Notes on a Case of Obsessional Neurosis," 10:113.

29. Gendlin, "Befindlichkeit."

30. From this point forward I will usually speak of the mother-child relationship (as opposed to mother/children). This is for the sake of simplicity, and not intended to imply that there is always necessarily only *one* child involved. Having more than one child obviously adds more complexity to the family dynamics. For example, sometimes a mother must decide between meeting the needs of

one child versus another, or sometimes a mother's ambivalence is split between children (one child is experienced as only loved, the other as only hated). In spite of my nominal reference to the relationship as a dyad, I will also explore the dynamics involving more than two people.

31. Damasio, *The Feeling of What Happens*, 145.

32. Ibid., 142.

33. Ibid., 135–136.

34. Young, *Throwing Like a Girl*, 50.

35. Ibid., 160.

36. Steingraber, *Having Faith*, 215.

37. Simms, "Milk and Flesh," 25–26.

38. Lazarre, *The Mother Knot*, 28.

39. Shields, *Down Came the Rain*, 81.

40. Steingraber, *Having Faith*, 225.

41. Moses, "A Mother's Body," 177.

42. Weaver-Zercher, "Afterbirth," 42–44.

43. Steingraber, *Having Faith*, 248.

44. Kristeva, "Stabat Mater," 315, 316, 324, and 325.

45. Quoted in Ballou, *The Psychology of Pregnancy*, 90.

46. Stringer.

47. Quoted in Ballou, *The Psychology of Pregnancy*, 97.

48. Rich, *Of Woman Born,* 63.

49. Trevarthan, "The Self Born"; Piontelli, "Infant Observation."

50. Stringer.

51. Bondas and Eriksson, "Women's Lived Experiences of Pregnancy," 836.

52. Wynn, "The Early Relationship," 6.

53. De Marneffe, *Maternal Desire*, 90–91.

54. Simms, "Milk and Flesh," 33–34.

55. Quoted in de Marneffe, *Maternal Desire*, 93–94.

56. Ibid., 94.

57. Damasio, *The Feeling of What Happens*, 226.

58. Simms, "Milk and Flesh," 31.

59. When her infant son will not stop crying at dinner, an older child gives words to what the mother is feeling. Jones, "Love with Teeth," 40.

60. Chodorow, *The Reproduction of Mothering*, viii.

61. Ballou, *The Psychology of Pregnancy*,161.

62. Maushart, *The Mask of Motherhood*, 49.

63. Wolf, *Misconceptions,* 2–3.

64. Parker, *Torn in Two*, 81.

65. Ibid., 44.
66. http://www.whattoexpect.com/first-year/breastfeeding/breastfeeding-guide/tackling-the-technique.aspx (accessed December 8, 2009).
67. Wolf, *Misconceptions*, 200 (emphasis added).
68. Shields, *Down Came the Rain*, 41 and 45.
69. Quoted in Hays, *The Cultural Contradictions of Motherhood*, 137. Hays remarks: "Mothers, she seems to be saying, are like confections that the kids just gobble down—and then they ask for more."
70. Quoted in Parker, *Torn in Two*, 131–132.
71. Quoted ibid., 120.
72. Wolf, *Misconceptions*, 247.
73. Quoted in Brown et al., *Missing Voices*, 179.
74. Quoted in Oakley, *Becoming a Mother*, 144.
75. Quoted in Wolf, *Misconceptions*, 247.
76. Shields, *Down Came the Rain*, 131.
77. Quoted in Brown et al., *Missing Voices*, 182.
78. Lazarre, *Mother Knot*, 29.
79. Lamott, "Maternal Anger," 90.
80. Kessler, "Epidemiology of Women and Depression," 5–13.
81. Robins and Regier, *Psychiatric Disorders in America*; Burke et al. "Comparing Age at Onset of Major Depression"; Gaynes, "Perinatal Depression."
82. Harris, "Biological and Hormonal"; O'Hara, *Postpartum Depression*.
83. Goodman, "Paternal Postpartum Depression." Also Wolff, "Secret Thoughts of an Adoptive Mother."
84. See, for example, www.rainbowkids.com/expertarticledetails.aspx?id=272; www.adoptionissues.org/post-adoption-depression.html; http://library.adoption.com/articles/post-adoption-depression-.html.
85. Wolff, "Secret Thoughts of an Adoptive Mother."
86. Parker, *Torn in Two*, 5.
87. Oakley, "Normal Motherhood," 89.
88. Ibid., 99–100; Oakley, *Becoming a Mother*, 13.
89. Rich, *Of Woman Born*, 23.
90. Quoted in Hays, *The Cultural Contradictions of Motherhood*, 136.
91. Quoted in Oakley, *Becoming a Mother*, 252
92. Quoted in Lazarre, *Mother Knott*, 68.
93. Rich, *Of Woman Born*, 29.
94. Lazarre, *Mother Knot*, 28.
95. Wolf, *Misconceptions*, 60 and 106.
96. Ibid., 211.

97. Lazarre, *Mother Knot*, 50 and 56.

98. McMahon, *Engendering Motherhood*, 168.

99. De Marneffe, *Maternal Desire*, 49.

100. Ibid., 52.

101. Liss, "Maternal CARE," 43–67.

102. Ibid., 65.

103. Tisdale, "Double Dare," 253–254.

104. Moses, "A Mother's Body," 179.

105. Keller, "You'll Get Used to It," 119.

106. Moses, "A Mother's Body," 180.

107. Peri, "Dancing with Death," 271.

108. Moses "A Mother's Body," 176.

109. Keller, "You'll Get Used to It," 11.

110. Chandler writes, "[Mothering] is a series of responses to the fundamental needs of another who is so interconnected with the self that there exists no definitive line of differentiation. When one mothers one is not one's own person. This is most acute when mothering an infant. Although one is not one's own person, one is not someone else's person either, for the infant is both neither 'other' than the mother nor the same thing. . . . In summation, 'mother' is an identity formed through a repetition of practices which constitute one as so profoundly interconnected that one is not one, *but is simultaneously more and less than one.*" Chandler, "Emancipated Subjectivities," 274.

111. Irigaray, "On the Maternal Order," 39.

112. Rouch quoted ibid., 39.

113. Ibid., 41.

114. Steingraber, *Having Faith*, 32.

115. Ibid., 31.

116. Ibid.

117. Ibid., 32.

118. Irigaray, "On the Maternal Order," 41.

119. Maushart, *The Mask of Motherhood*, 40–41.

120. Dunlop, "Child," 105.

121. Dunlop, "Written on the Body," 106.

122. Nemzoff, "Untitled Poem," 20.

123. Frye. "Making a Living," 21.

124. Chandler, "Emancipated Subjectivities," 271.

125. Consider, for example, Margaret Mahler, Fred Pine, and Anni Bergman's *The Psychological Birth of the Human Infant*, where they chronicle the "individuation-separation" process in infant development.

126. Rich, *Of Woman Born*, 36–37.

127. Parker, *Torn in Two*, 121.

128. Ibid., 22.

129. Smith, *The Daddy Shift*, 129.

130. Quoted in Ruddick, *Maternal Thinking*, 65.

131. Ibid., 67.

132. Ibid. Next to this account, Noddings's theory is a gross oversimplification. In particular, this statement: "Responding to my own child crying in the night may require a physical effort, but it does not usually require what might be called an ethical effort. I naturally want to relieve my child's distress." Noddings, *Caring*, 17.

133. De Marneffe, *Maternal Desire*, 199 and 200.

134. Martin Buber, "Distance and Relation," in *Martin Buber*, 4.

135. Ibid., 6.

136. Ibid., 15.

4. MATERNITY AS VULNERABILITY IN THE PHILOSOPHY OF EMMANUEL LEVINAS

Some of these ideas appeared previously in LaChance Adams, "The Pregnable Subject."

1. This interpretation is owed, at least in part, to Nancy Tuana's suggestions on how to "read philosophy as a woman" in *Women and the History of Philosophy*.

2. Levinas, *Time and the Other*, 57.

3. Levinas, *Totality and Infinity*, 263.

4. Ibid., 155.

5. See, for example, Ainley, "Levinas and Kant"; Chanter, "Introduction"; Brody, "Levinas's Maternal Method"; Perpich, "From the Caress to the Word."

6. Levinas, *Time and the Other*, 68.

7. Perpich, "From the Caress," 47.

8. Levinas, "Judaism and the Feminine," 33, *Difficile liberté*, 53–54.

9. This critique is parallel to that of social contract origin myths in Carole Pateman's *The Sexual Contract*. Pateman argues that, according to social contract, it is only through subjugating a woman that a man can gain status as an individual.

10. Levinas, *Totality and Infinity*, 263.

11. Irigaray, "Questions to Emmanuel Levinas," 113.

12. Chanter, "Introduction," 17.

13. Chanter, "Feminism and the Other," 36.

14. Levinas, *Time and the Other*, 86.
15. This problem has been thoroughly documented. See, for example: Beauvoir, *The Second Sex*; Bernasconi and Critchley, *Re-reading Levinas*; Chanter, *Feminist Interpretations of Emmanuel Levinas*; Irigaray, "The Fecundity of the Caress" and *An Ethics of Sexual Difference*.
16. Levinas, *Time and the Other*, 78 (emphasis added).
17. Levinas, *Otherwise Than Being*, 104.
18. Guenther, *The Gift of the Other*, 95.
19. Ibid., 95–96.
20. It is worth noting that many women do not experience such happenings as an example of the generosity of the maternal body, but instead as a parasitic leaching by the fetus. Furthermore, as discussed in the previous chapter, in cases of denied pregnancy, a fetus may be deprived of nutrients even when they are available. This suggests that a woman's conscious acknowledgment of her pregnancy (even if not her deliberate *choice*) is central to the "generosity" of the pregnant body.
21. Sikka, "The Delightful Other," 109.
22. Willett, *Maternal Ethics*, 84–85.
23. Taylor, "Levinasian Ethics," 222.
24. Ibid., 229. Taylor quotes Willett, *Maternal Ethics*, 84; Levinas, *Otherwise Than Being*, 49–51; and Levinas, *Entre Nous*, 49.
25. Levinas, *Time and the Other*, 86.
26. Some examples include Kittay, *Love's Labor*, and Noddings, *Caring*. Still, it is important to note some important differences between these theorists, such as Noddings's affirmation of caregiving as women's role versus Kittay's extension of caregiving responsibilities to men. The actual content of what is meant by the value of feminine caretaking will differ among these theorists.
27. See, for example, Bartky, "Feeding Egos and Tending Wounds"; Card, "Gender and Moral Luck"; MacKinnon, *Feminism Unmodified*; Puka, "The Liberation of Caring."
28. Levinas, *Otherwise Than Being*, 116.
29. Levinas, *Totality and Infinity*, 278, 267, and 277.
30. Guenther, *The Gift of the Other*, 92.
31. Ibid., 94.
32. Ibid., 6–7.
33. Guenther, "Like a Maternal Body," 119.
34. Ibid., 131.
35. Ibid., 128 and 132.
36. Thanks to Lisa Guenther for pointing out this possible critique of my work.

37. Derrida, "White Mythology," 209.
38. Ibid., 223.
39. Ibid., 221–222.
40. Derrida, "At this Moment," 19.
41. Guenther, "Like a Maternal Body," 124.
42. Brody, "Levinas's Maternal Method," 74.
43. Hardy, "Yogurt Couvade," 22.
44. Levinas, *Otherwise Than Being*, 83, 99, 100, and 112.
45. "Sensibility is exposedness to the other." Ibid., 75.
46. Ibid.
47. Ibid., 83.
48. Peri, "Dancing with Death," 271.
49. Levinas, *Otherwise Than Being*, 109.
50. Wolf's description of the appearance of her abdomen during her cesarean section in progress. Wolf, *Misconceptions*, 141.
51. Levinas, *Otherwise Than Being*, 92.
52. Levinas, *Totality and Infinity*, 199.
53. Shields, *Down Came the Rain*, 59–60.
54. Kittay, "Not *My* Way Sesha," 12.
55. Levinas, *Totality and Infinity*, 199-200.
56. Kunz, *The Paradox of Power and Weakness.*
57. Ibid., 133.
58. Levinas, *Totality and Infinity*, 84.
59. Ibid., 83.
60. Ibid.
61. Kittay, "'Not *My* Way Sesha," 12.
62. Levinas, *Otherwise Than Being*, 100–101.
63. Wolf, *Misconceptions*, 200 (emphasis added).
64. Lazarre, *Mother Knot*, 28.
65. Levinas, *Otherwise Than Being*, 76.
66. Levinas, *Totality and Infinity*, 232.
67. Levinas, "Peace and Proximity," 167.
68. Levinas, *Totality and Infinity*, 199.
69. Bergo, "Emmanuel Levinas."
70. Klein, "Love, Guilt and Reparation," 318.
71. Guenther, "Like a Maternal Body," 128.
72. Miller, *For Your Own Good*, 258.
73. Quoted in Parker, *Torn in Two*, 23.
74. Ibid., 8–9.

75. Tsing, "Monster Stories," 284.
76. Ibid., 283.
77. Gentleman, "Cameron to Look at Case of Mother."
78. Arcana, "Abortion Is a Motherhood Issue," 226.
79. Levinas, *Otherwise Than Being*, 112.
80. Consider, for example, the Tennessee woman who sent her adoptive Russian son back.
81. Levinas, *Otherwise Than Being*, 105.
82. Winnicott, "Transitional Objects," 202.

5. MATERNITY AS DEHISCENCE IN THE FLESH IN THE PHILOSOPHY OF MAURICE MERLEAU-PONTY

1. He writes, "a sort of dehiscence opens my body in two." Merleau-Ponty, *The Visible and the Invisible*, 123.
2. Merleau-Ponty, *Phenomenology of Perception*, 278.
3. Karen, *Becoming Attached*, 143–161; and Ainsworth et al., *Patterns of Attachment*.
4. Ibid.
5. Karen, *Becoming Attached*, 13–25; and James, *Handbook for the Treatment of Attachment-Trauma*.
6. De Marneffe, *Maternal Desire*, 90.
7. Moses, "A Mother's Body," 77.
8. Ibid.
9. Merleau-Ponty, "The Child's Relations with Others," 119.
10. It is not entirely clear if Merleau-Ponty gets the idea that the child has an anonymous relation to the mother from psychoanalysis or if he has simply found a like-minded theory here. In "Anonymity and Sociality," Stawarska argues that the developmental psychology of Merleau-Ponty's day influenced his theory of intersubjectivity. "Specifically, the psychological hypothesis about the anonymous and fusional form initially taken by human sociality appears to play a determining role in his conception of interpersonal life formulated on the ontological plane" (1).
11. Simms, "Milk and Flesh," 29. Simms cites Ayers, "Sensory Integration and the Child"; and Dennis, *Children of the Creche*.
12. Merleau-Ponty, "The Child's Relations with Others," 100.
13. However, as I argue in chapter 2, the "integrity" of the body can vary dramatically from one person to another, both in its distinctness from others and in its sense of internal unity.
14. Merleau-Ponty, *The Visible and the Invisible*, 10.

15. Lisa Guenther provides a thorough account and analysis of these metaphors in her essay "The Birth of Sexual Difference." She writes:

> On a number of occasions throughout his work, Merleau-Ponty compares the relation between self and other to a pregnancy. In 'The Philosopher and his Shadow,' for example, he claims that 'each one of us is pregnant with the others and confirmed by them in his body.' In 'Dialogue and the Perception of the Other,' Merleau-Ponty describes the other as 'reproduced from me,' born through 'that strange filiation which makes the other forever my second, even when I prefer him to myself.'" The Birth of Sexual Difference," 89. In "Dialogue," he asks: "To the infinity that was me something else still adds itself; a sprout shoots forth, I grow; I give birth, this other is made from my flesh and blood and yet is no longer me. How is that possible? How can the cogito emigrate beyond me, since it is me?"

Ibid., 90.

Merleau-Ponty's use of maternity as a metaphor is not so obnoxious as with the typical philosopher, probably because Merleau-Ponty did some research on the experiences of mothers. I will refer to some of this research further on in this chapter.

16. Trevarthan, "The Self Born"; and Piontelli, "Infant Observation from Before Birth."
17. Sears, Sears, and Holt, *The Pregnancy Book;* and Sears et al., *The Baby Book.*
18. Simms, "Milk and Flesh," 23.
19. Ibid., 26.
20. Ibid., 27.
21. Ibid., 35.
22. Olkowski, "Only Nature Is Mother to the Child," 51.
23. Irigaray, "The Invisible of the Flesh," 154.
24. See Guenther quoted in "The Birth of Sexual Difference," 88–94.
25. Butler, "Sexual Ideology and Phenomenological Description," 95.
26. Allen, "Through the Wild Region," 245.
27. Sullivan, *Living Across and Through Skins,* 66.
28. Grosz, "Merleau-Ponty and Irigaray in the Flesh," 155.
29. Stawarska, "From the Body Proper to Flesh," 104, 103.
30. Ibid., 92.
31. Ibid., 93.
32. Interestingly, Levinas has the same reading of reversibility in "Intersubjectivity."
33. Stawarska, "From the Body Proper to Flesh," 94.
34. Stoller, "Reflections on Feminist Merleau-Ponty Skepticism," 176.

35. Weiss, "The Anonymous Intentions of Transactional Bodies," 194.

36. Grosz, "Merleau-Ponty and Irigaray in the Flesh," 155.

37. See, for example, Beauvoir, *The Second Sex*; Bigwood, "Renaturalizing the Body"; Grosz, *Volatile Bodies*; Guenther, *The Gift of the Other*; Heinämaa, *Toward a Phenomenology of Sexual Difference*; Simms, "Milk and Flesh"; Wynn, "The Early Relationship of Mother and Pre-Infant"; and Young, *Throwing Like a Girl*.

38. Al-Saji, "Vision, Mirror, and Expression," 53.

39. Weiss, "*Ecart*," 205.

40. Ibid., 214.

41. Ibid., 208.

42. Fielding, "Grounding Agency in Depth," 180.

43. Fielding, "Envisioning the Other," 194.

44. Some of these ideas appeared previously in LaChance Adams, "The Need of Philosophy in Hegel."

45. Merleau-Ponty, "Hegel's Existentialism," 656.

46. Ibid., 64.

47. "The bad dialectic is that which thinks it recomposes being by a thetic thought, by an assemblage of statements, by thesis, antithesis, synthesis." Merleau-Ponty, *The Visible and the Invisible*, 94.

48. See for example Hegel, *The Encyclopedia Logic*, 127–128.

49. Hegel, *Phenomenology of Spirit*, 123.

50. Deleuze, *Difference and Repetition*.

51. Desmond, *Beyond Hegel and Dialectic*, 2.

52. See part 1 of Grier, *Identity and Difference*.

53. Maker, "Identity, Difference, and the Logic of Otherness," 15.

54. Ibid., 18.

55. Damasio, *The Feeling of What Happens*, 142.

56. Ibid., 145.

57. Levinas, *Otherwise Than Being*, 124.

58. Ibid., 83.

59. Ibid., 84.

60. Sartre, *Being and Nothingness*, 288.

61. As I argue in "Becoming with Child," Sartre provides us with a manner of understanding these conflicts in a positive light in *Notebooks for an Ethics*.

62. Merleau-Ponty, "The Child's Relations with Others," 105.

63. Taminiaux, "Merleau-Ponty."

64. Weaver-Zercher, "Afterbirth," 42–44.

65. Peri, "Dancing with Death," 271.

66. Quoted in Yusa, "Women Rocking the Boat," 155.
67. Tuvel, "Exposing the Breast."
68. Ibid.
69. Thanks to Bonnie Mann for this point.
70. Moses, "A Mother's Body," 177.
71. Merleau-Ponty, *Child Psychology and Pedagogy*, 78.
72. Note the difference between this statement and Carol Bigwood's appropriation of Merleau-Ponty in "Renaturalizing the Body (with the Help of Merleau-Ponty)." She claims that Merleau-Ponty's *chiasm* or *intertwining* provides a helpful alternative to the subject-object dichotomy in making sense of the mother's relation to her fetus. She states that "it becomes especially clear in the case of pregnancy that, as Merleau-Ponty argues, the metaphysical dichotomous categories of subject and object, and self and other, fail to describe the incarnate situation, for the 'subject' is blurred and diffused in pregnancy. A woman is inhabited by a growing sentience that is not truly 'other' to herself." Ibid., 68.
73. Andrews, "Vision, Violence, and the Other," 177.
74. Low, "The Foundations of Merleau-Ponty's Ethical Theory," 181.
75. Gantt and Reber, "Sociobiological and Social Constructionist Accounts," 26.
76. Waldenfels, "Responsivity of the Body," 94.
77. Ibid., 99.
78. Ibid., 102.
79. Al-Saji, "Vision, Mirror, and Expression," 54.
80. Ibid., 56.
81. Murphy, "All Things Considered," 436.
82. Ibid., 447.
83. Merleau-Ponty, "An Unpublished Text," 11.
84. Merleau-Ponty, *Child Psychology and Pedagogy*, 83.
85. Merleau-Ponty, *Hegel's Existentialism*, 65.
86. Carbone, "FLESH," 57.
87. Merleau-Ponty, "An Unpublished Text," 6.
88. Merleau-Ponty, *Signs*, 35.
89. Merleau-Ponty, *Child Psychology and Pedagogy*, 68.
90. Beauvoir, *The Second Sex*, 566.

6. MATERNITY AS NEGOTIATING MUTUAL TRANSCENDENCE IN THE PHILOSOPHY OF SIMONE DE BEAUVOIR

1. Beauvoir, "Introduction to an Ethics of Ambiguity," 292.
2. Beauvoir, *The Ethics of Ambiguity*, 9.

3. As Beauvoir writes,

> One cannot fulfill a man; he is not a vessel that docilely allows itself to be filled up. His condition is to surpass everything given. . . . Since man is project, his happiness, like his pleasures, can only be projects. The man who has made a fortune immediately dreams of making another. Pascal said it perfectly: it is not the hare that interests the hunter, it is the hunt. . . . A goal is always the meaning and the result of an effort. Separated from that effort, no reality is a goal but only a given made to be surpassed. . . . The notion of end is ambiguous since every end is a point of departure at the same time. But this does not prevent it from being seen as an end. Man's freedom resides in this power.

Beauvoir, "Pyrrhus and Cineas," 98–99.

4. "And it is not true that the recognition of the freedom of others limits my own freedom: to be free is not to have the power to do anything you like; it is to be able to surpass the power given toward an open future; the existence of others as a freedom defines my situation and is even the condition of my own freedom." Beauvoir, *The Ethics of Ambiguity*, 91.

5. Ibid., 72.

6. "As soon as a child has finished a drawing or a page of writing, he runs to show them to his parents. He needs their approval as much as candy or toys; the drawing requires an eye that looks at it. These disorganized lines must become a boat or a horse for someone. . . . By himself, he would not have dared to put confidence in those hesitant lines." Beauvoir, "Pyrrhus and Cineas," 116.

7. Ibid., 109.

8. "Men are free, and I am thrown into the world among these foreign freedoms. I need them because once I have surpassed my own goals, my actions will fall back upon themselves, inert and useless, if they have not been carried off toward a new future by new projects." Beauvoir, "Pyrrhus and Cineas," 135. "What is mine is therefore first what I do. But as soon as I have done it, the object goes and separates itself from me; it escapes me. The thought that I expressed a moment ago, is it still my thought? In order for it to be mine, I must make it mine again each instant by taking it toward my future." Ibid., 93.

9. Beauvoir, *The Ethics of Ambiguity*, 67.

10. "The sick man who wears himself out by struggling against sickness or the slave against slavery care for neither poetry, nor astronomy, nor the improvement of aviation. They first need health, leisure, security, and the freedom to do with themselves what they want." Beauvoir, "Pyrrhus and Cineas," 137).

11. "A man alone in the world would be paralyzed by the manifest vision of the vanity of all his goals. He would undoubtedly not be able to stand living. But man is not alone in the world." Ibid., 115.

12. Beauvoir, *The Ethics of Ambiguity*, 24.
13. Beauvoir, "Pyrrrhus," 93.
14. Beauvoir, *The Ethics of Ambiguity*, 156.
15. Ibid., 24.
16. Beauvoir, *The Second Sex*, 159.
17. Ibid.
18. Beauvoir, *The Ethics of Ambiguity*, 25.
19. Beauvoir, "Pyrrhus and Cineas," 131.
20. Ibid., 127.
21. Beauvoir, *The Ethics of Ambiguity*, 61, 65–66, 83, and 96.
22. Beauvoir, "Pyrrhus and Cineas," 126.
23. I claim that *The Second Sex* is the most mature of Beauvoir's ethical texts be-cause she is the least moralistic in tone (a tone that she herself found irritating in her earlier work) and more understanding of the power of situation over an individual's ability to be ethical in her sense of the term.
24. Beauvoir, *The Second Sex*, 16.
25. Beauvoir, *The Ethics of Ambiguity*, 96.
26. Ibid., 37.
27. Ibid., 76.
28. Ibid., 82.
29. Beauvoir, *The Second Sex*, 159–160.
30. Beauvoir, "Pyrrhus and Cineas," 124.
31. See Andrew, "Care, Freedom, and Reciprocity"; Gothlin, "Beauvoir and Sar-tre on Appeal"; Kruks, "Teaching Sartre About Freedom"; Scarth, *The Other Within;* Tidd, "The Self-Other Relation"; Ward, "Reciprocity and Friendship in Beauvoir's Thought."
32. Andrew, "Care, Freedom, and Reciprocity," 291.
33. Ibid., 290.
34. Ibid.
35. Tidd, "The Self-Other Relation," 230.
36. Scarth, *The Other Within*, 7.
37. Ward, "Reciprocity and Friendship in Beauvoir's Thought," 41.
38. Kruks, "Teaching Sartre About Freedom," 88.
39. See, for example, Simons, "Confronting an Impasse" and "Beauvoir's Philo-sophical Independence in a Dialogue with Sartre."
40. See, for example, Collins and Pierce, "Holes and Slime"; Gatens, *Feminism and Philosophy* and "Toward a Feminist Philosophy of the Body"; Greens, "Sartre, Sexuality and *The Second Sex*"; Lloyd, *Man of Reason;* Spelman, "Woman as Body" and *Inessential Woman;* Suleiman, *The Female Body in Western Culture;* Strickling, "Simone de Beauvoir and the Value of Immanence."

41. Lloyd, *Man of Reason*, 99–100.

42. Ibid., 101

43. Jardin, "Death Sentences, 90.

44. Scarth, *The Other Within*, 156. This is Scarth's own description of her project.

45. Ibid., 140 and 165.

46. Ibid., 156.

47. Ibid., 140.

48. Bergoffen, *The Philosophy of Simone de Beauvoir*, 207.

49. Ibid., 208.

50. Ibid., 209.

51. Ibid.

52. Beauvoir, *The Second Sex*, 159 (emphasis added).

53. Beauvoir, *The Ethics of Ambiguity*, 73.

54. Iris Marion Young, "Pregnant Embodiment: Subjectivity and Alienation," in *Throwing Like a Girl*, 46.

55. Beauvoir, *The Second Sex*, 531.

56. Ibid., 524.

57. Ibid., 539.

58. Simons, "Two Interviews with Simone de Beauvoir," 18.

59. Beauvoir, *The Ethics of Ambiguity*, 55.

60. Ibid., 48–49.

61. Beauvoir, *The Second Sex*, 554.

62. Ibid., 524.

63. Ibid., 525.

64. The same critique is often made regarding current discourse on children and abortion.

65. Lerner, *The War on Moms*, 63.

66. U.S. Dept of Health and Human Services, "Indicators of Welfare Dependence."

67. Lerner, *The War on Moms*, 70.

68. MTV, *No Easy Decision.*

69. Beauvoir, *The Second Sex*, 540.

70. Ibid., 533.

71. Ibid.

72. Beauvoir, "Pyrrhus and Cineas," 117.

73. Freud, *Totem and Taboo*, 66.

74. Beauvoir, *A Very Easy Death*, 71.

75. Levine, "Throwing the Book," 20.

76. Ibid., 21.

77. Ibid., 21–22.

78. Ibid., 22.

79. Beauvoir, "Pyrrhus and Cineas," 119.
80. Ibid., 118.
81. Beauvoir, *The Ethics of Ambiguity*, 142.
82. Beauvoir, *The Second Sex*, 539.
83. Sartre, *Notebooks for an Ethics*, 194.
84. Mirvish, "Sartre, Embodied Minds, Authenticity, and Childhood," 27.
85. Beauvoir, "Pyrrhus and Cineas," 138.
86. Ibid., 117.
87. Ibid., 121.
88. Ibid., 123.
89. Beauvoir, *The Second Sex*, 569.
90. Lerner, *The War on Moms*, 2, 39, 63.
91. Mezey, Greenberg, and Schumacher, "The Vast Majority."
92. Lerner, *The War on Moms*, 20.
93. Beauvoir, *The Second Sex*, 556.
94. Parker, *Torn in Two*, 121.
95. Rich, *Of Woman Born*, 36–37.
96. Parker, *Torn in Two*, 22.
97. Beauvoir, *The Ethics of Ambiguity*, 71.
98. Kovacic, "Salvation Road," 61.
99. "Without failure, no ethics. For a being who, from the outset, is an exact coincidence with himself, a perfect plenitude, the notion 'ought to be' [*devoir être*] would not make sense. One does not propose ethics to a god. It is impossible to propose one to man if he is defined as nature, as given. . . . This means that there can be an 'ought to be' [*devoir être*] only for a being who, according to the existentialist definition, questions himself within his being." Beauvoir, *The Ethics of Ambiguity*, 291.
100. Beauvoir, "Moral Idealism and Political Realism,"187.
101. Ibid., 188.
102. Beauvoir, "Introduction to an Ethics of Ambiguity," 292.
103. Ibid.
104. Beauvoir, *A Very Easy Death*, 108.
105. Beauvoir, *The Ethics of Ambiguity*, 134.

CONCLUSION

1. http://blogs.seattleweekly.com/dailyweekly/2011/02/angela_mcanulty_eugene_mom_ple.php.
2. http://www.klcc.org/Feature.asp?FeatureID=2246.

3. http://special.registerguard.com/csp/cms/sites/web/news/cityregion/242 49180–41/maples-family-jeanette-mcanulty-death.csp.

4. Ibid.

5. Ibid.

6. http://blogs.seattleweekly.com/dailyweekly/2011/02/angela_mcanulty_eugene _mom_ple.php

7. Meyer and Oberman, *Mothers Who Kill Their Children*, 175.

8. Nietzsche, *Thus Spake Zarathustra*, 112.

BIBLIOGRAPHY

Ainley, Alison. "Levinas and Kant: Maternal Morality and Illegitimate Offspring."
In *Feminist Interpretations of Emmanuel Levinas*, ed. Tina Chanter, 203–223. University Park: Pennsylvania State University Press, 2001.

Ainsworth, Mary, M. C. Blehar, E. Waters, and S. Wall, *Patterns of Attachment: A Psychological Study of the Strange Situation*. Hillsdale: Lawrence Erlbaum, 1978.

Alcoff, Linda Martin. "Merleau-Ponty and Feminist Theory on Experience." In *Chiasms: Merleau-Ponty's Notion of Flesh*, ed. Fred Evans and Leonard Lawlor, 251–271. Albany: State University of New York Press, 2000.

———. "Phenomenology, Post-Structuralism, and Feminist Theory on the Concept of Experience." In *Feminist Phenomenology*, ed. Linda Fisher and Lester Embree, 39–56. Dordrecht: Kluwer Academic, 2000.

Allen, Jeffner. "Motherhood: The Annihilation of Women." In *Mothering: Essays in Feminist Theory*, ed. Joyce Trevilcot, 315–330. Totowa, NJ: Rowman and Allanheld, 1983.

———. "Through the Wild Region: An Essay in Phenomenological Feminism." *Review of Existential Psychology and Psychiatry: Merleau-Ponty and Psychology* 18 (1982–83): 241–256.

Al-Saji, Alia. "Vision, Mirror, and Expression: The Genesis of the Ethical Body in Merleau-Ponty's Later Works." In *Interrogating Ethics: Embodying the Good in Merleau-Ponty*, ed. James Hatley, Janice McLane, and Christian Diehm, 39–63. Pittsburgh: Duquesne University Press, 2006.

Andrew, Barbara S. "Care, Freedom, and Reciprocity in the Ethics of Simone de Beauvoir." *Philosophy Today* 42.3 (1998): 290–300.

Andrews, Jorella. "Vision, Violence, and the Other: A Merleau-Pontian Ethics." In *Feminist Interpretations of Maurice Merleau-Ponty*, ed. Dorothea Olkowski and Gail Weiss, 167–182. University Park: Pennsylvania State University Press, 2006.

Arcana, Judith. "Abortion Is a Motherhood Issue." In *Women's Lives: Multicultural Perspectives*, 4th ed., ed. Gwyn Kirk and Margo Okazawa-Rey, 225–227. Boston: McGraw Hill, 2007.

Attridge, Harold W, ed. *Harper Collins Study Bible*. San Francisco: Harper San Francisco, 1989.

Ayers, A. J. *Sensory Integration and the Child*. Los Angeles: Western Psychological Services, 1979.

Badinter, Elisabeth. *Mother Love: Myth and Reality*. New York: Macmillan, 1981.

Ballou, Judith W. *The Psychology of Pregnancy: Reconciliation and Resolution*. Lexington: Lexington, 1978.

Bartky, Sandra. "Feeding Egos and Tending Wounds: Deference and Disaffection in Women's Emotional Labor." In *Femininity and Domination: Studies in the Phenomenology of Oppression*, 99–119. New York: Routledge, 1990.

Beauvoir, Simone de. *The Ethics of Ambiguity*. Trans. Bernard Frechtman. New York: Philosophical Library, 1949.

———. *Force of Circumstances*. Trans. Richard Howard. New York: Paragon House, 1992.

———. "Introduction to an Ethics of Ambiguity." Trans. Marybeth Timmerman. In *Simone de Beauvoir: Philosophical Writings*, ed. Margaret Simons, 289–298. Urbana: University of Illinois Press, 2004.

———. "Moral Idealism and Political Realism." Trans. Anne Deing Cordero. In *Simone de Beauvoir: Philosophical Writings*, ed. Margaret Simons, 175–193. Urbana: University of Illinois Press, 2004.

———. "Pyrrhus and Cineas." Trans. Marybeth Timmerman. In *Simone de Beauvoir: Philosophical Writings*, ed. Margaret Simons, 89–149. Urbana: University of Illinois Press, 2004.

———. "A Review of *The Phenomenology of Perception* by Maurice Merleau-Ponty." Trans. Marybeth Timmerman. In *Simone de Beauvoir: Philosophical Writings*, ed. Margaret Simons, 151–164. Urbana: University of Illinois Press, 2004.

———. *The Second Sex*. Trans. Constance Borde and Shelia Malovany-Chevallier. New York: Knopf, 2010.

———. *She Came to Stay*. New York: Norton, 1999.

———. *A Very Easy Death*. Trans. Patrick O'Brian. New York: Warner, 1973.

Bergo, Bettina. "Emmanuel Levinas." In *Stanford Encyclopedia of Philosophy*, http://plato.stanford.edu/entries/levinas/. Accessed March 3, 2010.

Bergoffen, Debra B. *The Philosophy of Simone de Beauvoir: Gendered Phenomenologies, Erotic Generosities*. Albany: State University of New York, 1997.

Bernasconi, Robert, and Simon Critchley, eds. *Re-reading Levinas*. Bloomington: Indiana University Press, 1991.

Bigwood, Carol. "Renaturalizing the Body (With the Help of Merleau-Ponty)." *Hypatia* 6.3 (1991): 54–73.

Bondas, Teresa, and Katie Eriksson. "Women's Lived Experiences of Pregnancy: A Tapestry of Joy and Suffering." *Qualitative Health Research* 11.6 (2001): 824–840.

Bordo, Susan. "Are Mothers Persons? Reproductive Rights and the Politics of Subjectivity." In *Unbearable Weight: Feminism, Western Culture, and the Body*, 71–97. Berkeley:University of California Press, 1993.

Bowlby, John. *The Making and Breaking of Affectional Bonds*, London: Tavistock/Routledge, 1979.

Brody, Donna. "Levinas's Maternal Method from 'Time and the Other' Through *Otherwise Than Being*: No Woman's Land?" In *Feminist Interpretations of Emmanuel Levinas*, ed. Tina Chanter, 53–77. University Park: Pennsylvania State University Press, 2001.

Brown, Stephanie, Judith Lumley, Rhonda Small, and Jill Astbury. *Missing Voices: The Experience of Motherhood*. Oxford: Oxford University Press Australia, 1994.

Buber, Martin. *Martin Buber on Psychology and Psychotherapy*, ed. J. A. Buber. New York: Syracuse University Press, 1999.

Burke, K. C., J. D. Burke Jr., and D. S. Rae. "Comparing Age at Onset of Major Depression and Other Psychiatric Disorders by Birth Cohorts in Five US Community Populations." *Archives of General Psychiatry* 48.9 (1991): 789–795.

Butler, Judith. *Precarious Life: The Powers of Mourning and Violence*. London: Verso, 2004.

———. "Sexual Ideology and Phenomenological Description: A Feminist Critique of Merleau-Ponty's *Phenomenology of Perception*." In *The Thinking Muse: Feminism and Modern French Philosophy*, ed. Jeffner Allen and Iris Marion Young, 85–100. Bloomington: Indiana University Press, 1989.

Carbone, Mauro. "FLESH: Towards the History of a Misunderstanding." *Chiasmi International* 4 (2002): 49–64.

Card, Claudia. "Against Marriage and Motherhood." *Hypatia* 11.3 (Summer 1996) 1–23.

———. "Gender and Moral Luck." In *Justice and Care: Essential Readings in Feminist Ethics*, ed. Virginia Held, 79–89. Boulder: Westview, 1995.

Chalier, Catherine. "The Exteriority of the Feminine." Trans. Bettina Bergo. In *Feminist Interpretations of Emmanuel Levinas*, ed. Tina Chanter, 171–179. University Park: Pennsylvania State University Press, 2001.

Chandler, Mielle. "Emancipated Subjectivities and the Subjugation of Mothering Practices." In *Redefining Motherhood: Changing Identities and Patterns*, ed. Sharon Abbey and Andrea O'Reilly, 270–286. Toronto: Second Story, 1998.

Chanter, Tina. *The Ethics of Eros*. New York: Routledge, 1995.

———. "Feminism and the Other." In *The Provocation of Levinas*, ed. Robert Bernasconi and David Wood, 32–56. New York: Routledge, 1988.

———, ed. *Feminist Interpretations of Emmanuel Levinas*. University Park: Pennsylvania State University Press, 2001.

———. Introduction to *Feminist Interpretations of Emmanuel Levinas*, ed. Tina Chanter, 1–27. University Park: Pennsylvania State University Press, 2001.

———. "Wild Meaning : Luce Irigaray's Reading of Merleau-Ponty." In *Chiasms: Merleau-Ponty's Notion of Flesh*, ed. Fred Evans and Leonard Lawlor, 219–236. Albany: State University of New York Press, 2000.

Chodorow, Nancy J. *The Reproduction of Mothering: Psychoanalysis and the Psychology of Gender*. Berkeley: University of California Press, 1999.

Collins, Margery, and Christine Pierce. "Holes and Slime: Sexism in Sartre's Psychoanalysis." In *Women and Philosophy: Toward a Theory of Liberation*, 112–127. ed. Carol Gould and M. Wartofsky. New York: Putnam, 1976.

Dally, Ann. *Mothers: Their Power and Influence*. London: Weidenfeld and Nicholson, 1976.

Damasio, Antonio. *The Feeling of What Happens*. San Diego: Harvest, 1999.

Deleuze, Gilles. *Difference and Repetition*. Trans. Paul Patton. New York: Columbia University Press, 1994.

De Marneffe, Daphne. *Maternal Desire: On Children, Love, and the Inner Life*. New York: Back Bay, 2004.

Dennis, W. *Children of the Creche*. New York: New York: Appleton-Century-Crofts, 1973.

Derrida, Jacques. "At This Very Moment in This Work Here I Am." In *Re-reading Levinas*, ed. Robert Bernasconi and Simon Critchley, 11–48. Bloomington: Indiana University Press, 1991.

———. "Violence and Metaphysics." In *Writing and Difference*, 79–183. Trans. Alan Bass. Chicago: University of Chicago Press, 1978.

———. "White Mythology: Metaphor in the Text of Philosophy." In *Margins of Philosophy*, 207–271. Trans. Alan Bates. Chicago: University of Chicago Press, 1982.

Desmond, William. *Beyond Hegel and Dialectic*. Albany: State University of New York Press, 1992.

Deutsch, Helene. *The Psychology of Women*, vol. 2: *Motherhood*. New York: Grune and Stratton, 1945.

Dunlop, Rishma, "Child." In *Redefining Motherhood: Changing Identities and Patterns,* ed. Sharon Abbey and Andrea O'Reilly, 103–123. Toronto: Second Story, 1998.

———. "Written on the Body." In *Redefining Motherhood: Changing Identities and Patterns*, ed. Sharon Abbey and Andrea O'Reilly, 103–123. Toronto: Second Story, 1998.

Ehrenreich, Barbara, and Deirdre English. *For Her Own Good: Two Centuries of the Experts Advice to Women*. Garden City, NY: Anchor, 2005.

Fielding, Helen. "Envisioning the Other: Lacan and Merleau-Ponty on Subjectivity." In *Merleau-Ponty, Interiority and Exteriority, Psychic Life and the World*, ed. Dorothea Olkowski and James Morley, 185–199. Albany: State University of New York Press, 1999.

———. "Grounding Agency in Depth: The Implications of Merleau-Ponty's Thought for the Politics of Feminism." *Human Studies* 19 (1996): 175–184.

Fisher, Linda. "Feminist Phenomenology." In *Feminist Phenomenology*, ed. Linda Fisher and Lester Embree, 1–15. Dordrecht: Kluwer Academic, 2000.

Fraiberg, Selma. "Blind Infants and Their Mothers: An Examination of the Sign System." In *Before Speech the Beginning of Interpersonal Communication*, ed. Margaret Bullowa, 149–170. New York: Cambridge University Press, 1979.

Freud, Sigmund. "Notes on a Case of Obsessional Neurosis." In *The Standard Edition of the Complete Psychological Works of Sigmund Freud*, 10:153–250, ed. James Strachey. London: Hogarth and the Institute of Psychoanalysis, 1953.

———. "The Interpretation of Dreams." *The Standard Edition of the Complete Psychological of Sigmund Freud*, 5:339–621, ed. James Strachey. London: Hogarth and the Institute of Psychoanalysis, 1953.

———. "Thoughts for the Times on War and Death." *The Standard Edition of the Complete Psychological Works of Sigmund Freud*, 14:273–302, ed. James Strachey. London: Hogarth and the Institute of Psychoanalysis, 1953.

———. *Totem and Taboo*. Trans. A. A. Brill. Toronto: Vintage, 1946.

Friedan, Betty. *The Feminine Mystique*. New York: Laurel, 1984.

Friedman, Marilyn. "Beyond Caring: The De-Moralization of Gender." In *An Ethic of Care: Feminist and Interdisciplinary Perspectives*, ed. Mary Jeanne Larrabee, 258–273. New York: Routledge, 1993.

Frye, Joanne S. "Making a Living, Making a Life." *Journal of the Association for Research on Mothering: Mothering in the Academy*, 5.2 (2003): 21–28.

Fullbrook, Edward. "She Came to Stay and Being and Nothingness." In *The Philosophy of Simone de Beauvoir*, ed. Margaret Simons, 42–64. Bloomington: Indiana University Press, 2006.

Fullbrook, Kate, and Edward Fullbrook. "Sartre's Secret Key." In *Feminist Interpretations of Simone de Beauvoir*, ed. Margaret Simons, 120–144. University Park: Pennsylvania State University Press, 1995.

———. *Simone de Beauvoir and Jean-Paul Sartre: The Remaking of a Twentieth-Century Legend.* New York: Basic Books, 1994.

Gadamer, Hans-Georg. *Truth and Method.* New York: Continuum, 2004.

Gantt, Edwin, and Jeffrey Reber. "Sociobiological and Social Constructionist Accounts of Altruism: A Phenomenological Critique." *Journal of Phenomenological Psychology* 30 (1999): 14–39.

Gatens, Moira. *Feminism and Philosophy: Perspectives on Difference and Equality.* Bloomington: Indiana University Press, 1991.

———. "Toward a Feminist Philosophy of the Body." In *Crossing Boundaries: Feminisms and the Critique of Knowledges*, 23–43, ed. E. Caine, E. Grosz, and M. de Lepervanche. Sydney: Allen and Unwin, 1988.

Gaynes B. N., N. Gavin, S. Meltzer-Brody, K. N. Lohr, T. Swinson, G. Gartlehner, S. Brody, and W. C. Miller. "Perinatal Depression: Prevalence, Screening Accuracy, and Screening Outcomes Summary." http://www.ahrq.gov/clinic/epcsums/peridepsum.htm.

Gendlin, Eugene. "Befindlichkeit: Heidegger and the Philosophy of Psychology." *Review of Existential Psychology and Psychiatry* 16 (1978–79): 43–71.

Gentleman, Amelia. "Cameron to Look at Case of Mother Who Asked for Daughter to Be Put Into Care." *Guardian.* Accessed January 25, 2011, http://www.guardian.co.uk/society/2011/jan/20/riven-vincent-disabled-daughter-support.

Gibbs, Lois. "'What Is Your Wife Trying to Do—Shut Down the Chemical Industry?': The Housewives of Love Canal——an Interview with Lois Gibbs." In *The Politics of Motherhood: Activist Voices from Left to Right*, ed. Alexis Jetter, Annelise Orleck, and Diana Taylor, 28–43. Hanover: University of New England Press, 1997.

Gilligan, Carol. "A Reply to Critics." In *An Ethic of Care: Feminist and Interdisciplinary Perspectives*, ed. Mary Jeanne Larrabee, 207–215. New York: Routledge, 1993.

———. *In A Different Voice.* Cambridge: Harvard University Press, 1982.

Goodman, J. H. "Paternal Postpartum Depression, Its Relationship to Maternal Postpartum Depression, and Implications for Family Health." *Journal of Advanced Nursing* 45 (2004): 26–35.

Gordon, Suzanne. "Feminism and Caring." In *Caregiving: Reading in Knowledge, Practice, Ethics, and Politics*, ed. Suzanne Gordon, Patricia Benner, and Nel Noddings, 256–277. Philadelphia: University of Pennsylvania Press, 1996.

Gothlin, Eva. "Beauvoir and Sartre on Appeal, Desire and Ambiguity." In *The Philosophy of Simone de Beauvoir*, ed. Margaret Simons, 132–145. Bloomington: Indiana University Press, 2006.

Greens, Naomi. "Sartre, Sexuality and *The Second Sex.*" *Philosophy and Literature* 4.2 (1980).

Grier, Phillip, ed. *Identity and Difference: Studies in Hegel's Logic, Philosophy of Spirit, and Politics*. New York: State University of New York, 2007.

Grimshaw, Jean. *Philosophy and Feminist Thinking*. Minneapolis: University of Minnesota Press, 1986.

Grosz, Elizabeth. "Merleau-Ponty and Irigaray in the Flesh." In *Merleau-Ponty, Interiority and Exteriority, Psychic Life and the World*, ed. Dorothea Olkowski and James Morley, 145–166. Albany: State University of New York Press, 1999.

———. *Volatile Bodies: Toward a Corporeal Feminism*. Bloomington: Indiana University Press, 1994.

Guenther, Lisa. "The Birth of Sexual Difference: A Feminist Response to Merleau-Ponty." In *Coming to Life: Philosophies of Pregnancy, Childbirth, and Mothering*. ed. Sarah LaChance Adams and Caroline Lundquist, 88–105. New York: Fordham University Press, 2013.

———. *The Gift of the Other: Levinas and the Politics of Reproduction*. Albany: State University of New York Press, 2006.

———. "'Like a Maternal Body': Emmanuel Levinas and the Motherhood of Moses." *Hypatia* 21.1 (2006): 119–136.

Haas, Lawrence. "Sense and Alterity: Rereading Merleau-Ponty's Reversibility Thesis." In *Merleau-Ponty, Interiority and Exteriority, Psychic Life and the World*, ed. Dorothea Olkowski and James Morley, 99–105. Albany: State University of New York Press, 1999.

Hardy, Rob. "Yogurt Couvade: Mr. Thirty-Eight Weeks." *Brain, Child* 5.3 (Summer 2004): 21–23.

Harris, B. "Biological and Hormonal Aspects of Postpartum Depressed Mood: Working Towards Strategies for Prophylaxis and Treatment." *British Journal of Psychiatry* 164 (1994): 288–292.

Hays, Sharon. *The Cultural Contradictions of Motherhood*. New Haven: Yale University Press, 1996.

Hegel, G. W. F. *The Encyclopedia Logic*. Trans. T. F. Geraets, W. A. Suchting, and H. S. Harris. Indianapolis: Hackett, 1991.

———. *Phenomenology of Spirit*. Trans. A. V. Miller. Oxford: Oxford University Press, 1977.

Heinämaa, Sara. *Toward a Phenomenology of Sexual Difference: Husserl, Merleau-Ponty, Beauvoir*. Lanham, MD: Rowman and Littlefield, 2003.

Held, Virginia. "Care and Justice in a Global Context." *Ratio Juris* 17.2 (2004): 141–55.

———. *Feminist Morality: Transforming Culture, Society, and Politics*. Chicago: University of Chicago Press, 1993.

Hoagland, Sarah Lucia. "Some Concerns About Nel Nodding's *Caring*." *Hypatia* 5.1 (1990): 107–112.

———. "Some Thoughts About '*Caring*.'" In *Feminist Ethics*, ed. Claudia Card, 246–263. Lawrence: University Press of Kansas, 1991.

hooks, bell. *Feminist Theory from Margin to Center*. Boston: South End, 1984.

Houston, Barbara. "Caring and Exploitation." *Hypatia* 5.1 (1990): 113–119.

Hrdy, Sarah Blaffer. *Mother Nature: A History of Mothers, Infants and Natural Selection*. New York: Pantheon, 1999.

Irigaray, Luce. *An Ethics of Sexual Difference*. Trans. Carolyn Burke and Gillian C. Gill. Ithaca: Cornell University Press, 1993.

———. "The Fecundity of the Caress: A Reading of Levinas, *Totality and Infinity*, 'Phenomenology of Eros.'" In *An Ethics of Sexual Difference*, 185–217. Trans. Carolyn Burke and Gillian C. Gill. Ithaca: Cornell University Press, 1993.

———. "The Invisible of the Flesh: A Reading of Merleau-Ponty, *The Visible and the Invisible*, 'The Intertwining—the Chiasm.'" In *An Ethics of Sexual Difference*, 151–184. Trans. Carolyn Burke and Gillian C. Gill. Ithaca: Cornell University Press, 1993.

———. "On the Maternal Order." In *Je, Tu, Nous: Toward a Culture of Difference*, 37–44. Trans. Alison Martin. New York: Routledge, 1993.

———. "Questions to Emmanuel Levinas on the Divinity of Love." In *Re-reading Levinas*, ed. Robert Bernasconi and Simon Critchley, 109–118. Bloomington: Indiana University Press, 1991.

———. *Sexes and Genealogies*. Trans. Gillian C. Gill. New York: Columbia University Press, 1993.

Jagger, Alison. "Feminist Ethics: Projects, Problems, Prospects." In *Feminist Ethics*, ed. Claudia Card, 79–95. Lawrence: University Press of Kansas, 1991.

James, B. *Handbook for the Treatment of Attachment-Trauma Problems in Children*. New York, Lexington, 1994.

Jardin, Alice. "Death Sentences: Writing Couples and Ideology." In *The Female Body in Western Culture*, ed. Susan Rubin Suleimen. Cambridge: Harvard University Press, 1986.

Jones, Adrienne. "Love with Teeth," *Brain, Child* 2.1(2010): 36–41.

Karen, Robert. *Becoming Attached*. Oxford: Oxford University Press, 1994.

Karp, Harvey. *The Happiest Baby on the Block*. New York: Bantam, 2003.

———. *The Happiest Baby on the Block*. Starlight Home Entertainment, 2002.

Karr, Mary. *Lit*. New York: Harper, 2009.

Katz, Claire Elise. "The Significance of Childhood." *International Studies in Philosophy* 34.4 (2002): 77–101.

Keller, Nora Okja. "You'll Get Used to It." In *Mothers who Think*, ed. Camille Peri and Kate Moses, 114–120. New York: Pocket, 1999.

Keltner, Stacy. "Beauvoir's Idea of Ambiguity." In *The Philosophy of Simone de Beauvoir*, ed. Margaret Simons, 201–213. Bloomington: Indiana University Press, 2006.

Kerr, Michael, and Murray Bowen. *Family Evaluation*. New York: Norton, 1988.

Kessler, R. C. "Epidemiology of Women and Depression." *Journal of Affective Disorders* 74.1 (2003): 5–13.

Kirk, Douglas. *Little Miss Spider*. New York: Scholastic, 1999.

Kittay, Eva Feder. *Love's Labor: Essays on Women, Equality, and Dependency*. New York: Routledge, 1999.

———. "'Not *My* Way Sesha, *Your* Way, Slowly': 'Maternal Thinking' in the Raising of a Child with Profound Intellectual Disabilities." In *Mother Troubles*, ed. Julia Hanigsberg and Sara Ruddick, 3–27. Boston: Beacon, 1999.

Klein, Melanie. "Love, Guilt and Reparation." In *Love, Guilt and Reparation and Other Works,* 306–343. New York: Free Press, 1975.

———. *The Writings of Melanie Klein*. New York: Free Press, 1961.

Kovacic, Kristin. "Salvation Road." *Brain, Child* 2.2 (2010): 56–61.

Kristeva, Julia. "Sabat Mater." In *The Portable Kristeva*, ed. Kelly Oliver, 310–332. New York: Columbia University Press, 2002.

Kruks, Sonia. "Merleau-Ponty and the Problem of Difference in Feminism." In *Feminist Interpretations of Maurice Merleau-Ponty*, ed. Dorothea Olkowski and Gail Weiss, 25–47. University Park: Pennsylvania State University Press, 2006.

———. "Teaching Sartre About Freedom." In *Feminist Interpretations of Simone de Beauvoir*, ed. Margaret Simons, 104–130. University Park: Pennsylvania State University Press, 1995.

Kunz, George. *The Paradox of Power and Weakness*. Albany: State University of New York Press, 1998.

LaChance Adams, Sarah. "Becoming with Child: Pregnancy as a Provocation to Authenticity." In *New Perspectives on Sartre*, ed. Adrian Mirvish and Adrian van den Hoven, 25–36. Cambridge: Cambridge Scholars, 2010.

———. "The Need of Philosophy in Hegel." *Southwest Philosophy Review: The Journal of the Southwestern Philosophical Society* 23.1 (January 1, 2007): 89–96.

———. "The Pregnable Subject: Maternity and Levinas' Relevance to Feminism." *PHENOMENOLOGY 2010*, vol. 5: *Selected Essays from North America*, part 1: *Phenomenology Within Philosophy*, ed. Michael Barber, Lester Embree, and Thomas J. Nenon, 333–355. Bucharest: Zeta/Paris: Arghos-Diffusion, 2010.

———. "Reconsidering the Political Individual: Responding to Carole Pateman's Critique of Social Contract Theory with Help from Developmental Psychology and Care Ethics," *Journal of the Association for Research on Mothering* 10.1 (Spring/ Summer 2008): 233–242.

———, and Paul Burcher. "Communal Pushing: Childbirth and Intersubjectivity." In *Feminist Phenomenology and Medicine*, ed. Kristin Zeiler and Lisa Krall, 69–80 Forthcoming from SUNY press in 2014.

———, and Caroline Lundquist. "Introduction: The Philosophical Significance of Pregnancy, Childbirth, and Mothering." In *Coming to Life: Philosophies of Pregnancy, Childbirth, and Mothering*, ed. Sarah LaChance Adams and Caroline Lundquist, 1–28. New York: Fordham University Press, 2013.

Lamott, Ann. "Maternal Anger: Theory and Practice." In *Mothers Who Think*, ed. Camille and Kate Moses, 89–96. New York: Washington Square, 1999.

Lauritzen, Paul. "A Feminist Ethic and the New Romanticism—Mothering as a Model of Moral Relations." *Hypatia* 4.3 (1989): 29–44.

Lazarre, Jane. *The Mother Knot*. Durham: Duke University Press, 1997.

Leonard, Victoria Wynn. "Mothering as Practice." In *Caregiving: Reading in Knowledge, Practice, Ethics, and Politics*, ed. Suzanne Gordon, Patricia Benner, and Nel Noddings, 124–140. Philadelphia: University of Pennsylvania Press, 1996.

Lerner, Sharon. *The War on Moms: On Life in a Family-Unfriendly Nation*. Hoboken: Wiley, 2010.

Levinas [Lévinas], Emmanuel. *Difficile liberté: Essais sur le judaïsme*. Paris: Albin Michel, 1970.

———. *Entre Nous: Thinking-of-the-Other*. Trans. M. Smith and B. Harshav. New York: Columbia University Press, 1998.

———. *Ethics and Infinity*. Trans. Richard A. Cohen. Pittsburgh: Duquesne University Press, 1985.

———. "Intersubjectivity: Notes on Merleau-Ponty." In *Ontology and Alterity in Merleau-Ponty*, ed. Galen A. Johnson and Michael B. Smith, 55–60. Evanston, IL: Northwestern University Press, 1990.

———. "Judaism and the Feminine." In *Difficult Freedom: Essays on Judaism*. Trans. Seán Hand. Baltimore: Johns Hopkins University Press, 1990.

———. *Otherwise Than Being or Beyond Essence*. Trans. Alphonso Lingis. Pittsburgh: Duquesne University Press, 1998.

———. "Peace and Proximity." In *Basic Philosophical Writings*, ed. Adriaan Peperzak, Simon Critchley, and Robert Bernasconi, 161–169. Bloomington: Indiana University Press, 1996.

———. *Time and the Other*. Trans. Richard A. Cohen. Pittsburgh: Duquesne University Press, 1987.

———. *Totality and Infinity*. Trans. Alphonso Lingis. Pittsburgh: Duquesne University Press, 1969.

Levine, Sara. "Throwing the Book." *Brain, Child* 2.4 (2010): 18–23.

Lindemann, Nelson, Hilde, and James. "Cutting Motherhood in Two: Some Suspicions Concerning Surrogacy." *Hypatia* 4.3 (1989): 85–94.

Liss, Andrea. "Maternal CARE: Mierle Laderman Ukele's Maintenance Art," In *Feminist Art and the Maternal*, 43–67. Minneapolis: University of Minnesota Press, 2009.

Llewelyn, John. *Emmanuel Levinas: The Genealogy of Ethics*. London: Routledge, 1995.

Lloyd, Genevieve. *Man of Reason: Male and Female in Western Philosophy*. London: Routledge, 1993.

Low, Douglas. "The Foundations of Merleau-Ponty's Ethical Theory." *Human Studies* 17 (1994): 173–187.

Lundquist, Caroline. "Being Torn: Toward a Phenomenology of Unwanted Pregnancy." *Hypatia* 23.3 (2008): 136–155.

MacKinnon, Catherine. *Feminism Unmodified: Discourses on Life and Law*. Cambridge: Harvard University Press, 1987.

Mahler, Margaret, Fred Pine, and Anni Bergman. *The Psychological Birth of the Human Infant*. New York: Basic Books, 1975.

Maker, William. "Identity, Difference, and the Logic of Otherness." In *Identity and Difference: Studies in Hegel's Logic, Philosophy of Spirit, and Politics*, ed. Phillip Grier. New York: State University of New York, 2007.

Manninen, Bertha Alvarez. "The Pro-Choice Pro-Lifer: Battling the False Dichotomy." In *Coming to Life: Philosophies of Pregnancy, Childbirth and Mothering*, ed. Sarah LaChance Adams and Caroline Lundquist, 171–192. New York: Fordham University Press, 2013.

Manning, Robert J. S. "Thinking the Other Without Violence? An Analysis of the Relation Between the Philosophy of Emmanuel Levinas and Feminism." *Journal of Speculative Philosophy* 5.2 (1991): 132–143.

Matustik, Martin J. "Merleau-Ponty's Phenomenology of Sympathy," *Auslegung* 17.1 (1991): 41–65.

Maushart, Susan. *The Mask of Motherhood: How Becoming a Mother Changes Everything and Why We Pretend It Doesn't*. New York: New Press, 1999.

McMahon, Martha. *Engendering Motherhood: Identity and Self-Transformation in Women's Lives*. New York: Guilford, 1995.

Merleau-Ponty, Maurice. *Child Psychology and Pedagogy: The Sorbonne Lectures, 1949–1952*. Trans. Welsh. Evanston, IL: Northwestern University Press, 2010.

———. "The Child's Relations with Others." Trans. William Cobb. In *The Primacy of Perception*, ed. James M. Edie, 96–155. Evanston, IL: Northwestern University Press, 1964.

———. "Hegel's Existentialism." In *Sense and Non-Sense*, 63–70. Trans. Hubert Dreyfus and Patricia Allen Dreyfus. Evanston, IL: Northwestern University Press, 1964.

———. *Phenomenology of Perception*. Trans. Colin Smith. London: Routledge, 1958.

———. *Signs*. Trans. Richard McCleary. Evanston, IL: Northwestern University Press, 1964.

———. *The Structure of Behavior*. Trans. Allen Fisher. Pittsburgh: Duquesne University Press, 2002.

———. "An Unpublished Text by Maurice Merleau-Ponty: A Prospectus of His Work." Trans. Arleen B. Dallery. In *The Primacy of Perception*, ed. James M. Edie, 3–11. Evanston, IL: Northwestern University Press, 1964.

———. *The Visible and the Invisible*. Trans. Alphonso Lingis. Evanston, IL: Northwestern University Press, 1968.

Meyer, Cheryl L., and Michelle Oberman. *Mothers Who Kill Their Children*. New York: New York University Press, 2001.

Mezey, Jennifer, Mark Greenberg, and Rachel Schumacher. "The Vast Majority of Federally Eligible Children Did Not Receive Childcare Assistance in FY 2000: Increased Child Care Funding Needed to Help More Families." Center for Law and Social Policy, 2002. www.clasp.org/admin/site/publications_archive/files/0108.pdf.

Miller, Alice. *For Your Own Good: Hidden Cruelty in Childrearing and the Roots of Violence*. New York: Farrar, Straus, Giroux, 1983.

Milner, Larry S. *Hardness of Heart/Hardness of Life: The Stain of Human Infanticide*. Lanham: University Press of America, 2000.

Mirvish, Adrian. "Sartre, Embodied Minds, Authenticity, and Childhood." *Man and World* 29 (1996): 19–41.

———. "Sartre on Friendship: Promoting Difference While Preserving Commitment." *Journal for the British Society for Phenomenology* 33.3 (2002): 260–272.

Moses, Kate. "A Mother's Body." In *Mothers Who Think: Tales of Real-Life Parenthood*, ed. Camille Peri and Kate Moses, 176–181. New York: Washington Square, 1999.

MTV. *No Easy Decision*. First aired on December 28, 2010. http://www.mtv.com/videos/no-easy-decision-special/1654990/playlist.jhtml.

Murphy, Anne. "'All Things Considered': Sensibility and Ethics in the Later Merleau-Ponty and Derrida." *Continental Philosophy Review* 42 (2010): 435–447.

Nemzoff, Ruth. "Untitled Poem." *Journal of the Association for Research on Mothering: Mothering in the Academy* 5.2 (2003): 20.

Nietzsche, Friedrich. *Thus Spake Zarathustra*. Trans. Thomas Common. Hazelton: Pennsylvania State University, 1999.

Noddings, Nel. *Caring: A Feminine Approach to Ethics and Moral Education*. Berkeley: University of California Press, 1984.

Nussbaum, Martha. "The Future of Feminist Liberalism." In *The Subject of Care: Feminist Perspectives on Dependency*, ed. Eva Kittay and Ellen Feder, 186–214. Lanham: Rowman and Littlefield, 2002.

Oakley, Ann. *Becoming a Mother*. New York: Schocken, 1979.

———. "Normal Motherhood: An Exercise in Self-Control?" In *Controlling Women: The Normal and the Deviant*, ed. Bridget Hutter and Gilliam Williams, 79–107. London: Croom Helm, 1981.

O'Hara, M. W. *Postpartum Depression: Causes and Consequences*. New York: Springer, 1995.

Oksala, Johanna. "Female Freedom: Can the Lived Body Be Emancipated?" In *Feminist Interpretations of Maurice Merleau-Ponty*, ed. Dorothea Olkowski and Gail Weiss, 209–228. University Park: Pennsylvania State University Press, 2006.

Oliver, Kelly. "Ecological Subjectivity: Merleau-Ponty and a Vision of Ethics." *Studies in Practical Philosophy* 4.1 (2004): 102–125.

———. *Family Values: Subjects Between Nature and Culture*. New York: Routledge, 1997.

———. "Paternal Election and the Absent Father." In *Feminist Interpretations of Emmanuel Levinas*, ed. Tina Chanter, 224–240. University Park: Pennsylvania State University Press, 2001.

———. *Womanizing Nietzsche: Philosophy's Relation to the Feminine*. New York: Routledge, 1995.

Olkowski, Dorothea. "Only Nature Is Mother to the Child." In *Feminist Interpretations of Maurice Merleau-Ponty*, ed. Dorothea Olkowski and Gail Weiss, 49–70. University Park: Pennsylvania State University Press, 2006.

Parker, Rozsika. *Torn in Two: The Experience of Maternal Ambivalence*. London: Virago, 1995.

Pateman, Carole. *The Sexual Contract*. Stanford: Stanford University Press, 1988.

Peri, Camille. "Dancing with Death." In *Mothers Who Think*, ed. Camille Peri and Kate Moses, 255–272. New York: Washington Square, 1999.

Perpich, Diane. "From the Caress to the Word: Transcendence and the Feminine in the Philosophy of Emmanuel Levinas." In *Feminist Interpretations of Emmanuel Levinas*, ed. Tina Chanter, 28–52. University Park: Pennsylvania State University Press, 2001.

———. "Moral Blind Spots and Ethical Appeals: A Response to Bernhard Waldenfels." In *Interrogating Ethics: Embodying the Good in Merleau-Ponty*, ed. James Hatley, Janice McLane, and Christian Diehm, 107–131. Pittsburgh: Duquesne University Press, 2006.

Piontelli, A. "Infant Observation from Before Birth." *International Journal of Psycho-analysis* 68 (1987): 453–463.

Plutarch. *Life of Lycurgus.* Trans. John Dryden. London: Tonson, 1758.

Puka, Bill. "The Liberation of Caring: A Difference Voice for Gilligan's 'Different Voice.'" *Hypatia* 5.1 (1990): 58–82.

Radbill, Samuel X. "A History of Child Abuse and Infanticide." In *Violence in the Family,* ed. Suzanne K. Steinmetz and Murray A. Straus, 173–179. New York: Dodd, Mead, 1974.

Rich, Adrienne. *Compulsory Heterosexuality and Lesbian Existence.* Denver: Antelope, 1980.

———. *Of Woman Born.* New York: Norton, 1986.

Robins, Lee, and Darrel Regier. *Psychiatric Disorders in America.* New York: Free Press, 1991.

Ruddick, Sara. *Maternal Thinking: Toward a Politics of Peace.* New York: Ballantine, 1989.

Sakiko, Kitagawa. "Living as a Woman and Thinking as a Mother in Japan: A Feminine Line of Japanese Moral Philosophy." In *Frontiers of Japanese Philosophy 6: Confluences and Cross-Currents*, ed. Raquel Bouso and James W. Heisig, 141–154. Nagoya: Nanzan Institute for Religion and Culture, 2009.

Sartre, Jean-Paul. *Being and Nothingness.* Trans. Hazel E. Barnes. New York: Washington Square Press, 1956.

———. *Notebooks for an Ethics.* Trans. David Pellauer. Chicago: University of Chicago Press, 1992.

Scarth, Fedrika. *The Other Within: Ethics, Politics, and the Body in Simone de Beauvoir.* Lanham: Rowman and Littlefield, 2004.

Sandford, Stella. "Masculine Mothers? Maternity in Levinas and Plato." *Feminist Interpretations of Emmanuel Levinas*, ed. Tina Chanter, 180–202. University Park: Pennsylvania State University Press, 2001.

Scott, Joan. "Experience." In *Feminists Theorize the Political*, 22–40. ed. Judith Butler and Joan W. Scott. New York: Routledge, 1992.

Sears, William, Martha Sears, and Linda Hughey Holt. *The Pregnancy Book.* New York: Little, Brown, 1997.

Sears, William, Martha Sears, Robert Sears, and James Sears. *The Baby Book.* New York: Little, Brown, 2003.

Shields, Brooke. *Down Came the Rain: My Journey Through Postpartum Depression.* New York: Hyperion, 2005.

Sikka, Sonia. "The Delightful Other: Portraits of the Feminine in Kierkegaard, Nietzsche, and Levinas." In *Feminist Interpretations of Emmanuel Levinas*, ed. Tina Chanter, 96–118. University Park: Pennsylvania State University Press, 2001.

Simms, Eva-Maria. "Milk and Flesh: A Phenomenological Reflection on Infancy and Coexistence." *Journal of Phenomenological Psychology* 32.1 (2001): 22–40.

Simone, Maggie Lamond. *From Beer to Maternity.* New York: Brodman, 2009.

Simons, Margaret. "Beauvoir's Philosophical Independence in a Dialogue with Sartre," *Journal of Speculative Philosophy* 14.2 (2000): 87–103.

———. "Confronting an Impasse: Reflections on the Past and Future of Beauvoir Scholarship." *Hypatia* 25.4 (2010): 909–926.

———. "Two Interviews with Simone de Beauvoir." Trans. Jane Marie Todd. *Hypatia* 3.3 (1989): 11–27.

Smith, Jeremy Adam. *The Daddy Shift.* Boston: Beacon, 2009.

Spelman, Elizabeth. *Inessential Woman: Problems of Exclusion in Feminist Thought.* Boston: Beacon, 1988.

———. "Woman as Body: Ancient and Contemporary Views." *Feminist Studies* 8.1 (1982): 109–131.

Stawarska, Beata. "Anonymity and Sociality: The Convergence of Psychological and Philosophical Currents in Merleau-Ponty's Ontological Theory of Intersubjectivity." *Chiasmi International* 2 (2004): 295–399.

———. "From the Body Proper to Flesh: Merleau-Ponty on Intersubjectivity." In *Feminist Interpretations of Maurice Merleau-Ponty,* ed. Dorothea Olkowski and Gail Weiss, 91–106. University Park: Pennsylvania State University Press, 2006.

Steinbeck, John. *The Gapes of Wrath.* New York: Penguin, 1999.

Steingraber, Sandra. *Having Faith: An Ecologist's Journey to Motherhood.* Cambridge: Perseus, 2001.

Stoller, Silvia. "Reflections on Feminist Merleau-Ponty Skepticism." *Hypatia* 15.1 (2000): 175–182.

Strickling, Bonelle. "Simone de Beauvoir and the Value of Immanence," *Atlantis* 13.2 (1988): 36–43.

Stringer, Kristan, personal communication, 2005.

Suleiman, Susan, ed. *The Female Body in Western Culture.* Cambridge: Harvard University Press, 1986.

Sullivan, Shannon. "Domination and Dialogue in Merleau-Ponty's *Phenomenology of Perception.*" *Hypatia* 12.1 (1997): 1–19.

———. *Living Across and Through Skins.* Bloomington: Indiana University Press, 2001.

Taminiaux, Jacques. "Merleau-Ponty: From Dialectic to Hyperdialectic." *Research in Phenomenology* 10 (1980): 58–76.

Taylor, Chloé. "Levinasian Ethics and Feminist Ethics of Care." *Symposium* 9.2 (2005): 217–239.

Taylor, Diana. "Making a Spectacle: The Mothers of Plaza de Mayo." In *The Politics of Motherhood: Activist Voices from Left to Right*, ed. Alexis Jetter, Annelise Orleck, and Diana Taylor, 182–197. Hanover: University of New England Press, 1997.

Tidd, Ursala. "The Self-Other Relation in Beauvoir's Ethics and Autobiography. In *The Philosophy of Simone de Beauvoir*, ed. Margaret Simons, 228–240. Bloomington: Indiana University Press, 2006.

Tisdale, Sallie. "Double Dare." In *Mothers Who Think*, ed. Camille Peri and Kate Moses, 250–254. New York: Washington Square, 1999.

Tong, Rosemarie. *Feminine and Feminist Ethics*. Belmont: Wadsworth, 1993.

Toombs, S. Kay. "Disability and the Self." In *Changing the Self: Philosophies, Techniques, and Experiences*, ed. Thomas M. Brinthaupt and Richard P. Lipka, 337–356. Albany: State University of New York Press, 1994.

Trainer, Mark. "Don't Try This at Home." *Brain, Child* 11.4 (2010): 47–54.

Trevarthan, Colwyn. "The Self Born in Intersubjectivity: The Psychology of an Infant Communicating." In *The Perceived Self: Ecologies and Interpersonal Sources of Self Knowledge*, ed. V. Neisser, 121–173. Boston: Cambridge University Press, 1993.

Tronto, Joan C. *Moral Boundaries: A Political Argument for an Ethic of Care*. New York: Routledge, 1993.

———. "Women and Caring: What Can Feminists Learn About Morality from Caring?" *Justice and Care: Essential Readings in Feminist Ethics*, ed. Virginia Held, 101–115. Boulder: Westview, 1995.

Tsing, Anna Lowenhaupt. "Monster Stories: Women Charges with Perinatal Endangerment." *Uncertain Terms: Negotiating Gender in American Culture*, ed. Faye Ginsberg and Anna Lowenhaupt Tsing. Boston: Beacon, 1990.

Tuana, Nancy. *Women and the History of Philosophy*. St. Paul: Paragon House, 1998.

Tuvel, Rebecca. "Exposing the Breast: The Animal and the Abject in American Attitudes Towards Breastfeeding." In *Coming to Life: Philosophies of Pregnancy, Childbirth and Mothering*, ed. Sarah LaChance Adams and Caroline Lundquist, 263–279. New York: Fordham University Press, 2013.

Ueland, Brenda. *If You Want to Write*. St. Paul: Graywolf, 1987.

U.S. Department of Health and Human Services. "Indicators of Welfare Dependence." Washington, DC: DHHS, 1998.

Vasey, Craig R. "Faceless Women and Serious Others: Levinas, Misogyny, and Feminism." In *Ethics and Danger*, ed. Arleen B. Dallery and Charles E. Scott with P. Holley Roberts, 317–330. Albany: State University of New York Press, 1992.

Waerness, Kari. "The Rationality of Caring." In *Caregiving: Reading in Knowledge, Practice, Ethics, and Politics*, ed. Suzanne Gordon, Patricia Benner, and Nel Noddings, 231–255. Philadelphia: University of Pennsylvania Press, 1996.

Waldenfels, Bernhard. "Responsivity of the Body: Traces of the Other in Merleau-Ponty's Theory of Body and Flesh." In *Interrogating Ethics: Embodying the Good in Merleau-Ponty*, ed. James Hatley, Janice McLane and Christian Diehm, 91–106. Pittsburgh: Duquesne University Press, 2006.

Ward, Julie. "Reciprocity and Friendship in Beauvoir's Thought." *Hypatia* 14.4 (1999): 36–49.

Weaver-Zercher, Valerie. "Afterbirth." *Brain, Child* 11.1 (2010): 42–44.

Weiss, Gail. "The Anonymous Intentions of Transactional Bodies." *Hypatia* 17.4 (2002): 187–200.

———. "Écart: The Space of Corporeal Difference." In *Chiasms: Merleau-Ponty's Notion of Flesh*, ed. Fred Evans and Leonard Lawlor, 203–216. Albany: State University of New York Press, 2000.

Whitbeck, Caroline. "The Maternal Instinct." *Philosophical Forum* 6.2–3 (1974–1975): 321–332.

Willett, Cynthia. *Maternal Ethics and Other Slave Moralities*. New York: Routledge, 1995.

Winnicott, D. W. "Hate in the Countertransference." In *Through Paediatrics to Psycho-Analysis*, 194–203. New York: Brunner-Routledge, 1992.

———. "Transitional Objects and Transitional Phenomena." In *Through Paediatrics to Psycho-Analysis*, 229–242. New York: Brunner-Routledge, 1992.

Wolf, Naomi. *Misconceptions: Truth, Lies, and the Unexpected on the Journey to Motherhood*. New York: Doubleday, 2001.

Wolff, Jana. "Secret Thoughts of an Adoptive Mother." http://www.adoptivefamilies.com/articles.php?aid=184. Accessed November 22, 2012.

Woolf, Virginia. *A Room of One's Own*. San Diego: Harcourt Brace, 1929.

Wynn, Francine. "The Early Relationship of Mother and Pre-Infant: Merleau-Ponty and Pregnancy." *Nursing Philosophy* 3 (2002): 4–14.

Wyschogrod, Edith. "Exemplary Individuals: Towards a Phenomenological Ethics." *Philosophy and Theology* 1.1 (1986): 9–32.

Young, Iris Marion. "Gender as Seriality: Thinking About Women as a Social Collective." In *Feminist Interpretations of Jean-Paul Sartre*, ed. Julien S. Murphy, 337–357. University Park: Pennsylvania State University Press, 1999.

———. *Throwing Like a Girl and Other Essays in Feminist Philosophy and Social Theory*. Bloomington: Indiana University Press, 1990.

Young, Philip E. "The Ineradicable Danger of Ambiguity at Ch[i]asm's Edge." In *Merleau Ponty's Later Works and Their Practical Implications: The Dehiscence of Responsibility*, ed. Duane Davis, 101–137. New York: Humanity, 2001.

Yusa, Michiko. "Women Rocking the Boat: A Philosophy of the Sexed Body and Self Identity." In *Frontiers of Japanese Philosophy 6: Confluences and Cross Currents*, ed. Raquel Bouso and James W. Heisig, 155–169. Nagoya: Nanzan Institute for Religion and Culture, 2009.

INDEX